The Evolution of a Revolution:

An Attack upon Reason, Compromise, and the Constitution

by

Lance Simmens

The Evolution of a Revolution:

An Attack upon Reason, Compromise, and the Constitution

by

Lance Simmens

ISBN: 978-1-939625-74-8

Library of Congress Control Number: 2014934506

Published by Inkwell Productions
10869 N. Scottsdale Road # 103-128
Scottsdale, AZ 85254-5280

Tel. 480-315-3781
E-mail   info@inkwellproductions.com
Website   www.inkwellproductions.com

Printed in the United States of America

The Evolution of Revolution:
An Attack upon Reason, Compromise, and the Constitution

This work, which has been four years in the making, represents an attempt to chronicle various points in the evolution of the Obama policy agenda through two elections, as seen through the lens of the author's nearly four-decade long career in political and public service. It also traces the evolution of the "new opposition", one based on obstruction and rejection of compromise. The advent of the blogosphere and, more specifically, the Huffington Post, has afforded those of us who observe and practice the art of public policy an opportunity to both voice and vent our opinions through the written word. But every bit as important is that it allows a discussion of remedies to the current miasma that is preventing the nation from moving forward.

The traditional option of writing journal articles and opinion-editorial pieces has usually been reserved for academics and principal policymakers, with only occasional input from those who toil in the vineyards of the policymaking process or, even more likely, the province of words written by staff and attributed to their principals. But the new world of communication allows for diversity and an ever-expanding universe of thought that can help broaden knowledge and enlighten a growing audience.

I have carefully negotiated these new currents by not abusing the privilege of exposure, and sincerely hope that such caution will have enhanced the value of the opinions expressed in these eighty-six articles published between September 25, 2008 and December 28, 2012. And while the articles were written at random in concert with unfolding events I found compelling enough to comment upon, I believe there is a discernible thread connecting them which helps to elucidate a theory and conviction that validates my professed and oft-stated belief—that public service is a noble profession, and that government can be a venerable and important contributor to the benefit of society as a whole.

One needs only the most precursory look at some of government's achievements in the last century alone to validate this notion. Consider the establishment of the Food and Drug Administration; the Glass-Steagall financial reforms; the alphabet agencies of the New Deal; Social Security; the Interstate Highway System; the programs of the Great Society, including Medicare, Medicaid, Head Start, the Civil Rights Act of 1964, and the Voting Rights Act of 1965; the Clean Water

Act; and the Clean Air Act, among others.

Today we are faced with a system of governance that is dysfunctional. Some scholars, such as Thomas Mann of the Brookings Institution and Norman Ornstein of the American Enterprise Institute, make the intellectually valuable argument that this dysfunction is asymmetrical. They place almost complete blame on the Republican Party's virtual abandonment of compromise, a concept inextricably woven into the sinew and fabric of the guiding document which gave birth to this republican form of government. It is difficult to disagree with this assessment.

We must figure out a way to surmount these counterproductive and self-destructive barriers to progress. Currently, there is a reassessment underway within the Republican Party regarding whether or not it makes sense, from either the perspective of self-preservation or good governance, to continue their scorched-earth campaign of obstruction and obfuscation. However, nothing short of the continued prominence of the country on the world stage is at risk.

Politics has always been a tough business, but now it has become downright ugly. The vehemence directed at the Obama Administration from an increasingly vitriolic and mean-spirited, ultra-conservative element within the opposition party shakes even hardened political veterans to the core. My belief is that race plays a major role, and not a concealed one, in the abject hatred harbored by many political opponents of the president.

I may be wrong, but having spent a good deal of my career working for southern-elected and non-elected officials and having attended college in south Georgia, it never seems to be too far beneath the surface. No matter what Obama has done or can do, the one thing he cannot do is change the color of his skin. And while I have been disappointed at the centrist nature of some of his positions, like health care, and chagrined at the apparent abandonment of others, like climate change, I fully appreciate the insanely difficult position in which he finds himself.

He has inherited an incredibly mismanaged economic collapse, an intransigent and obstructionist Congress, the most activist and profoundly political Supreme Court in history, and an accumulated popular anger and frustration that finds expression on both the right and the left. He inherited two wars which were inadequately funded, a nation still wounded by 9/11, a three-decades-long attack on the integrity and value of public service and government itself, and a growing level of income inequality which is leading the nation into feudalism.

At the same time, the nation is changing in other ways as well. Of course, the changing demographics within the country played a major role in Obama's reelection in 2012. It is a very difficult pill for the angry old-white-male power structure to swallow. But it is real and it will not be reversed, so let us hope that in the 2012 election we have seen the last vestiges of concerted cultural and racial bigotry reflected in the national electorate. I strongly believe that the election of 2012 was a watershed event in the sense that a torch has been passed to the newly emerging character of a nation that will, each year, become more diverse, younger, and more tolerant.

Between 2000 and 2008, the country witnessed cavalier, reckless, and inept leadership which drove the nation to the brink of financial catastrophe. It also did enormous damage to the national psyche by hoodwinking a populace stunned by the horrendous events of September 11, 2001 into an ill-advised and purposefully deceitful war, which remains with us to this day. The fiscal insanity pursued by those professing to be stewards of the country's economic health turned a huge budget surplus into a staggering deficit, and brought the nation to the brink of financial collapse while leaving the economy weakened by the deepest recession since the Great Depression. The political corruption of influence-peddling reached new heights.

In fact, the election of this gang of incompetents was seen by the majority of citizens as validation that politics had trumped fairness in the electoral process. And the cabal was sanctioned by no less an authority than the United States Supreme Court. In the *Citizens United v. Federal Election Committee* case, the highest court in the land essentially sanctioned pervasive, systematic corruption in our political system by opening the door to a strategy of policy being sold to the highest bidder.

After eight years of ineptitude, the prospect of intellectual competence and an agenda of hope and change, epitomized by the historic election of America's first Black president, gave rise to a profound sense of optimism and excitement that was immediately tempered and ultimately dashed by the convergence of two destructive forces: first, the aforementioned economic and financial collapse; and second, an intransigence to compromise, based upon a concerted strategy of obstruction unlike anything in US history, which ultimately spread like a cancer into the processes of legislative protocol.

Against this backdrop, Obama labored to find a formula that would both mitigate a floundering economy and adapt to the new political reality by attempting to appeal to a national consciousness, which had traditionally proved successful in averting disasters. Unfortunately, politics reared its ugly head in an unprecedented show of recklessness which placed party above country. It was against this backdrop that the new administration found itself trying to forge an alliance for moving forward.

I believe that government can work, that it can provide an effective counterbalance to the negative consequences that often affect large swaths of the nation's citizenry. But if the barriers to solving problems are large enough, particularly in a system of checks and balances in which minority rights are fairly protected, and those rights are abused, such as has happened with the pervasive use of the filibuster, then problems can fester and worsen. And that is exactly what has happened.

So while the compilation of these works reflects what happened, it also reflects a fervent belief that we can solve and overcome these problems. Underlying each of these reflections is a premise, starting from the idea that certain inviolable precepts can and should govern our actions and, if followed, will render an acceptable outcome. For instance, focusing on the long-term welfare of the government and its citizens with vision and wisdom, considering the larger picture, and, most importantly, striking a balance in the pursuit of problem solving are all basic ideals that should guide our policymaking processes.

It is my hope that these works will help foster the hope that our broken system can be fixed. We have kicked the proverbial can a long way down the road on a path filled with potholes and landmines. Now we must proceed boldly yet smartly, with a firm resolve and the understanding that compromise plays a crucial role in our ultimate success. That is how our system is constructed. The so-called patriots who insist we must follow our founding documents literally, and then proceed to carelessly reject the major tenets upon which those documents are based, delude themselves and contribute to the dysfunction we all decry.

The articles presented here are chronologically configured to track events as they occurred. Some of the issues discussed have a broader application which transcends any particular point in time, and are as valid today as they were then. But the important thing is to approach problems that may appear to be intractable with a sense and resolve that together, we can solve them.

It is often useful to revisit past writings to attain perspective on how time has treated thoughts of the moment. Time not only has a way of encouraging us to reassess and evaluate our original views, but it also reignites the passions and emotions that sparked their creation.

The reader will note fundamental concepts throughout the writings which reflect the author's beliefs of what is important to a functioning political and policy process. First and foremost among those beliefs is a focus on broader-picture issues and long-term thinking. While the concept of long-term planning does not fit well into a political system geared to immediate gratification and a horizon that does not stretch beyond the next election, we now, more than ever, need leaders who use vision and wisdom which may not be readily apparent to the population at large. Statesmanship is the product of vision and wisdom, and today we are sorely in need of statesmen and women who are wired to make difficult decisions which may not be apparently or immediately popular. We elect followers, not leaders, and we get mercurial and inconsistent policies and laws as a result. We need to reorient ourselves on this fundamental issue.

Our system is built upon compromise. Today the connotation of that word is toxic to a broad and loud section of the populace. Ironically, the same individuals who reject compromise yell loudest in proclaiming their adherence to the precepts laid out by the Founding Fathers. Even a cursory examination of the philosophical intentions and written documents reveal a system predicated on and dependent upon consensus and comprise. Our system is founded on the idea that incremental change helps insulate us from radical swings which may jeopardize the stability of the system. We must return to a system of governance that moves the nation forward—even if at a slower pace than liberals or conservatives wish—but forward nevertheless.

A disturbing element of the current dysfunction is the notion that we need to go backwards, to return to a mythical time which, in nearly all instances, never existed except in minds clouded by nostalgic misperception, or fabricated as a deliberate appeal to a romantic vision warped by age. In many instances, those promoting this return to a simpler time yearn for days in which their responsibilities were considerably less than those that come with maturity. Regardless, we must progress as a nation and society, utilizing the benefits of greater understanding, knowledge, and experience, while taking maximum advantage of technological advances that enlighten us and make us more productive.

When I think back over the past half century and measure the technological and intellectual advances I have witnessed and benefitted from, I marvel at the opportunities that avail themselves to me and generations that will follow. Besides, the world is advancing, not retreating, and for those who wish to maintain or develop a cutting edge or even keep par with a more competitive global marketplace, going backwards is not a viable or wise option.

We are witnessing the disintegration of the middle class, and growing economic and income inequality is threatening one of the most valuable contributions American society has made to the world; opportunity for all. As a nation, we are envied for the opportunities we have created for our citizens and the quality and standard of living we provide to our population. As a society, we are deviating from this path, and the statistics which illustrate this are staggering, demonstrating the degree and speed of disintegration in progress.

Many of the writings contained herein are directed at what I perceive to be the most serious issue facing generations of individuals who will be forced to assume the legacies we leave them—the issue of climate change. We may not be threatening the survival of the planet, but we are certainly experimenting with the survival of the species. The planet will most likely survive no matter what we do to it; whether the same can be said for humankind is another question. If we do not begin to regard this issue seriously and take action, we are condemning future generations to a life of adaptation that will very well make them resent us forever—and rightfully so.

In this arena, my generation has done a tremendous collective disservice to future generations, and there is little to suggest that we will attempt to mitigate the damage we are inflicting upon our children and grandchildren. This is a human tragedy of the highest magnitude, and I have devoted a large part of the last two decades trying to draw attention to the need to address this critical issue. I am disheartened and saddened by the collective resistance to face up to the realities and consequences of our actions. Unless we move immediately to arrest our inexorable appetite for fossil fuels, we are forcing our progeny into an environmental disaster that will make their lives harsher and more difficult. What kind of a legacy is that? Is that how we want to be remembered? I hope not.

It is always a difficult proposition to identify the most pressing needs of individuals or societies. There are so many competing interests and issues that vie for our attention, so many levels of comprehension, differing levels of cultural and religious variables, and, of course, the differences contained in value systems ingrained through our individual upbringings and educational achievement, that it is often nearly impossible to identify the most serious and pressing problems which span all these variables.

However, I firmly believe that the most fundamental threat to us as a species in the long term is continuing environmental degradation and the massive changes that global warming and climate change will have on all of us. Thus, in a large portion of the writings, the reader will see a decided bias toward this issue. My standpoint is that there is no more important issue facing the survival of humans than survival itself. It affects all of us and, if we do not start to incorporate this concept into our overall policies, we run the very real risk of passing a point of no return, a tipping point after which our attempts to address the issue will have lesser effect—or no effect at all.

Last but not least, we are in the throes of an internal revolution over the role of government in our society. Since the 1980 election of Ronald Reagan, which brought with it the "Reagan Revolution," we have witnessed a steady deterioration in the public's perception of government and its role as a problem solver. Reagan ran on a platform of government as the problem, not the solution, and then initiated a set of policies which sought to prove that point. People who did not believe in government were put in positions within the government to fulfill the prophecy.

It was a deviously clever strategy to starve the beast, and remnants of that built-in dysfunction have festered and grown stronger over the years. Unfortunately, that steady deterioration was aided and abetted by many Democrats. The evolution of the revolution referred to in the title is a direct indictment of the advent of Tea-Party politics, which have taken this cynical and dismal view of government and elevated it to inviolable dogma. Traditional Republican conservatism certainly reflected a strong belief in limited or smaller government, but today's ultra-conservative bravado asserts that government, except for national defense, is the problem. If today's conservatives were presented with President Dwight D. Eisenhower's farewell address of 1961, they would roundly and soundly reject it as liberal drivel, and maybe even socialist propaganda. Even the Republican patron saint, Ronald Reagan, might encounter resistance among current right wing ideologues.

Suspicion of intellectualism and science has replaced our Cold War obsession with communism; the new enemy is reason. We are in dire need of robust debate and a degree of civility in our policymaking apparatus which allows us to agree to disagree, make decisions, and move on. That does not happen in the current political environment, and thus, as a society, we have become fractured and intolerant. The media consolidation that has overtaken dissemination of information has totally abdicated their responsibility to inform. Control of information is a powerful inducement to a split society, and today we are split in a way not seen since the days leading up to the Civil War.

Unless we correct these structural flaws, we will continue to drift in a sea of uncertainty and inaction, which will have serious adverse consequences not only for our own citizens, but for the world. We are still a leader on the world stage, and our actions are admired and scrutinized by our allies and adversaries alike. As the most prosperous, as well as the most destructive, nation on the planet, we have a solemn responsibility to help set a course to be followed by the rest of the world. At this point we are floundering, and it is not out of the question for others to step into the void. We run the risk of squandering the moral compass we once had or were perceived to have had.

The reflections outlined in the following pages are snapshots in time which reflect the emotionalism and vigor of the moment in which they were written. Reviewing these writings was a cathartic experience for me; beyond that, however, it gave me a fuller appreciation for the evolution of events that characterized the first Obama Administration. I truly hope they serve as a benchmark for historians and others interested in history, and as a microscope to view our growth over those four years.

The articles that comprise this book are arranged chronologically, and chart what I viewed as significant flashpoints during this time period. When viewed in hindsight, they paint a very clear picture of my thinking at the time and why I thought weighing in important. But more important is the fact that, when taken as a whole, they capture a fluid timeline containing snapshots, not unlike photo albums of your kids growing up.

The reader will find six themes running through these pages that form the core concepts I believe are necessary to right the dysfunctional nature of the current political and policy systems. Each article adheres to these core concepts and I believe they lay a foundation for a more effective and rational model for governance. The core concepts include the following:

1. A renewed commitment to the value of public service.

2. A focus on the importance of statesmanship versus leadership.

3. Acknowledgement and acceptance of the notion that government can work.

4. A shift in emphasis away from short-term to long-term thinking.

5. Promotion of public interests over special interests.

6. Removing the corrupting influence of money in electoral politics and our system of governance.

Now we will embark on a voyage that hopefully will reveal whether or not those concepts will stand the test of time. Let the journey commence.

Prelude to Election 2008

Article 1

September 25, 2008
Anger Management

As the presidential election of 2008 entered the final stretch, it had become obvious to me that two distinctly different emotions were competing for Americans' attention: anger and fear. Surely the country had been wracked with fear since that autumn morning seven years prior. On September 11, 2001, the country was brought face to face with an attack on our soil so bold, so striking, so audacious, and so unexpected that, for a few long days, it seemed the world was in a state of suspended animation. And while these two emotions find differing forms of expression, they are a toxic combination when they occur simultaneously. It was against this backdrop that the 2008 election unfolded.

I was in New York City that morning, and the bustling energy which characterizes the most exciting city in the world went into freeze frame. In a contemporary context, it was as though the citizens of that city, as well as the nation as a whole, entered a zombie-like trance, struggling mightily to make sense of or comprehend what had just hit us. In my lifetime, spanning six decades, I had only witnessed one incident that rivaled the seeming deconstruction of life that occurred that day and in the days that followed, and that was the assassination of President John F. Kennedy in 1963. My vivid recollection of that event, which happened when I was ten years old, was a slow, agonizing death march accompanied by numbness which was captured and choreographed on our small black and white television sets. But in that instance, we were assured that an individual had attacked our leader. On 9/11, something much larger and more sinister had attacked us, the people, and the visceral reaction indicated that there was a national emotional attachment to the families and individuals directly affected by the actions of that day. This was personal, because it could have been any one of us in harm's way on that magnificent autumn day in New York City.

The chaos that surrounded the Oswald assassination on live

television—the stricken first lady still clad in her blood-stained pink suit standing next to now-President Lyndon Baines Johnson on the airplane which carried the body of our beloved president back to Washington, the grief on her face, the numbness that replaced the vivacious character of Camelot, showed it all—emptiness, shock, disbelief, and loss. Those emotions encapsulated the feeling of a nation and those of many parts of the world. It was all followed by the most solemn funeral procession to Arlington cemetery, the slow-motion roll of the caisson carrying the president's body from the Capitol where an even slower procession of individuals patiently waited just to gather one last glimpse of their fallen leader. Days seemed like weeks, and then, magically, the schools opened again and life went on.

After the attack on the World Trade Center and subsequently on our national psyche, the clean-up magically commenced and life somehow resumed. But the days seemed like weeks, and for those of us caught in Manhattan that day, struggling to get back to our families a continent away, the ordeal stretched out for five days—an eternity to those like me with young children on the opposite coast.

But the fear provided if not a convenient, at least an appropriate, rationale for actions that would dominate both George W. Bush Administrations, and would cast the world into a dark period of revenge and destruction labeled the War on Terror. Certainly this is a strange concept in the grammatical sense alone, but that never was a strong suit of either the president or those around him, who propagated a wide-ranging assault on civil liberties in the name of national security.

Fear is a great motivator, and can elicit the most irrational actions from individuals who ordinarily would act rationally. The country was afraid and the remedy was revenge, the political palliative that would see us through the illness regardless of its ultimate potential to harm. Seemingly it did not matter whether those responsible were targeted or not; revenge for the sake of revenge was good enough.

And so for eight years we embarked on a vengeful mission of cleansing the fear that affected not only our international affairs, but our domestic affairs as well. Fear was used as a defense when it came to justifying curtailed civil liberties on the home front, and those restrictions were generally accepted as the price of doing business in a world now viewed as dangerous and threatening. The Bush-Cheney strategy turned Franklin Delano Roosevelt's admonition that "The only thing we have to fear is fear itself" on its head. Fear was exploited politically to promote a neo-conservative agenda that otherwise might not have passed congressional or constitutional muster. Fear is a powerful weapon, and its manipulation produces powerful results. The harnessing of fear and anger together inhibited criticism of what would have seemed irrational actions in a more stable national emotional state.

To the world, it must have appeared as though we, as a country, had lost a piece of our soul, and the most basic premise upon which this democratic experiment is predicated—freedom—took a major hit. But to those who saw America as an imperialist empire determined to secure whatever resources were necessary to support its way of life as well as its global hegemony, the actions undertaken in the name of defense, revenge, fear, and/or anger have been viewed with hatred and disdain. This is particularly true given the overtly religious connotations carelessly tossed out by the then-leader of the free world in characterizing this thing called the War on Terror. To the Muslim world, our ignorance of the cultural, historical, and religious differences that play such a large role in the Middle East could easily be translated into a modern-day Crusade, particularly after the American president used that word himself to defend our actions.

After a costly adventure in Iraq, with massive casualties and a largely discredited rationale for the initiation of hostilities under the guise of weapons of mass destruction, there was an escalating war on a second front in Afghanistan, a war that carries on to this day and into an undefined future. It seemed that nothing had been learned from the Russian debacle there a decade earlier, and there was even less appreciation for the culture, history, religious and tribal configurations, and geopolitical significance of the region by Americans. And now a confused and exhausted populace was being asked to choose a direction for the future.

As Election Day neared, it became quite evident that fear has lost its luster. Riding a wave of optimism, hope, and change was an African-American legislator from Illinois who had burst onto the scene with a riveting keynote speech at the Democratic National Convention in Boston just four years earlier. And as improbable as it seemed, with the name Barack Hussein Obama, he had captured a longing in the hearts and minds of the country's citizens to break away from the politics of fear and focus on their anger at what that fear had produced—a bankrupt political system and an economy on the verge of collapse.

The politics of anger proved to be a stronger motivator than fear. Anger, when properly managed, can spur great awareness and accomplishment. Obama capitalized on a collective desire to rid ourselves of the destructive forces that had created in the nation and the world a dark side, a pernicious ugliness that allowed us to do things of which we did not approve.

In "Let the Politics of Anger Prevail," I attempted to capture this change in society, which would allow a reawakening of our core values and would set us on the path to redemption and righteousness. Supplanting the politics of fear with the politics of anger would allow us to refocus our energy and direction to the future and away from the past. At this point, I could sense that the country yearned for a redefinition of who and what we were. I was hopeful that Obama had tapped into a vein of character that would allow hope and change to trump revenge and retribution. But the election was still a month and a half away, and the only thing I was certain of was that I hoped for change.

Posted September 25, 2008
Let the Politics of Anger Prevail

Here in Pennsylvania, a critical battleground state, I sense the election will hinge on the strongest emotion evident on Election Day, with the two competing emotions on trial: namely, fear versus anger. Republicans have deftly exploited the politics of fear. Of course, 9/11 touched the fears in all of us, but was shamelessly exploited as leverage for a host of immoral and undemocratic policies that have come to define us in the eyes of the world as imperialist hypocrites.

Human nature seems to dictate that irrationality is a perfectly acceptable response to fear, and we currently are now at our irrational worst, thrashing around in the currents of uncertainty and squandered opportunities desperately in search of a life raft, a buoy, a piece of driftwood, anything that will allow us to keep our heads above water, if only temporarily, hopefully long enough for us to be rescued.

On the other hand, there are those among us who survey the scorched landscape and are angry. Democrats, particularly Sen. Barack Obama, skillfully exploited the politics of anger during the primary season and until the "Great Distraction" (read: Sarah Palin), successfully managed to transform that anger into a program of progressive policy prescriptions that Americans could identify with and relate to.

It harkens back to the age old sports conundrum: what is more effective, a good offense or a good defense? Fear is premised on defensive strategies to protect us from the future. Anger is premised on offensive strategies designed to project us into the future and divorce us from the past. I have always opted for offense because if executed properly it does not allow for the 0-0 score. But then again, the trick is to always stay one step ahead of your opponent by scoring more than s/he. With Obama as the quarterback, I like my chances.

Fear versus anger, defense versus offense, past versus future, insecurity versus hope. These are the trademarks of the current decisions Americans must make in the next six weeks. The choices really could not be starker. And yes, lest we not forget, because it is the sleeping giant in this election: black versus white. Forget the experience issue; the cynical choice of Gov. Palin takes that off the plate.

The question really should not be whether or not we are better off than we were four or eight years ago, but are we better? Is the world a better place? Are we a better society? Are there better opportunities? Are our kids better positioned to take advantage of those opportunities?

Constructive anger can be a positive motivator and make us better. Fear is negative and makes us bitter. Whether it is the economy or the environment; our international prestige or our domestic failures; the loss of civil liberties or the gross specter of increasing intolerance be it racial, religious and/or cultural; health care inequality or a decrepit national infrastructure; mounting debt or the crumbling of our retirement savings and pensions, we truly cannot say we are either better off or better.

Change for the better will not be accomplished by wielding the axe of fear but rather through the dynamic forces of anger, properly crafted and carefully harnessed. Some of us are, and all of us should be, "Mad as hell and not going to take it anymore," so let's work to ensure that the politics of anger prevails over the politics of fear. We will be better for it.

The Evolution of Revolution:
An Attack upon Reason, Compromise, and the Constitution

Article 2

September 26, 2008
Not Your Average Guy

In my years in politics, I had come across an intriguing notion that permeated practically every election I'd been involved in. And that is the attractiveness of a candidate who seemed to be just a regular guy— and most of them were guys—the guy you'd most want to have a beer with. It always seemed a little odd to me that we were willing to put our faith in an individual who was so, well, ordinary. It seems that if there is ever a time when we need someone who possesses an above-average, if not superior, intellect and comprehension of the art of governance, it is when we elect a president. Likeability is one thing, and I understand how important a role it plays in elections, but it seems to have taken on an overblown quality through the years. A little goes a long way when electing the top dog.

It may attest to our general insecurity that we would entrust the reins of power to someone we would hang with, and maybe even get drunk with. I'd certainly had more than my fair share, and maybe even your fair share, of drunken nights followed by a lost day dealing with the aftereffects. I enjoyed these experiences with friends and acquaintances, but would not want to see these folks running the country. My first experience with this phenomenon was the 1980 election, when the country, in its inimitable wisdom, decided to go with the "aw–shucks" persona of a B-list movie actor who came across as a real guy. Now let me be perfectly clear that I am biased; after all, I worked for the guy he beat. But seriously, this was a rather important decision, don't you think?

From a political perspective, selling a candidate as a regular guy has a proven track record of success; likeability is an important element of an individual's candidacy. But I'm secure enough with my strengths and weaknesses to know that if I am going to trust someone to make momentous decisions on my behalf, I want them to be smarter, more clever, and strong enough to avoid the types of mistakes I might make.

Every time I hear someone talk about electing someone you would most like to have a beer with, I cringe. Not me; I want someone to whom I'd most likely lose an intellectual argument. Ideally, I would want someone who understood my shortcomings and difficulties, but who is level-headed enough to know when to leave the bar—more like a one-drink thing. But, of course, when most people talk of wanting someone to have a beer with, what they mean is someone to get drunk with. A one-drink guy is no fun to hang out with, and the people who insinuate that this character trait is desirable in an elected leader do not go to the bar for one drink.

More importantly, what I have witnessed over time is a steady diminution of the intellectual capacity we demand of our elected officials. Anti-intellectualism has become a steadily growing assessment tool in our arsenal of reasons for choosing a candidate. A close cousin to this phenomenon is the current anti-science wave that has swept through the conservative movement, particularly regarding climate change. It seems as though we'd dumbed-down for the 1980 and 1984 elections, and certainly for the 2000 and 2004 elections. The results were disastrous. After the sophomoric hijinks of the previous eight years, now was a time for a serious-minded and intellectually capable candidate to emerge. Looking at issues in simplistic terms, seeing only black and white, good and bad, with little variations on those themes, had become all too familiar in many elections in my lifetime.

This disturbing development has acted as an escape valve for those struggling to cope with complex and technically challenging issues. Whether or not this is a product of an educational system that has ignored science and mathematics and subordinated our graduates to a very low place on the world's educational totem pole is ripe for discussion, but there can be little doubt that Americans have a difficult time with complex problems.

Having worked for President Jimmy Carter and witnessed, first-hand, a summary rejection of his call for a forward-looking energy policy which he referred to as "the moral equivalent of war," I have seen a steady deterioration in the level of discourse on policy issues which are extremely complex and difficult. Reagan took the solar panels off the White House roof, and his "morning in America" rose-colored-glass-es-depiction of the problems facing the nation provided ample evidence of this phenomenon.

Reagan was likeable enough, but he and his policies were like applying a salve to a wound that required surgery. Life was wonderful,

America was the best, and we could solve any problem just because we were who we were. Sure, you would probably rather have a beer with him because Carter was intelligent and serious and, yes, wonkish, and had a deeper appreciation of both the past and the future and was, well, boring. That we make decisions based on this type of thinking should give us pause to rethink and recalibrate the basis upon which we make them when the consequences are so great.

At this point in the 2008 campaign, I was beginning to worry that Obama's intelligence might be used against him. McCain was a war hero and surely would have interesting stories to tell at the bar; Obama might be likely to launch into a dissertation on social policy and the urban condition. I was a little concerned that intelligence was a liability. This was a sad state of affairs, but it had happened in four of the previous six elections. (I purposely discount the 1988 election, because both candidates were intellectually capable. I had been involved in each of the other campaigns—1980 and 1984—and was all too aware that both smart guys lost.)

In "On Principle, The Presidency Is Not for Average Folk," I attempted to draw attention to what I felt should be an immutable fact in choosing a president—go with the smart guy.

Posted September 26, 2008
On Principle, the Presidency Is Not for Average Folk

Speaking plainly, why is it that a large swath of the American electorate has become enamored with the notion that entrusting the levers of power of the free world to someone ought to be contingent upon whether or not that person would be fun to have a beer with? As one who considers himself to be sufficiently well-versed in the activity of imbibing alcohol, having lived long enough to carry the mantle of experience deemed necessary to make one an expert in this particular activity, I am dumbfounded that such criteria even ranks in the top ten, let alone seemingly occupies top billing in people's minds with respect to selecting our next leader.

Now don't get me wrong, I certainly don't hold this qualification against a candidate; it's just that it seems to me to be incidental to the job at hand. In my foggiest of memories, it seems to me that once upon a time serious and right-minded individuals cherished the thought that it might be prudent to elect individuals who know more than you do about their jobs, since by its very nature, running for office enables one to have more time and information to make responsible decisions affecting the greater society and hence the greater good.

Logically, this makes sense. Tragically, however, we as a society seem to have abandoned logic. We have become a wistful electorate, intoxicated by the elixir of irresponsibility that I can only guess traces back to the gee-whiz, by-golly folksiness of Gerald Ford. True, not even in our post-Watergate-, post-Vietnam-induced trauma could we bring ourselves to vote him into the White House, but it was close. You know the rest of the story.

This is not meant to be an indictment of either political party, but rather a depressing observation about the political system we the people seem to be most comfortable with. We value personality over experience, style over substance, conventionality over change, regardless of how insistent if insincere claims about change might be. We are far too easily swayed by sound bites, commercials, and bumper stickers, and almost contemptuous of facts.

After nearly eight years of universally accepted policy failures and incompetence bordering on criminality, the ability of political strategists to use fear and complacency as tools upon which to construct a structure worthy of a Hollywood studio set—all show, no functionality—is quite simply astonishing.

I sincerely hope that rationality and logic prevail in the upcoming election. But in order for that to happen, we must first demolish this myth, perpetrated by those whose only goal is to prevail, for better or worse, that we need to identify with the individual(s) who are most like us. Speaking for myself, I prefer to hold our elected leaders to a higher standard. I want them to think in a way that I cannot. I want them to act in a way I might not see immediately is in our best interest, but is. I want them to be intelligent. No, America, that is not a dirty word. I respect people more intelligent than myself, and can bring myself to admit that someone knows more than I do. I also respect someone who can do things I cannot, whether in the world of athletics or politics.

Lest I sound apocalyptic, two terms of the Bush idiocracy should disabuse us of the notion that the world will end. But—and this is important—the accumulation and continuation of missed opportunities will portend disastrous consequences for someone, whether or not it is our generation or those that follow. No, the world will not stop turning, but a more practical question is whether or not it will be a better place. That, after all, is what we can truly ask of our leaders—to make this world a better place.

So as you weigh your choices this fall, do not allow yourself to be fooled by the false choice of whether or not this or that individual is more like yourself. In fact, just the opposite; you should be looking for someone who is most unlike yourself, but willing to place greater interests above self-interest. If you use this as your barometer, I am convinced that the outcome will make this world a better place. And that, I believe, is the best we can do.

The Evolution of Revolution:
An Attack upon Reason, Compromise, and the Constitution

Article 3

September 26, 2008
Sarah Who?

Cynicism has played an inordinately large role in contemporary politics. There is a valid and valuable role for skepticism, but cynicism is especially dangerous. When combined with fear, it can wildly distort perspective. Cynicism was pervasive during the 2008 campaign, and it was manifested clearly in the selection of an unknown governor from Alaska to be a potential heartbeat away from the presidency. This might have not been such a prominent concern if it had not been for the precariousness of John McCain's health, both physical and mental. Certainly the choice alone gave rise to serious questioning of the legitimacy of his judgment.

Who in the world was this woman, and what in the world qualified her to be considered for the position? What scared me the most was how unexpected McCain's choosing her was, and how a political operative always fears that someone must know something more than they do. Unknowns can either be extraordinarily good or incredibly bad. This was a gamble for sure, and I hoped it was one worth taking.

Palin proved to be a major liability and embarrassment for the Republican Party. What was most unsettling was the short span between her selection and Election Day. At first it appeared to rival the boneheaded decision of George H. W. Bush who, in 1988, picked an obscure, unserious, and curiously unengaged young senator from Indiana named Dan Quayle. Palin soon eclipsed the Republican nominee's credibility altogether.

Since the election of Reagan in 1980, I'd been intrigued by the decision of legions of young Republicans who steadfastly professed their disgust with government in general and, more specifically, a dripping disdain for federal service, who were very willing to join the ranks of political appointees populating the federal bureaucracy. Surely their love affair with the private sector would guide their career decisions away from public service, yet there they were, lined up for the opportunity to take on these relatively well-paying positions with generous benefit packages, prestigious titles, and great responsibilities.

It did not cross my mind at that relatively early time in my life and career that there might have been a collectively sinister effort to definitively prove that, in fact, government did not work because they were determined to infiltrate and wreck the system from within. How dastardly, I thought; the evil genius of it. I was first introduced to this concept as I daily watched and listened to New York Senator Patrick Moynihan while a staff member of the Senate Budget Committee. What would eventually be labeled as the strategy of "starving the beast"—in this case, starving it of dedication, commitment, and raw talent—might be an effective strategy of achieving what the traditional Republican establishment cherished most of all, which was validating the need for smaller government.

This, however, would be the height of cynicism. And whether or not it was a large-scale and deliberately malicious strategy or merely the byproduct of disinterested and sub-par personnel matters little. The end result was the same: the dismantling of trust and confidence in the institutions of government perpetuated by a cadre of individuals who had no use for them. What a shame, what a pity, what a waste, and what a lack of respect for the millions of people who depended upon government in the course of their daily lives. But to the victor goes the spoils.

As one who views public service as a noble occupation and an honorable profession, the damage done by these anti-government, anti-science, and anti-intellectual adherents is antithetical to the notions of community, shared sacrifice, and unity we know as the United States. What hypocrites; what traitors in our midst. Yet these are the self-professed patriots who cling to literal interpretations of both the Bible and the Constitution, and who eschew any conception of evolution, mental or physical. The large-scale betrayal of the public is one of the most disconcerting long-term trends I have experienced in my political career, and I believe it has led to a pervasive corrosion and lack of confidence in our governmental institutions.

In "Cynicism Versus Commitment," I take a stab at presenting the vice-presidential pick as a cynical attempt to again try to connect with the common man—or, in this case, woman—in a desperate attempt to win at any cost. It dovetails with the previous article in that it demonstrated the dumbing-down of the importance of candidates and the positions they are trying to secure. Luckily, in this instance, it did not work. But the fact that desperation would lead to such a potentially disastrous miscalculation underscores the degree of cynicism that permeates our political system.

Posted September 26, 2008
Cynicism versus Commitment

I guess I will never cease to be amazed at the gross and unadulterated hypocrisy spawned by some politicians. And, of course, in the minds of the citizenry, seemingly incapable of discerning between change agents and cynics, politics and all politicians simply get thrown into the dung heap of self-serving opportunists. Hence, the public, over time, loses interest in the people and processes that effectively govern their lives. In this environment, cynics thrive and prosper. It is this environment that has existed over the nearly past eight years, and it is this environment that truly needs cleaning up.

I vividly recall the 1980 election, one arguably defined by the anti-government rhetoric of the Reagan campaign, in which the public made a conscious decision to turn government over to those most fervently opposed to the fundamental role of government itself. I recall asking several acquaintances who had enlisted with the Reaganistas and then immediately sought to secure government jobs why they were so interested in participating in the governmental bureaucracies they had so little faith in, especially those who joined agencies they sought to eliminate. I figured that, as a true believer, they would want to make a principled stand and refuse to engage in such blasphemous activity. Yet I suppose the allure of an appointed federal position, a high-level federal paycheck, and the excitement of Washington, DC was just too strong to let principle get in the way.

Of course, maybe it was a sign of true commitment to prove that government does not work, and who better to populate the senior levels of bureaucratic decision-making than those who believed this. If that is the case, they should have worked for free. You see, I don't have a problem with those who say we can make it work better. More power to you, have at it. But those who maintain that government is the enemy are the people we ought to be most afraid of.

This is what scares me most about the current election campaign. The proverbial "throwing the baby out with the bathwater" mentality finds security and comfort in a cynical electorate. Throw in a healthy dose of fear, and you have a combustible mixture. And God knows we certainly have seen an overdose of fear these past eight years or so.

What disturbs me most about the Palin pick is not so much the woman's lack of experience, judgment, honesty, or intelligence, but rather the cynical calculation that these things really don't matter. If it helps you capture the prize, we will worry about those things later—or maybe not; winning is all that matters. The Republican Party has shown an amazing ability to manipulate the electorate and the processes of choosing a president. They have been very successful at convincing the American people that government is the problem and not the solution over the past thirty years. Hence, when people become desensitized to the notion that their elected leaders can perform their jobs in a competent manner and in a way that maximizes the public interest, they lose trust in the institutions and people who run them and become cynical.

The current Republican campaign is forthrightly designed to exploit this cynicism, it is clearly evident in the Palin pick, and it harkens back to the very incompetence that such a movement engenders, eg, the Iraq War, the assault on civil liberties, torture, rendition, evisceration of environmental regulations, politicization of the Justice Department, the Federal Emergency Management Agency follies, Halliburton, Enron, the housing crisis, subprime mortgages, mountains and mountains of public debt, devaluation of the currency, and last but certainly not least, the squandering of our international prestige and the loss of our moral leadership worldwide.

This is the legacy of cynicism. It is ugly, demoralizing, and dangerous. It is unsustainable, unsettling, and unacceptable. We must, as a nation, put an end to the culture of cynicism that pervades our politics and our political institutions. Thus, the real choice this year is to reject cynicism and usher in a renewed commitment to improving government. Stop bashing and start building. We must fight, but we must fight for the positive choice. The time for positive choice is long overdue.

Article 4

October 16, 2008
A Statement about Statesmen

This article was a revised op-ed I'd penned over twenty years prior when I was a staffer on the United States Senate Budget Committee, but had no luck getting published. I kept a copy and used the argument I'd advanced in many speeches, both written and delivered, in the subsequent two decades. I was and am particularly enamored with the concept even to this day.

It was originally intended to be a response to David Stockman's book *The Triumph of Politics*, in which he outlined exactly how Reagan-era "supply-side economics" came to overtake the budget. Many of us who were, at the time, adamantly opposed to and confounded by the concepts embodied in that sham masquerading as economic policy were eventually vindicated by the incredibly disastrous consequences these policies had upon our economy and the budget deficits and debt they engendered. I'd argued that Stockman, who was by all accounts one of the brightest stars in the Reagan constellation, had to have known better that what was to become known as Reaganomics was a fraud and a hoax, and that he had failed in his duty as a trusted adviser to the president to not advise or at least caution against its application. In recent interviews, it seems as though he has seen the error of his ways. But as a conscientious staffer, I never backed away from imparting my best judgment to whomever I have worked for. That, in the end, is the true value of public service. If you get rebuffed too many times, leave; but at least do your best.

Stockman was a formidable director of the Office of Management and Budget in the early years of the Reagan presidency. It is not a stretch to say that he intimidated senators serving on the Senate Budget Committee into submission on both sides of the aisle. Today he has become a rather forceful critic of both the policies he once peddled and the subsequent budgetary and fiscal chicanery which followed in the

George W. Bush years.

The crux of the argument is that we need to seek out and elect dedicated stewards of the public good with long-term vision, rather than short-sighted snake-oil salesmen who tell you what you want to hear or parrot what you are saying. Contemporary politics rewards those who can most convincingly mirror what people say and want, rather than delve into the seriousness of complex policy analysis which is in the best interest of all. How unusual it is to hear our so-called leaders espouse ideas and make reasoned arguments for ideas and programs that the people do not readily see or accept.

I have assiduously argued over the years that we need statesmen and women who have qualities not necessarily defined as those required of a leader in the contemporary political environment. You can be a good leader or a bad leader, but a leader nevertheless. George Custer was a leader, yet he took his troops into Little Big Horn. Ronald Reagan was a leader, yet he trebled the national debt in a little under a decade.

A statesperson, on the other hand, differs from a leader in that s/he possesses vision and wisdom. Jimmy Carter may not have registered high on the leadership scale by contemporary standards, but his vision and wisdom in warning the American people about the energy crisis was an act of statesmanship that resonates to this day. We have become a short-term-oriented, disposable society, and we need to exercise vision, wisdom, and a willingness to make long-term commitments in order to maintain our legitimacy on the world stage.

I have posited this idea to leaders throughout the years, and point-blank asked individuals of considerable stature to identify and name contemporary statesmen and women. Invariably, they draw a blank. It is startling to see, but not unpredictable. I recall, during my early days in Washington, DC, being able to identify leaders, even when I did not agree with them. In one instance I was on the Senate floor when a vote was held on whether to pass a constitutional amendment to balance the federal budget. Superficially, this was an absurd proposition for many reasons, but politically, it was very popular with those who have nary a clue as to the nature of budgets and budget processes.

I remember when the US Senate debated a constitutional amendment to balance the Federal budget in 1986. Passage required two-thirds affirmative vote for passage and I was involved in an extensive back and forth between Senator Gore and Senate Leader Dole on compromise language after being summoned to the floor by the Senator from Tennessee. Ultimately we failed to reach compromise language, much to my relief. However, after an impassioned speech by Republican Senator Mark Hatfield from Oregon stating his opposition to the proposed language on the floor, thus depriving the Republicans of the 67th vote needed for passage, I made sure that I would have a chance to talk with him as he exited the Chamber.

Meeting up with him in the Senate anteroom I extended my hand and told him that as a Democrat I sincerely respected the courage he exhibited in letting his convictions override the partisan pressure he was surely under to provide the deciding vote. He stopped, stood in front of me and with a smile told me that that meant a great deal to him and he thanked me for taking the time to mention it to him.

I had just witnessed a concrete example of statesmanship and it was a modern day profile in courage. He was the Chairman of the powerful Senate Appropriations Committee and there were threats that if he bucked his party leadership he could lose that powerful position. On that day I was truly proud to be part of an institution that restored my faith in what I believed to be the primary responsibility of those who were a part of it: namely, the preservation of the public interest.

We need more statespersons and visionaries in politics, and we need intellectuals with wisdom to run our institutions of government. We need long-term thinking and people who are unwilling to pander to their constituencies. We need persons who take seriously their roles as senators and congressmen, not merely state or district leaders who act as ward heelers within a larger polity. It was a Republican—Abraham Lincoln—who risked everything to preserve and strengthen the Union, and we have systematically deserted that cherished ideal over the years, except in times of national crisis and wars. President Obama comes close to encapsulating this message when he talks of not red states and blue states, but the United States.

I believe this to be one of the most important concepts I have learned over my thirty-six years in politics and government. It is needed now more than ever, but most importantly for future generations. It represents a systemic challenge of the first order.

Posted October 16, 2008
Time for Statesmanship

Here's a novel idea: how 'bout we consider electing statesmen and women instead of politicians? Now this is not to say we cannot have both, but foremost in our thinking, regardless of the severity of the current economic crisis confronting us, ought to be the thought that we need to turn to leaders who exercise vision and wisdom, not merely leadership qualities.

Let me explain further. For most of my life, I have listened to men and women extol the virtues of their leadership qualities, and in times of crisis I constantly hear folks talk about the need for leadership. Our elected leaders are leaders by virtue of their election. This, however, does not mean they are effective leaders. The thing about leaders is they can be either good or bad leaders.

I do not quarrel with John McCain's claim of possessing leadership qualities; he does. But to witness the rudderless direction of his leadership over the past week or so, or for that matter the past decade or so, is to question whether this is what is either needed or desired. John McCain is about change all right, but his backsliding, flip-flopping reversal on principle is the worst kind of change.

Statesmanship, on the other hand, by its very definition, entails possessing wisdom and vision. It requires one to think and act in a way that may not be popular in the short-term, but required in the long-term. It requires a steady hand on the rudder to guide the ship of state through perilous shoals. It also demands a steely resolve to execute a long-term plan for achieving desired goals. As a military man, McCain ought to understand and accept this as a given. However, McCain's actions over the past week, reflexively darting from fundamental economic soundness to economic crisis, from suspension of his campaign to suspension of disbelief, casts great doubts upon his comprehension of either the problem or the solution. Senator McCain does not understand.

And to those who have been critical of Sen. Obama's cool and calm demeanor as though it smacks of aloofness or elitism, I offer that, in times of genuine crisis, this temperament is both needed and desirable. People need to seriously ask themselves who is better capable of making decisions and judgments that carry long-term consequences for the future. I believe that the answer is becoming readily apparent to more and more Americans, and the answer is clearly that Sen. McCain is a leader, but Sen. Obama is a statesman.

We need to restore confidence in both the economic and political systems in this country. It will take someone with extraordinary foresight and the ability to make unpopular decisions. Such decisions will be acceptable to people who have confidence that they will help us reach our goals. Leadership without statesmanship is a gamble, whereas statesmanship accompanied by leadership inspires to achieve great things. The past week very well may be a watershed event in the course of this election.

Article 5

October 17, 2008
The Child and the Adult

This article chronicles the physical antics of the recently concluded McCain-Obama debate, in which the elderly and self-ordained mature politician and candidate exhibited childlike reactions to obvious points scored by his opponent during and after the debate. It harkened back to the advent of the televised debates in 1960, when a nervous, sweating, and shifty-eyed Richard Nixon was bested—on television—by the cool, unflappable demeanor of his opponent, John F. Kennedy. Had no lessons been learned of the importance of television presence in the preceding half-century?

McCain was visibly shaken, and his reactions were captured by cameras positioned to catch every movement. This should not have come as a surprise to the elder politician. What is incomprehensible is that he either could not contain himself, or thought the effect of his reactions might be positive, either his judgment was seriously flawed or he had lost control of his emotions—neither appealing qualities in a person wishing to be leader of the free world.

In "Maturity and Age Are Not Synonymous," I attempted to outline that it was becoming increasingly clear that age does not necessarily equal maturity. In fact, dementia and senility are a reversal of maturity; in many instances, the adult reverts to a childlike persona. I am not asserting that McCain was suffering from either senility or dementia, but certainly his temperament in this debate did not demonstrate a reassuring maturity, and this at a time when increasingly loud rumors asserted that he did and does have a problem with his temper. All this, coupled with increasing criticism regarding his flawed judgment in picking Sarah Palin as a running mate, only exacerbated the perception problem that was growing among the electorate.

The practical impact of his antics more clearly demonstrated not just differences in personal temperament, but drew a stark contrast between these two individuals from distinctly different generations.

Clinton used this contrast to his advantage in both the 1992 and 1996 elections; first against George H.W. Bush, and later Bob Dole. Now Obama was being handed a golden opportunity to contrast youth and vibrancy with old age and crankiness. It was likely not the deciding issue, but it helped.

Posted October 17, 2008
Maturity and Age Are Not Synonymous

I could not put my finger on it, but something struck me as particularly odd about the way John McCain acted during the debate the other night. As a caretaker for an eighty-five-year-old parent, it suddenly hit me; McCain is reverting to childhood, while Obama is maturing into the role of president.

For anyone who is tasked with taking care of their parent(s), at some point it becomes painfully obvious that the ultimate role reversal is inevitable; namely, the child assumes the role of parent and the parent assumes the role of child. It can be a daunting and challenging metamorphosis, fraught with contradiction, frustration, stubbornness, and plain childishness.

The erratic behavior we have all witnessed over the past month or so, I believe, is attributable largely to the realization by McCain that on issues of substance, demeanor, and temperament, Obama is the adult. The not-so-veiled tantrum McCain exhibited the other evening— the eye-rolling, blinking, blank stares, and exaggerated movements post-debate—all reminded me of the awkwardness of a teenager rather than those of a would-be world leader.

They are cute when the child is five or six, they are barely tolerable when the child is fourteen or sixteen, but they are pathetic when the individual approaches their twilight years.

More astonishing, however, than the physical antics is the lameness and absurdity of the rationale behind the professional judgments and actions of the person who would be responsible for leading this great nation, regardless of the condition we now find ourselves in. From Sarah Palin being a heartbeat away; to Joe the Plumber, who is not really a plumber; to being proud of all those who attend his and her rallies, regardless of whether or not they incite hatred and bigotry; to "since you have not traveled there you cannot possibly understand" to "well, you know, it is really all about taxes," and have we not heard this before from our Republican trickle down-supply-side-laissez-faire-government-is-the-problem-love it-or-leave it-flag-waving pseudo-patriots before. Please. Enough is enough.

And besides, what exactly is wrong with spreading the wealth? I thought that was the essence of capitalism. Isn't a vibrant middle class a noble byproduct of a capitalist economy? Oh, yeah, I forgot, he never mentioned the words middle class (air quotes).

This race started out to be about experience. I would argue that that notion has been abandoned by the Republicans because a large measure of experience is maturity, especially in times of crisis. Obama exudes maturity; McCain does not. So this election, let's place our future in the hands of an adult. McCain is right about one thing; the past eight years have been disastrous, but we placed our trust in a dolt.

Calmness, professionalism, reason, dialogue, diplomacy, flexibility—these are the hallmarks by which to judge our next president. Hands down, Obama has demonstrated that he possesses these qualities.

The Evolution of Revolution:
An Attack upon Reason, Compromise, and the Constitution

Article 6

October 28, 2008
Too Much for Traditional Republicans!

Sarah Palin was increasingly becoming not only a drag on the ticket, but a bona fide embarrassment. This was a real problem for the Republican Party's prospects, and it was also becoming evident that there was not just a lack of chemistry between her and the man at the top of the ticket, but real tension. The extent to which this was reflected in the ranks of more traditional Republicans was unclear, but it was becoming a discomforting possibility among party operatives.

There was a sense that momentum—"the big mo"—was decidedly on Obama's side, but hanging in the background like a nightmare that would not go away was the memory of how, in the 2000 election, defeat was snatched from the jaws of victory, and how no election in my lifetime would ever be final until all the ballots were counted. That painful memory will be with me for the rest of my days, and its impact on the fate of the nation and the world will assuredly be debated for many years to come. Never again will any of us who lived through that debacle and who were intimately affected by the outcome take for granted a political outcome until the proverbial fat lady sings.

From my vantage point in conservative central Pennsylvania, I was feeling more and more confident. Then, one day, I received a call from an old friend, a former Republican mayor of York, Pennsylvania, a small city just north of the Maryland border. Mayor Bill Althaus had risen to become president of the US Conference of Mayors during my time with that organization (1987–1993). Though he represented a conservative side by virtue of his party affiliation and geographical location, it was an open secret that Republican mayors were more liberal by virtue of their charge over urban areas than many, if not most, Democratic congressmen. Bill and I shared a respectful relationship, but had not talked in many years. He was one politician I looked forward to having not one, but many beers with. James Carville once remarked in his inimitable manner that Pennsylvania was a mixture of Philadelphia and Pittsburgh with Alabama in between. Others have remarked that the large rural configuration of the state lends itself to a more appropriate name change to "Pennsyltucky." Well, Mayor Bill came from Pennsyltucky, and would proudly proclaim it.

He had just returned from several years in the Baltics, helping build democratic governments there. We met in Harrisburg, the state capital, for lunch. During the course of our meal, I was pleasantly surprised to learn of his support and enthusiasm for Obama. Whether it was because he was no longer in office and therefore not constrained by party loyalty, or his international experience had engendered a broadening of his philosophical horizons I did not know, nor did I care. What was important to me was his stated position that his party had abandoned him, and that the ticket chosen to lead his party was more of a deadly than a dynamic duo.

If this thinking was prevalent among the more moderate faction of the Republican Party, then Election Day promised to have a positive outcome not only for Democrats, but for the country as a whole. Remember this was in advance of the Tea Party tsunami that was about to hit the Republicans; however, fraying was already evident. He confided to me that many of his friends and colleagues felt as he did, and I came away from lunch with both a newfound respect for my old friend and an upbeat, positive attitude.

In "Beyond the Palin," I tried to capture the optimism and positivity resulting from this encounter. The tide seemed to be shifting in the right direction. Check that—the correct direction.

Posted October 28, 2008
Beyond the Palin

One of the benefits of longevity is the ability to develop a broad network of friends and acquaintances. When you have spent the past thirty years in the political arena as I have, it allows one to build an extensive Rolodex, and if done correctly, it can include an impressive array of folks with differing backgrounds, opinions, and ideas.

Just yesterday I had occasion to have lunch with a former mayor from a mid-sized central Pennsylvania city who has been fond of telling people over the years that he represents Pennsyltucky, that T-section of the state that James Carville so aptly described once in this way; the state can be described as being Philadelphia and Pittsburgh, with Alabama in between.

It is a place I have called home for the past five plus years. It is staunchly conservative, and Republicans heavily out register and outvote Democrats. My old friend, the mayor, opened up our conversation with the following question, "So how are we doing?" This seemed odd to me given that even though we have been friends for nearly two decades now, it was always understood that politics was not fruitful territory for discussion.

"What's this 'we,' Kimosabe?" was my reply. The mayor has spent the greater part of the past eight years or so doing democracy-building work in foreign lands, and I immediately thought that the broadening of his horizons must have truly had a positive impact on his thinking abilities.

He proceeded to tell me of his support for Barack Obama, the positive impact it would have upon our international credibility, the potential it would have for addressing our domestic concerns, including the deteriorating infrastructure of our urban areas (an area where mayors and former mayors live and breathe), and the awful prospect of contemplating Sarah Palin anywhere near the White House. I was astounded, but happily so.

He then proceeded to tell me that the new John McCain and the new Republican Party were not the party he so loyally clung to for all these years. His was the party of Rockefeller, Lindsay, and Hugh Scott. Essentially, he feels that his party has abandoned him.

I wondered how widespread this attitude is, and suppose we will not accurately know for another week or so. But in a state like Pennsylvania, if moderate Republicans reflect this sentiment to any small degree, I believe it will blunt the negative impact of what remains of the so-called "Bradley effect," hence giving Obama a comfortable win here.

I have always respected my friend, even as I disagreed with his politics, but I found myself marveling at the changing dynamic that has taken place over the course of this presidential election. Whether this represents simply a maturation of political thought, or the hoped for liberation of entrenched biases—racial, political and/or ideological—it does provide hope and portend an excitement that has not captured the public imagination since the election of John F. Kennedy.

The troubled times we find ourselves in cry out for and demand creativity, ingenuity, and a new way of thinking. Obama/Biden offers at least the possibility of a new frontier. McCain/Palin offers no possibility other than a reckless tack into a mythical past that never existed.

I surely hope that my chat is a harbinger of a reawakening of the American spirit, an appeal to the very best that we have to offer, a challenge to the can-do attitudes that made this country great. The recent defection of conservative thinkers from the McCain/Palin vision for the country only serves to reinforce the radical nature of the current Republican Party. It is a vision that is short-sighted, dark, and dangerous. And, mercifully, it is a vision we will not be forced to deal with as we embark upon meeting the challenges of the contemporary world.

I felt better after lunch that day. I will feel better the day after Obama prevails.

Article 7

October 28, 2008
Can't We All Share?

As the campaign neared its end, the desperation of the floundering McCain-Palin campaign turned to a predictable, well-worn strategy of equating Democrats, liberals, progressives, and anyone who dared to argue with the failing conservative agenda as socialist. Obama and his ideas were virulently described as adhering to a program of inherently unfair redistribution of wealth. It is astonishing to me how violently Americans react to the word "socialism"; I think it is because few are familiar with or knowledgeable about the concept itself. But labeling Democrats as socialists is a tactic I have witnessed in every campaign I have worked in over the past thirty-six years. Luckily, as time goes on, it seems to have become less and less effective.

Disregarding the overwhelming economic data outlining an ever-widening level of economic inequality and a disappearing middle class, the Republicans once again pandered to fears that economically flourishing citizens would be deprived of their wealth by policies dedicated to free handouts for those who had been less successful in accumulating material goods. After all, had God not decreed that haves and have nots were the natural order of things? I mean, he did agree to have his name attached to the paper money that allows the free market to function.

The diabolical notion that an entire society would benefit from broader success was economic heresy to a party that worshiped laissez-faire capitalism. Of course, the silliness of the argument becomes apparent when considering that the broader the access to the market, the more profitable and successful the market becomes. Nevertheless, most any discussion of equal opportunities quickly degenerates into argument over redistribution of wealth with little regard for either, and social engineering is inevitably injected into the equation. Before you know it, you have a full-blown argument regarding the role of overbearing government intent on taking one's hard-earned money and handing it to lazy people. The inability to have a cogent and intelligent discussion of economic theory opens the door to such nonsense.

The country was quickly becoming mired in what would become the most serious economic disruption since the 1930s. People were already feeling the discomfort of a runaway economic train which had been engineered by reckless money mongers on Wall Street, with our money fueling it. Playing the redistribution-of-wealth card was a last-ditch act of desperation to woo undecided independent voters. But by this point in the campaign—entering the final week—they had played nearly all their other cards, and Obama had weathered those attacks. Accusing Obama of a reckless economic platform in light of the utter devastation wrought by eight years of Republican disregard, deregulation, deficits, and debt made the strategy that much more curious. It was becoming apparent that the McCain-Palin experiment had been a terribly flawed one, a monumental miscalculation, and this only reinforced the despair and desperation that had set in among Republican voters and operatives throughout the nation.

In "Redistribute This," I point out the fruitlessness of this tactic, and once again pinpoint the fear factor that seemed to be the centerpiece of the Republican strategy for electoral success. I felt very confident that the Republican juggernaut was unraveling.

Posted October 28, 2008
Redistribute This

As the presidential election of 2008 careens to an end, the party of McPain seems to have zeroed in on one last diabolically desperate attempt to paint Obama as a socialist, this of course to go along with his unpatriotic, Muslim, domestic terror, anti-white, elitist tendencies: namely, he is a proponent of redistribution of wealth.

The clarion call to those who have yet to make up their minds in this election is that he wants to rob you of your money and give it to those who are far less deserving than yourself. What group of voters, exactly, is this supposed to appeal to? It is the last vestige of fear in a campaign that has borrowed not ninety percent, but one hundred percent from the Bush Administration playbook. Say it ain't so, Joe! Forget about Joe the Plumber; this is Joe Stalin.

The idiocy of this campaign will pave the way for a truly historic outcome: the election of an African-American named Barack Hussein Obama to the Oval Office. For this, I suppose we owe a debt of gratitude to these fear mongers. However, the damage done through the use of such tactics, the divisiveness sown by these pseudo-patriots, the resurgence of bigotry and hatred enshrined in the dangerous and reckless use of a strategy designed to segregate the country into good and bad, Christians versus pagans, white versus all others, will be with us for quite some time, and the healing process will be painful. Mercifully, it will begin soon.

But back to my original thought about distribution of wealth; the concept is not a new one. In fact, the proposition of a government collecting revenue so that essential needs of society can be addressed is as old as humankind. There is nothing wrong with the concept itself, only its application. There will always be disputes about how much to collect and how to spread it around. The real issue here is who gets what. In the Bush/McCain world, corporate welfare is good, public welfare is bad. Redistribution of wealth when it is targeted to the wealthy is positive; redistribution of wealth to the poor is negative.

This perverse line of thought is largely responsible for a society where the income gap continues to widen, where the middle-class, a term that has been AWOL from the Republican discourse and seemingly removed from the Republican dictionary altogether at this juncture, continues to shrink under the weight of wrong-headed and senseless economic and fiscal priorities. Every tax credit deposited at the altar of small business represents redistribution of wealth, every tax dollar devoted to strengthening our military represents redistribution of wealth, every investment in the nation's social and physical infrastructure represents redistribution of wealth.

So the next time your conservative puppets talk about redistribution of wealth as though it were a totally abhorrent concept, ask them if they support a strong defense or a strong economy, then tell them the cornerstone to both is a redistributive economic system that creates incentives through investment of tax dollars. There can be no doubt that there are good and bad investments, depending upon your ideological framework, but to merely imply that the concept of redistribution of wealth is inherently evil (read: socialistic) is simplistic and absurd. It is symptomatic of the campaign itself. Fear is pervasive and paralyzing; hope is focused and liberating. Fear traps us in a time warp; hope opens up a new horizon. Fear is grounded in the certainty of the past; hope allows us to explore the uncertainty of the future. This is what this campaign is all about.

The Evolution of Revolution:
An Attack upon Reason, Compromise, and the Constitution

NOVEMBER 4, 2008: OBAMA WINS
AMERICA ELECTS FIRST BLACK PRESIDENT

Article 8

November 5, 2008
Public Service and the Public Good

While basking in the afterglow of the Obama victory the day before, I felt it important and necessary to sound a clarion call for all public servants to renew their vows, in a manner of speaking, and rededicate themselves to the original purpose for public service—to make things better for all people. The anti-government forces that had been spawned by the Reagan Administration in 1981 had had a particularly harsh impact upon the public's confidence in government institutions and elected officials, and not without good reason. In essence, the Reagan Revolution filled government positions with people who believed that government was the problem and not the solution. Is it any wonder that faith and confidence in those very institutions would deteriorate?

The hope and energy Obama infused into the populace was a reincarnation of the positivity and hope that had captured the nation in John F. Kennedy's 1960 campaign. There was a palpable feeling that we had passed through a very dark period, but were entering a period of brightness and enlightenment. Now would be the time to roll up our sleeves and do the massive cleanup work that was required. The enormity of the task was mind numbing. Certainly it would take time, and there would be no immediate turnaround, but as the Chinese proverb instructs, "A journey of a thousand miles begins with a single step."

The first priority would be a renewed emphasis on the positive things government could deliver, which would hopefully restore the value of public service. After all, Obama was a former community organizer, and even though his service was regularly decried during the campaign, what was needed most in the national and international community was a rebuilding effort geared to restoring trust and a feeling that we are all in this together. I must admit I took it on the chin on numerous occasions over the years for even attempting to make the argument that government can work. This moment provided an opportunity to prove it.

But cynicism, distrust, paranoia, and a track record of government failures—including the response to Hurricane Katrina, the collapse of financial institutions, and endless wars—had all taken their toll. It would require a massive effort to convince the public that government was there to help them in times of crisis. Additionally, the substantively chronicled runaway influence peddling and corruption in our institutions had disabused the average individual of the notion that anything good would come from their government or elected officials. The damage was significant, and had been building for several decades. In my lifetime, one could trace a general dissatisfaction with government leadership back to the Vietnam War and the Johnson Administration. The general anger at and distrust of our governmental institutions grew as the war wore on.

The Watergate scandal, which erupted shortly after the 1972 reelection of Richard Nixon, cemented a pervasive feeling in the country that our institutions of leadership and governance had totally collapsed under the weight of massive corruption and the loss of our moral compass. Carter tried to restore integrity to the system, but his administration failed to genuflect to the prevailing power relationships between the executive and legislative branches of government. Additionally, Carter had too much respect for the people's ability to comprehend the need for a long-term agenda. This was particularly true of the changing international dynamic regarding the oil resources which powered our economic and industrial engines, not to mention the automobiles that had become integral to our culture. Reagan did not believe that issues were complicated or complex, but rather was simpatico with Americans' belief that everything could be simplified into us versus them, right versus wrong, black versus white. Technical complexity was something for the technicians to worry about; it would be morning in America again.

But the world was changing, and had developed a complex web of interrelationships that defied simple solutions. The government's inability to simply fix problems without involving sacrifice and a matrix of variables further frustrated a populace watching their country's prominent position in the world begin to slip.

Frustration and anger had been building for a generation, and change was occurring at a faster pace than the slow, incremental rate which best fits our system of checks and balances and protects our government from wild swings in policy.

Our system is built upon stability, and we are not well equipped to deal with rapid changes in national or international affairs. This was complicated at this time by the fact that we had been involved, since 1946, in a Cold War that allowed us to focus almost entirely on one enemy—the Soviet Union, with its ideology of communism. With the end of the Cold War, we were forced into focusing on a world system that had many moving parts rather than one monolithic enemy. This necessitated a shift in our approach to world events, and our dependence upon oil made us vulnerable to powers in places we had not had to pay much attention to when there were only two major superpowers. And technological advances in the second half of the twentieth century and the first decade of the new millennium forced us to contend with a world changing so rapidly that it made one's head spin. It was a new world for sure, and we were struggling to adjust to it.

To say that Obama inherited a shitstorm would be an understatement. The cumulative damage that had been inflicted upon the nation during the preceding eight years, the injury to our esteem both at home and abroad, and the worsening condition of the economy, the virtual disappearance of the middle class, under- and unemployment, health care unaffordable to larger numbers of workers, lost pensions, unfathomable levels of home foreclosures, lack of public confidence, growing frustration, and a sizable portion of the electorate and workforce who had resigned themselves to the fact that things would never again be the same all accompanied the job he had applied for and won.

It would take a magician and a master politician to make even a dent in the problems facing the nation and subsequently the world. But I was and still am convinced that the most effective way to combat this miasma is a strong and effective federal government, working in conjunction with state and local entities to restore faith and trust in our collective ability to rebuild a sense of community which had been crushed by a regime that had little use and no respect for those very same institutions. Government is not the answer for everything that ails us, but a properly functioning set of government institutions can provide a framework and compass for success. The New Deal; *Brown v. Board of Education*; Social Security; The Great Society, including the Voting Rights Act, civil rights legislation, Medicare and Medicaid; affirmative action; and a whole host of safety-net programs to protect the most vulnerable among us are examples of government playing a constructive role in fashioning a society that was to be envied and emulated.

In "Government Can Work," I attempted to outline the justification for a recommitment to public service and a restoration of faith and confidence in government institutions that would inspire a generation which had lost trust in them. Unless we recapture the assurance and swagger that was a hallmark of our growth in the preceding century, we are destined to muddle through at a time when others are surging forward.

Posted November 5, 2008
Government Can Work

Ten years ago a friend and colleague of mine was teaching a course at the Kennedy School of Government and invited me to lecture his students. I gratefully accepted his challenge and titled my lecture "Government Can Work." For this I was rewarded by being introduced as an Irresolute Idealist.

Over the course of the last thirty years I have been involved in a myriad of public policy issues, a veritable generalist in a world of specialization. I have also had the unique honor and opportunity to speak before various elected officials' leadership training institutes in my current capacity as assistant for intergovernmental affairs for the Governor, a position that allows me to interact on a daily basis with local elected officials representing nearly 2,600 municipalities across the Commonwealth of Pennsylvania.

Each time I have an opportunity to address gatherings of students interested in public policy or elected officials, I preface my remarks by lauding the notion that public service is a noble profession. Similarly, I remind everyone within earshot on a daily basis that elected officials represent not special interests, but public interests. Unfortunately, this concept is too often lost upon our intergovernmental institutions and those who run them.

Also unfortunate is the idea that one who promotes the notion that government can work for the betterment of society and the greater good should or could be labeled as an irresolute idealist. I always remind people that the underlying rationale for involvement in public service or elective office ought to be to make things better for people. When this basic principle is lost or becomes clouded it demeans the purpose of government and those who have devoted their professional lives to make it effective.

Such is the case currently. Eight years of outright incompetence, indifference, and seeming contempt for the institutions of government itself have deepened the cynicism in the public at large towards its government and provided red meat to those constituencies who unconsciously benefit from government programs while decrying their availability to others. The contempt that many conservatives feel for government finds great comfort in attacks against the notion of progressive taxation, for instance, and the notion that redistributive schemes are anything more than merely setting priorities.

As this sorry Administration limps towards a merciful termination, as Dubya slinks back to Crawford to do whatever it is he does when not making the world a more dangerous and unsafe place, let us as a society renew our social contract with our government and its leaders.

Yesterday's historic election of Barack Obama as the forty-fourth president of the United States represents many magnificent things to many people, but to me it most importantly represents the triumph of a return to good government and public service. Not since John F. Kennedy's election in 1960 has the country been as energized or excited about charting a new course.

It is now time for those who have already dedicated their lives to the pursuit of public service to step up to the plate and make known their intentions to use their considerable skills and experience to make this government as efficient and as effective as it can be. This will be no simple task; the clean-up work that needs to be done is enormous. But I would argue that this is the true essence of patriotism. Restoring respect for and confidence in our government will require a rededication on behalf of all who believe in government as a solution not the problem.

I vividly remember President Clinton calling together a meeting of political appointees immediately after the Oklahoma City bombings. Nearly 3,000 strong gathered at Constitution Hall in Washington, DC to hear from the Commander in Chief that day and I will never forget him telling us that day that "You cannot love your country and hate your government."

Today begins a new chapter in the magnificent story that is this country. Of all the things for which we can be proud of, reconstituting the public consensus that public servants serve the public good must rank as one of our top priorities. It just might make irresolute idealists out of us all.

Article 9

November 11, 2008
It's About the Kids

A week after the election, I was excited to travel back to my undergraduate alma mater to address students on the importance of the election they had just witnessed. Although my travels would take me to a rural backwater in south Georgia—not the most hospitable place for a person with a liberal agenda or leanings—it was an institution of higher learning, and had steadily climbed in stature over the years. My faith in youth and education superseded geopolitical considerations. Sure, they were bound to be more conservative than college students elsewhere, but they were college kids who had yet to become jaded and cynical; thus, there was hope.

I had made several trips back to Georgia Southern University over the three decades since I'd graduated, and had thoroughly enjoyed the opportunity to talk with future generations of leaders who would soon be making their impact upon the world. Of course, the Obama campaign had made a concerted effort to draw younger voters into its orbit, a strategy that had traditionally met with little success. The strides made by the Obama campaign would most certainly lay the bedrock for the future, and its capture of youth turnout and the youth vote represented a significant shift in electoral campaigning.

As a father of two teenage sons, I have a special appreciation for the sheer physical and intellectual energy that resides in our youth, and this was enhanced by the volume of information and access to information readily available to them via the Internet and twenty-four-hour news cycles. I was absolutely enthralled by the reception I encountered and by the degree of participation and lines of questioning these students presented to me.

I came away from the experience convinced that the kids are indeed all right. They possess an incalculable wealth of knowledge and excitement that needs to be harnessed and redirected as we seek to build a better world for their future. To squander such an opportunity would border on criminality. I believe that we, as a society, must dedicate ourselves to fulfilling our responsibility to leave the world in better shape than we found it for the sake of generations to come.

On several fronts, particularly climate change, we have failed miserably to present our progeny with a fighting chance to live in a better environment than we did. By not providing our youth with an opportunity to participate in a vibrant economy having jobs which pay a living wage and the chance to do as well as we did, and access to education and the perpetuation of a middle class, we forfeit our solemn duties to our children.

It is fair for our youth to criticize many of the decisions we as a society have rendered, leaving the consequences to be shouldered by them. It is fair for them to question our commitment to their well-being, and to rework and reverse bad policies and decisions. We must encourage them to question aggressively, and then respond constructively and appropriately. Far too many of our youth, armed with information and keen insight that belies their ages, are legitimately concerned that their futures look bleak and that traditional avenues of success, such as education, offer little opportunity for them. It is a sad indictment indeed, and one that we must address with vigor and honesty.

In "The Kids Are All Right," my goal was to show that the hope and change that had just captured the nation was equally vibrant among our youth. It was an encouraging sign, and must be cultivated to its fullest. I came away from my engagement with a healthy dose of optimism.

Posted November 11, 2008
The Kids Are All Right

I came face to face with the future this past week, and I am as positive as at any point in my lifetime about it. If you have not been on a college campus lately, and if you don't truly believe that what has been missing from our politics and political debate has been an energy and enthusiasm for hopefulness and creativity, and if you still don't accept the idea that change and the need for it is more than an empty slogan, then do yourself a favor and connect with today's youth.

I had the distinct honor to travel to Statesboro, Georgia following last week's election to talk with students at my alma mater about politics and policies. Although I have addressed dozens of students on college campuses over the past twenty years or so, the level of engagement I witnessed this past week far surpasses any I have discerned since I was a college student in the early 1970s. And post-election analyses validate that the phenomena is widespread among our youth today.

To whatever or whomever you may attribute this surge of interest, it is critically important that our governmental institutions and leaders honor the trust that our youth has placed in them by delivering sound, effective, and forward-looking programs and policies that will address the problems that threaten our present and our future. It is our solemn responsibility to preserve and perpetuate their involvement.

Many of us have decried the pervasive cynicism that has captured the public's attention for far too long. Some, me included, have despaired of the lack of involvement and interest on the part of the electorate that has given rise to the hijacking of our processes and institutions by special interests.

Even among those who have remained involved in government for the purest of reasons, the line between public and special interest has blurred. Hence, you find competition between various levels of government (ie, federal, state, local) over scarcer and scarcer financial resources, rather than a truly intergovernmental partnership designed to maximize the public interest for all citizens.

The grass-roots nature of the Obama campaign has been wildly successful. It has surpassed the expectations of the most experienced political practitioners. It has connected on a level that has meaning and importance to most Americans, the local level. It is therefore critical that this connection not be severed or disrupted by drawing artificial distinctions between levels of government. We must ensure a seamless flow of functions and duties, a working partnership between federal, state, and local governments, a level of cooperation that enhances equity and efficiency that encourages our youth to remain engaged and involved and willing to offer resolutions rather than reticence.

And already, we must lay the foundation for the next generation of youth, so we can continue to capitalize on their energy, innovation, and creativity for the future. The kids are all right.

The Evolution of Revolution:
An Attack upon Reason, Compromise, and the Constitution

Article 10

November 14, 2008
Back in the Peach State

While visiting my alma mater in Georgia, I was drawn to the spectacle of a special runoff election to fill a US Senate seat that would occur in early December. It featured a character by the name of Saxby Chambliss, a fellow who had run an absolutely despicable campaign six years earlier to defeat Max Cleland. What made that election so appalling were the tactics employed. The Chambliss campaign suggested that because Cleland was a Democrat, he was not a patriot, despite the fact that Max had served his country with distinction in Vietnam and had left there a triple amputee.

Max had served his country in war and on the political battlefield, having been secretary of state in Georgia, head of the Veterans Administration in Washington, and a US Senator. But what made this current race more galling than most was the involvement of recently defeated presidential candidate John McCain, himself a war veteran, campaigning for Chambliss and against a fellow war hero. I realize that politics makes strange bedfellows, but when you disparage a patriot in the name of patriotism, something is dreadfully wrong.

Politics trumped patriotism six years earlier, and McCain should have refused to be a part of the current race. It seemed hypocritical that he would allow himself to participate in the situation given the circumstances that had led to Chambliss assuming the seat in the first place. So much for that well-advertised campaign slogan the Republicans trotted out, proclaiming "Country First."

This was similar to the swiftboating of Democratic presidential candidate John Kerry in 2004. These self-proclaimed patriots were openly defaming the sacrifices true patriots had made for their country. It was all for political gain, and totally contemptible. Chambliss was elected in the runoff, which was expected, but McCain could have showed a smidgeon of decency by refusing to be part of it. He didn't. The 2008 McCain was very different from the 2000 version, and it was little wonder that he had fared so badly in the recently concluded presidential election.

I guess I should be beyond taking any of this personally, and certainly should harbor no illusions that integrity plays a role in elections. But I'd hoped McCain would stand on principle. I had watched him up-close in the New Hampshire primary in 2000 while working for the Gore campaign, and I felt he would present the most difficult challenge to us. He seemed to be grounded and centered on issues and, while admittedly conservative, had demonstrated that he was willing to swallow pride for advancing policies and politics that were good for the country.

After the 2000 election, I was invited to a gathering at Arianna Huffington's house in Los Angeles where McCain was the featured attraction. I found his comments that evening encouraging, and given the turnout of Hollywood celebrities—a heartily liberal-leaning bunch—I was encouraged that he might be a person who would put country first. But that was the old McCain; this was the new one. I could stomach the old model, but the new model lacked style, class, and appeal. I guess old soldiers don't die, they just fade away.

In "Georgia on My Mind," I took a decidedly personal swipe at what I viewed as an act of hypocrisy. I had known Max Cleland since my days working in the Georgia State Senate, and you will not find a more honorable individual. To me, it was very personal.

Posted November 14, 2008
Georgia on My Mind

Although I am not a native Georgian, I hold fond affection for the place. I attended college there, worked in the Georgia State Senate, stumped in New Hampshire with the Peanut Brigade in January, 1976, for former Governor Carter, and worked in Washington for former Senator Herman Talmadge. Over the years, I have returned on occasion to visit friends I still have there, converse often with college professors at my alma mater, and I keep in touch with a mentor and friend of mine, a former state senator and lieutenant governor. So it is not far-fetched to say that Georgia is often on my mind.

During my early years in politics, I knew Max Cleland when he was [Georgia] secretary of state and later head of the Veterans Administration in the Carter Administration. I worked in Washington when he was first elected US Senator. If one strove to define the true meaning of sacrifice, Max stands as a living, breathing example of what it means to "leave it on the field." We often use that term to define athletic achievement, but in this case it applies to the field of battle. Max is a triple amputee with a heart of gold and a steely determination that defies description. He is truly the embodiment of an American hero.

Six years ago he was savaged in his reelection campaign by one of the most despicable acts of political opportunism I have seen in my thirty years in politics. The person directing these attacks was none other than current US Senator Saxby Chambliss, and today that individual finds himself in a tight reelection runoff that will not be decided until December 2.

The stakes could not be higher. In order for the Democrats in the US Senate to reach a filibuster-proof sixty votes; they need to capture that seat, along with Minnesota and Alaska. Georgia will be treated to a steady parade of political celebrities over the next three weeks or so. The carnival-like atmosphere began yesterday with the arrival of ringmaster John McCain, the 2008 version. Lest we not confuse the clown of today with the P.T. Barnum of 2000, there was John McCain, former prisoner of war, former disparager of the politics of personal destruction, former critic of the tactics and ads of the Chambliss campaign of 2002, speaking out forcefully for that very individual.

The transformation of John McCain is complete. Each time there is a glimpse of the old version, such as the most gracious concession speech just a little over a week ago, it is as if the devil himself snatches back his soul and he delivers on whatever Faustian pledge he made in his vain attempt to be something other than he actually is. Sometimes individuals are humbled by defeat; other times they are hardened by it. I had hoped that in McCain's case the former would apply, it seems not to be the case.

So I truly hope that the voters of Georgia rise to correct the injustice that was perpetrated upon them six years ago. You are in the spotlight, and it is your turn to show the world that politics as usual is no longer acceptable or desirable. As we enter into a new era of hopefulness and change, you can do your part and reject the desperation of a status quo that has ill served this nation and hardworking Americans who love their country.

Max Cleland paid another sacrifice six years ago, and politics trumped patriotism. We cannot allow that to stand. McCain should understand this far better than others, yet he has demonstrated that politics is more important than country and integrity.

I believe that the greatest sin that a politician can commit is that of hypocrisy. The hypocrisy of having John McCain weigh in on this race, hopefully, will resonate with the voters of Georgia and his impact will actually have a negative effect on the candidacy of Saxby Chambliss. If so, Max, this one is for you.

Article 11

November 19, 2008
Gracious in Victory

One of the cruelest ironies of the 2008 election was the involvement of Connecticut Senator Joe Lieberman in the McCain campaign—yes, the same man who was graced with the privilege of being Democrat Al Gore's running mate in the 2000 election. Enraged Democrats and progressive-minded partisans were ready for Obama to seek some degree of revenge upon the wayward Democratic senator once the election had concluded. Similarly, there was a question as to how Obama would relate to his two vanquished rivals for the presidency—New York Senator Hillary Clinton, whom he defeated in the primaries, and Arizona Senator John McCain, whom he defeated for the presidency.

Obama was facing the first real test of the post-partisanship he had called for in his quest for hope and change. He graciously reached out to both Lieberman and McCain, and of course he offered Hillary the most important job in his administration by making her secretary of state. The latter was brilliant, and she served with distinction. The president-elect's delicate handling of McCain and Lieberman reflected his intention to honor the words and ideas he represented on the campaign trail. Obama was absolutely convinced that through a willingness to work together, he could convince former foes and current opponents of the need to overcome the rancor of the campaign trail and roll up their sleeves to forward the interests of the country.

It is interesting to look back at this period to see how he pursued his post-election agenda through consensus, compromise, and a willingness to give the benefit of the doubt that once the game had ended, all could shake hands and move on. He would discover, however, that his desire for a post-partisanship presidency would have a very short shelf life indeed.

In "Obama Diplomacy," I made clear, as did he, what his preferred style would be in dealing with legislative opposition. I would be disingenuous if I did not interject that I was skeptical that the Obama prescription would work. I had spent over two decades in DC and had witnessed how much things had changed in my lifetime. The caliber of elected officials was different, partisanship was punctuated with shrillness to a much greater extent than when I started, comity and civility were disappearing at a rapid rate, and the infusion of large sums of money into the processes of government had changed the system in a very short period of time. But as a competitive human being, I was astounded at the restraint and calm demeanor of the president and was willing to sit back and admire him while giving him a chance to work his magic on the new world order. He should be lauded for his patience, perspective, and his overall willingness to deal with the vanquished as a gracious sportsman. In time his patience would test the patience of supporters like me, but at this point he would be afforded the benefit of the doubt.

Posted November 19, 2008
Obama Diplomacy

My natural inclination, like others who are still savoring the sweet taste of triumph on November 4, is to exact a pound of flesh from the vanquished. Eight years of thievery, deception, ineptitude, incompetence, anti-intellectual arrogance, and sheer stupidity will do that. The first opportunity for the president-elect to show there is a new sheriff in town would have been to hoist Joe Lieberman by his miserable petard and banish him from partaking in the spoils of victory. Make no mistake about it, I found his actions despicable, his words menacing, and his judgment terribly flawed. It would have delighted many on the left to make an example of this Democratic traitor.

But for all the short-term satisfaction such an act might have engendered, in the long run it would have been counterproductive and hypocritical. It would have cut against the grain of everything that the president-elect campaigned for under the rubric of change. Change not only implies, but demands, that we seek to accomplish our program and policy goals for the country utilizing a different process orientation. It is critically important that we divorce ourselves from the blood sport of politics and the impotence of partisan governance that has paralyzed our system and left us with the immense problems now facing the next administration. The key to leadership here is to take the anger and channel it into constructive energy, and that is exactly what Obama has done.

Similarly, Obama reaching out to Clinton and McCain, two former rivals, is also critically important to moving forward to address these problems. One might think that this requires Herculean inner strength on the part of the president-elect, but I tend to believe that it is totally in keeping with the cool and calm demeanor he demonstrated as the economy began imploding just a few months back. In my calculus, Obama's studious attention to that disaster, coupled with McCain's erratic overreaction, did more to swing undecided independent voters than anything else. Therefore, to succumb to the emotions of the moment with respect to Sen. Lieberman would have been out of character and legitimately raised questions as to who the real Obama is.

The most important variable in all of this is the ability to accomplish a change in the direction of the country. The course Obama has laid out will require consensus, an old-fashioned word that too often has not been invoked in the past eight years. The ability to achieve consensus is made all that more difficult if you divide up the world into red teams and blue teams. The president-elect understands this, and has understood it for some time. Sacrifice also requires consensus, and we simply cannot escape from the current problems facing our nation without a sense of commitment to our ideals that will force us to change our ways of doing things.

What we are witnessing is the first test of statesmanship from our new leader. We may not readily see it, but he does. We may struggle with the counter-intuitiveness of these actions, but he does not. What we are getting is exactly what we found so appealing about the candidate in the first place: namely, he actually believes in his words. That, in itself, is reason to celebrate. But far more importantly, the long term results we will experience from such dedication will be well worth the pain in achieving them.

The noble appeal of public service is to get things done. After a long period of unintended consequences, this is a refreshing ideal. So let us hold our powder and allow the man to get to the job of repairing our broken system. And as we should, we will let the people of Connecticut render their verdict come election time. For now, we must put that aside and set to work on the people's business. One must hope that in the process of his rehabilitation, the good senator might be more susceptible to return the favor of forgiveness on issues where he might be straddling the fence. In the end, the benefits of this decision will outweigh the costs and we surely do need a studious sense of cost-benefit analysis as we approach the difficult dilemmas facing our nation's future.

I believe that Obama has passed his first post-election test with flying colors. Now it is on to the next one, and the next one, and the next one…

Article 12

November 21, 2008
What Is Good for GM Is Good for America!

The transition from Bush to Obama seemed to take an agonizingly long time, and as in all transitions, the potential for last-minute mischief remained a great concern. This was particularly true considering the circumstances resulting in the hijacking of the 2000 election and the mean-spiritedness exhibited by the henchmen who were unfortunately charged with running the country during those eight woeful years.

As the economy tumbled into the Great Recession with the Bush administration still in nominal control of the government, an appropriate yet simultaneously sickening spectacle took place on Capitol Hill just two weeks after the election and two months ahead of the transfer of power. America's large automobile manufacturers had mismanaged their industry for decades, and the horrible consequences that would befall the millions of hardworking Americans who had toiled on the assembly lines and in ancillary businesses that supported this industry were raising their ugly head.

Congress, always vigilant after the fact, decided to bring the heads of these companies before them to see what the hell was going on. And there they sat, transported to DC via private jets, and pompously positioned at the witness table to explain themselves. These men—and yes, they were all men—should have been charged with criminal conspiracy against the American workers who relied upon their judgment to make a decent living.

But in a show of abject audacity, they proceeded to follow the predictable tactic of extorting Congress to bail them out of the dire straits they had created on behalf of the American economy, automobile industry workers, and supply firms dependent on the industry. There was not a scintilla of humility or remorse. An industry ruled by managers who, just a short time ago, had killed the electric car, who had assiduously buried their collective heads in the sand as a world running out of fossil fuels demanded their product adjust accordingly, and who failed to recognize that foreign competition was unmercifully rendering their products less acceptable to the consumer, sat there and, with straight faces, extorted the people's elected representatives into bailing their asses out of the disaster they had fomented.

Of course, only the most cynical among us would seriously consider allowing the industry to collapse. Not even the most ardent free-market capitalists, who constantly and consistently decry government welfare to those who really need it, would allow this giant business to fall under its own weight of mismanagement. These tyrants of industry hid behind the human shields of American workers, and demanded public monies to bail out their private sector misdeeds. It was a foregone conclusion that such assistance would be forthcoming, but as with the Wall Street tycoons and charlatans who were protected because they belonged to an industry deemed too big to fail, not one would go to jail for large-scale thievery and deception. Too big to fail—and too big to go to jail!

The sorry spectacle unfolded at a dizzying clip as George W. Bush prepared to head into the Texas sunset. And as is often the case, the cruel irony of passing the buck—and, in this case, the billions upon billions of bucks—to the new guy must have given even the most optimistic hope-and-change advocates in the soon-to-be-installed Obama administration pause and concern.

My father, who is not particularly political or cynical, always told me that if you were going to steal, steal in a big way. From his observations, he had learned that society and its protectors always went after the low-hanging fruit, and the old maxim "You can't fight city hall" applied to all—except those who owned city hall. I had learned the hard way, up close and personal, that the big-time crooks seemed to never get punished. Here again was another example of that unfortunate maxim. In "The Hits Just Keep Coming," I registered my disgust and amazement at how the biggest crooks not only seem to walk away from their crimes, but are also awarded with golden parachutes, promotions, and bonuses. Our system of incentives seems to be awfully cockeyed. But what do I know? I never have, nor will I ever, be a part of that crooked class.

Posted November 21, 2008
The Hits Just Keep Coming

In another time and another place, the captains of the automotive industry might be tried for crimes against humanity. This week, they paraded like mindless peacocks before Congress with arrogance, insolence, and a brazen audacity that is almost impossible to describe. Adding further insult to injury, with collective hats in their hands, they pleaded for a monetary reprieve that would allow them to continue to hold both the American economy and millions of workers hostage to the most pernicious mismanagement of our domestic manufacturing sector history has ever recorded.

So pathetic is this sorry story that Congress was left collectively scratching its head and wondering if, in fact, the American people could allow even this grossest level of malfeasance to go unpunished, while at the same time realizing that the costs of allowing the industry to self-destruct most likely far outweighs the benefits of rescuing it from an ignominious death.

While the stock market, and hence the bulk of middle-class retirement savings, cascades under the relentless waves of bad economic news, while the economy sputters to a virtual halt, while unemployment claims climb to stratospheric levels and layoffs mount at a dizzying pace, deep in our hearts we know that even this clueless and callous administration cannot afford to watch the unfolding economic apocalypse without dipping deeper into the seemingly inexhaustible money well that drains from our children's future.

It seems almost impossible to imagine a more debilitating ending to what will be one of the darkest periods in American electoral history. The hits just keep on coming. Jimmy Buffet sings "if we weren't all crazy we would all go insane." Well this seems like one of those times. It seems like the only good news we have had in a long time are the results of November 4. And keeping with the rock-lyric motif, maybe "the darkest hour is just before dawn."

We must and we will rise above it, but you simply cannot help but wonder how different things would have been had the great heist known as the 2000 election not happened. The lost lives, lost international integrity, lost savings, lost homes, lost jobs, lost momentum with respect to domestic programs, including alternative energy development, repair of our crumbling physical infrastructure, a broken health-care system, and a rapidly shrinking middle class all point toward a government on political autopilot. We have been rudderless for some time, and it shows. The cumulative toll in terms of dollars is staggering, but in terms of damage to the societal psyche it is incalculable.

The challenges ahead are so daunting as to make even the calmest and shrewdest heads spin. The call to public service is now more urgent than at any time in our nation's history. Obama is the right person at the right time, but he will need to summon legions of individuals dedicated to the prospect of toiling in the fields to resurrect and reconstruct a strong and vibrant society.

Placing aside our anger, we must strive above all things to do the right thing, and this means removing as many obstacles to progress as possible as we build a better world. It means setting aside our differences and our prejudices.

The lessons of the last eight years are harsh, yet we must learn from them and never allow them to be repeated. The next two months simply cannot go fast enough, for as we sit here today, the administration is plotting to undercut the wishes of the electorate, and the opportunities for last minute mischief remain. So put on your work boots and roll up your sleeves and join in the effort to reclaim our country. Can you think of a better way to spend the next four to eight years?

Article 13

December 3, 2008
Stimulating the Economy

As the Obama administration started to take form, it became painfully clear that time was of the essence. I will never forget the impatience felt by many, including myself, that the transition was simply too long; we had nary a minute to waste in correcting the missteps and recovering from the fumbles of the inept Bush administration. Yet it seemed like they would never leave.

It was clear that order number one would be a large fiscal-stimulus bill, a sufficiently strong jolt to an economy that was on life support. As the incoming administration started to assemble its team and prioritize its agenda, there were positive signs that, true to his campaign promises, this was a president who would be willing to keep his eyes fixed forward, to not let the past muddy the present waters or prevent what needed to happen from happening.

In putting together the stimulus bill, Obama reached out to all parties concerned. But particularly important from my perspective as one who had steadfastly tried to champion the need for intergovernmental cooperation, it appeared as though he was willing to involve governors, mayors, and other local elected officials; non-governmental organizations; community activists; and a broad array of bipartisan actors in the mix. Of course, this elicited groans from many circles, harkening back to the Jacksonian maxim that "To the victors belong the spoils."

But in the precariously balanced federalist system of government we call representative democracy, compromise and consensus is a highly valued and treasured commodity. Intergovernmental cooperation entails bipartisanship, as many officials at other levels of government compose a system of interconnectedness that defies partisan labeling. For instance, many Republican governors would be consulted. But this was the type of post-partisanship presidency that Obama had run on, and that would be how he would proceed.

Obama may have not been a creature of Washington, but this he understood well. I must admit I was heartened that after a hard-fought contest, he was willing to offer an olive branch, and felt that even though there would be a loyal opposition, there would be a sufficient number of reasonable elected officials from both parties to allow the people's will to be executed. Of course, this would prove to be an unfounded assumption for many reasons. But in the early days, it seemed like a fresh, new beginning, repairing the damaged machine that was the US economy.

In "No Rear-View Mirrors: Managing the Economic Crisis," I expressed my hope that change would come, and felt confident that, as always in times of crisis, we would transcend partisanship and act in the best interest of the country. It appeared as though we were headed in the right direction—forward. There was no time to look backward; it might have made some feel better, but would have been counterproductive and divisive in the long run. I thought it would have been perfectly acceptable to investigate and prosecute many in the Bush administration for war crimes, but did not expect it would happen. There was no time to waste on revenge. This was the attitude that prevailed leading up to Christmas, 2008. Joy to the world!

Posted December 3, 2008
No Rear-View Mirrors: Managing the Economic Crisis

The president-elect has, so far, shown an uncanny ability to bring all parties to the table as he carefully fills in the outlines of his broad policy agenda. Allies, adversaries, and agnostics all seem to be willing to follow his leadership as he aggressively seeks to quell the roiling seas and extinguish the burning fires that await his presidency. Beyond his cabinet assemblage, he has now ventured into the thicket of bailout politics with a vigor and sophistication not seen in many years.

Managing inclusion can be a tricky business, but it is crucial in times of crisis, and we are in a bona fide crisis with an economy spiraling deeper and deeper into the abyss, the recent events in Mumbai reminding us of just how precarious and dangerous a place the world actually is, a worsening situation in Afghanistan, and the continuing quagmire in Iraq.

With little time for recriminations against the woefully inept administration about to mercifully leave office, Obama is showing that his focus and concern is on moving forward, not looking backward.

And oh, how easy is would be to just look back and start casting blame. The only real lament seems to be that given the constitutional constraints of only allowing one president at a time, it is a shame that we have to wait until January 20 to actually start putting new policies and programs into place.

His latest mastery of difficulties involves ensuring that the nation's states and localities play a pivotal role in putting together an economic recovery program that will maximize the creation of jobs, repair a crumbling infrastructure, and minimize the burdens and hardships on individuals hardest hit by the now official recession.

Our federalist system is dependent upon a working relationship between the central government and state and local jurisdictions. Intergovernmental cooperation is a prerequisite for effective, efficient, and equitable governance. States and cities, counties and boroughs, townships and towns of all sizes and compositions, both rural and urban, are disproportionately adversely affected by economic downturns. Their collective ability to manage budgets as the economy worsens is constrained by balanced-budget requirements and often by state-imposed limits to raise revenues.

One of the unique aspects to the current reaction to our worsening economic troubles seems to be a national will, and a bipartisan one at that, to adopt a Keynesian approach to spending our way out of this mess. John Maynard Keynes believed that it was okay for the government to borrow money to lift the economy out of recession. Of course, the implicit agreement is that you pay it back once the economy recovers, and that will be a massive undertaking to be sure. Deficits do matter, and balanced budgets in times of prosperity are fiscally prudent and responsible. However, borrowing can also be prudent and responsible, assuming one has the will and the ability to repay the loans. At this point, we have little choice.

Having the nation's governors and mayors, Democrats and Republicans alike, join in the effort to create an effective infrastructure-led recovery program will further strengthen the hand the forty-fourth president will have to play after January 20. The times ahead will be difficult, and the economic hardships will be spread broadly. However, the foundation being laid at this point will help to shorten the time it will take for the economic recovery to take hold.

State and local officials are keenly aware of the needs and capabilities of their respective jurisdictions. They will be called upon to actively implement whatever recovery plan is put into place; thus they have a right and a need to be involved in its construction. Obama sees this and is acting upon his best instincts for bringing all working partners into the fold. This is not just smart politics, it is smart policy. He realizes he needs broad support for the tough decisions and hard choices that need to be made, and he is going about securing that support.

There is evidence of a pattern here: the need to engage partners, the need to garner the greatest degree of consensus possible, utilization of diplomatic skills to attack problems, and a vision and steadfast dedication to implement it. In a weaker moment, I could go on to say that has been missing for a long time, but that would be looking backward, and the mantra henceforth will be forward-looking and visionary.

But if only January 20 were tomorrow…

Article 14

December 7, 2008
Christmas Spirit

It was becoming painfully obvious that by virtue of an unyielding electoral calendar and an administration asleep at the wheel, the two-and-a-half month interval between Obama's victory at the polls and the assumption of office was too long. Imbued with Christmas spirit and a wistful and wishful deviousness, I wondered out loud if we might not be able to find an extraordinary solution to what were surely extraordinarily dire times, which would be to buy out George W. Bush's contract on America.

Realizing that the piece would be written tongue-in-cheek, there were some very real considerations. First, it was meant to dramatize the incredibly serious death spiral we were facing; second, it was meant to teach a lesson to all those who had blithely decided that their choice of president did not have serious consequences.

Elections do have consequences; this was the lesson from 2000. I had often found myself wondering how things might have been different if Gore had won that year. It is a painful exercise for those who care, and I do. We cannot waste time thinking about what should have or could have been, but I cannot believe that things would not have been better for the country and for the world. But that's the way it goes.

In "I Have a (Christmas) Dream," I intended to draw attention to the possibility that the transition process was insufficient in times when a headless and destructive administration had lost control of events and had no idea what to do about it. Seriously, I do not know if there has ever been consideration of changing the length of time between incoming and outgoing administrations, but maybe there should be.

Posted December 7, 2008
I Have a (Christmas) Dream

'Tis the season to be jolly, 'tis the season to be thankful, 'tis the season to give, 'tis the season to dream! I want to be the good team player, the magnanimous victor, the calm voice of reason above the din of the legitimately disgusted and angry patriots who have watched this idiotic administration run the ship of state aground, but alas I care too much about those who ultimately pay the price for such malfeasance: namely, the incredible shrinking middle class.

While the president has been mindlessly absent for the bulk of his tenure, his hand at the helm at this moment in time, asleep, blissfully ignorant, thirsting for the time he can return to Crawford, or Dallas, or wherever next he can be taken care of, as he has his entire life, seemingly tests the true strength of the glue that holds this country together.

If George W. Bush is truly looking at his legacy, I have a suggestion: your greatest contribution to the nation would be to magnanimously suggest that for the next six weeks or so the country will be guided by a co-presidency, one that allows you to continue to act like you are in control while actually allowing Obama to make decisions. After all, the only difference from the last eight years would be that Obama would replace Cheney, so really, Mr. President, there is no difference at all as far as you are concerned.

Of course, if you decide to take early retirement, I would gladly accede to allowing a portion of the economic recovery stimulus to be used as a golden parachute. This is one time when it actually would be a good investment to heap an obscene amount of cash on an unsuccessful executive in order to save the company, or in this case the country.

I try to catch myself and wonder if I am not overreacting, but seriously, how many people, both unemployed and underemployed, the latter being the great hidden secret the family does not want to face, sort of like Uncle John's drinking problem, or Aunt Millie's kleptomania, that is spinning exponentially out of control and threatens to accelerate the misery index beyond anything we are now facing.

The economic correction we are now looking at is a reaction to the carelessness of a deregulatory fervor that has been underway for some time now. It has been fueled by the darkest forces that justify the laissez-faire delusions certain conservatives have brought to the dismal science of economics. Trickle down is now cascading upon us, sweeping us further and further down the river. And to continue to scramble metaphors, if only to attempt to ease the pain, millions of Americans will be left up the creek without a paddle.

The need to act and act forcefully is now. Obama realizes this, the American people realize this, Congress realizes this, and sadly, even Dubya has an inkling that something is not right. So, Mr. President, you have sleepwalked through eight years; your administration has committed actions that few doubt should result in criminal prosecution; tens of thousands of people have died, many defending your decisions and honoring your high office; the world is a far more dangerous place than it was and it should be; you have squandered the Nation's moral authority on issues like human rights, civil rights, and climate change, have you not done enough?

You can save your pride, save your honor, save your proverbial rear end, you can play president for the rest of your time, but you have no right to make decisions that will hinder or impede the incoming administration in its efforts to try to put back together the broken mess you have created and will be leaving behind. You will live the rest of your life in taxpayer-funded comfort. When is enough, enough?

Do the right thing. Schedule a press conference immediately, announce that in an unprecedented move you and the president-elect will together guide the country through these difficult times, and you will defer to the incoming administration on matters that will be their responsibility on January 20, which is to say everything.

I realize that this will not happen, but sometimes you just have to take your shot. It is only a dream, but what a dream. Mr. President, you have lived a charmed life, you will continue to live a charmed life; you are a very lucky soul. But there are so, so many who work hard, strive to make life better for themselves and their families, find themselves living on the edge, from paycheck to paycheck, or worse yet find themselves falling behind, and then there are the unlucky ones who never had a chance. So this Christmas season, live out the dream, and just stay out of the way while the serious folks take over.

It could be the twenty-first-century version of *A Christmas Carol*, *It's a Beautiful Life*, and the Grinch all rolled up into one, but it's only a dream, right?

The Evolution of Revolution:
An Attack upon Reason, Compromise, and the Constitution

Article 15

December 19, 2008
Interminable

When George W. Bush traveled to the Middle East, a member of the foreign press showed the ultimate display of disgust and disrespect by throwing a shoe at the president. He missed. Subsequently, an electronic version titled sockandawe.com became the rage on computers everywhere, registering some 46 million hits. The object was to see how many hits one could inflict upon Dubya. It was all quite hilarious and innocent. From my perch in the governor's office, I would take a break and test my skills. I took great pleasure in perfecting my expertise at this game, and found it very therapeutic.

It did, however, mask a much more serious and discomforting reality; our image and level of respect internationally had suffered tremendously during the previous eight years. It is hard to conceptualize the degree of hatred that our misadventures in Iraq and Afghanistan have engendered over that period of time, and that continues until this day. Elections do have consequences. Neo-conservative policies that took hold early in the Bush administration will haunt us for decades. The amount of damage and destruction done in the aftermath of 9/11 will surely be the subject of volumes of study by historians, and I will leave the judgment and verdict to those who have the luxury of time to study them. But I cannot help but feel that we have paid and will pay heavily for these actions.

As I look back on this collection of articles, I realize how interminable the transition between Bush and Obama seemed. This is the third article I'd penned in a little over two weeks, moaning that the days dragged on like months. What particularly sparked my angst at this moment, however, was the fact that both Bush and Cheney had commenced something approaching a victory tour touting their—and I use this term advisedly—"accomplishments."

This gave new meaning to Nero fiddling while Rome burned. These comrades in criminality were either so hopelessly out of touch that they had no concept what they were doing, or had made a deviously conscious decision to put the icing on the cake of big lies they'd baked. My guess is that Dubya was out of touch and Cheney was the devious one, once again constituting the deadly mix which had characterized their time in office.

They would not go away. They were like hemorrhoids; eventually they would go away, but waiting for it to happen was so painful. Their show of defiance, like landing on an aircraft carrier in a flight suit where a huge banner proclaimed "Mission Accomplished" after exposing and continuing to expose thousands of troops and hundreds of thousands of Iraqi citizens to death and pain after the photo op only served to reinforce the perception that we had endured a dark period that had not totally ended. Merciful God in heaven, please put an end to this nightmare.

In "Sock and Awe(ful)," I once again registered my frustration that this sorry chapter in American history could not end soon enough.

Posted December 19, 2008
Sock and Awe(ful)

Does it seem to you that November 4 was a long, long time ago? Does it also seem to you that the interregnum between November 4 and January 20 is an interminably long period of time? Does it seem almost as though time is standing still?

If the answer to all three questions is yes, then you are most likely among the overwhelming majority of people who are, one, surprised that we actually made it through the Bush years, two, concerned over the damage they can still do on their way out the door, and three, beyond anxious awaiting the arrival of the new order.

I have tried very hard to focus on the future and not waste time lamenting the squandered opportunities of the past eight years. Each time I believe I have gotten to that magical place where my mind is at peace, these clowns plunge us right back into the spider hole they have occupied for so long. This past week our mad political scientist, Dr. Dick Cheney, emerged from an unannounced location to remind us how proud he is of the role he played in lowering the standards of decency and democracy by committing others to fight a war with no apparent justification other than his warped conception of the world, and the subsequent actions defying the Geneva convention that opened the way for torture to be the operative norm for treatment of prisoners by the leading nation of the free world.

I recall vividly a documentary on the bombing of Tokyo during the closing days of World War II and a comment by future General Curtis Le May in which he told the brass planning the assault that it was a good thing we were going to win this thing because otherwise they, the brass in the room, would be treated as war criminals. That has stuck with me; it is clear demonstration of the axiom "Where you stand depends upon where you sit."

I find this legacy tour the Bush administration is conducting an abomination. It is sickening to watch the president and vice president so desperate to claim some degree of perceived moral authority over the dastardly formulation and disastrous implementation of the most vile, evil, and profoundly unsuccessful military adventure in history. Normally I am inclined to offer that there is room for reasonable people to disagree; however, in this case, what is missing is a voice of reason. It is a deadly perversion of the old parental exasperation "Because I said so."

Well, we as a free society should strengthen our resolve that "never again" will we allow our leaders a free pass on such weighty matters of life and death. We are owed an explanation, we are owed a well-defined and reasoned justification for action, our elected representatives at all levels owe us a return on the trust investment we place in them, and further, we demand accountability for subsequent actions taken on our behalf.

We can "handle the truth"; we must, or else the justification for our existence as a free society crumbles. In a discussion with my good friend, the distinguished actor Ed Asner, he described an unquestioning public as "sheeple." Well, Bush and Cheney were the herdsmen, and they led us to the slaughterhouse.

So where is the accountability? Those of us who are parents constantly remind our children that there are consequences for actions. If that is the case, what are the consequences of these actions?

What makes me so angry is that these people are not only not held accountable, but allowed to attempt a very public showing of vindication. It is truly theatre of the absurd. If there were any degree of self-respect whatsoever they would merely bow out, go away, slink into their very cushy retirements, accumulate even more wealth on the lecture circuit, play golf, clear brush, whatever.

Reinstituting trust in the institutions and personalities of government is going to be difficult enough, and President-elect Obama is striving mightily to do just that. But the actions of the outgoing president and vice president continue to rub salt into still fresh wounds. We talk of making the moguls of industry accountable for the economic catastrophe they have wreaked on the American people, and they should be made to answer.

Is the best we have to offer sockandawe.com, the game of electronically throwing shoes at the president? I must admit, I derive great pleasure in participating in this exercise, and obviously I am not alone, when last I checked in excess of 46 million shoes has found the mark and the number grows by the second. Is this the best we can do?

I am grudgingly willing to allow these crooks to merely go away, but if they insist on taking advantage of the good nature of all of us by insulting our integrity then at some point we need to say *no mas*, enough is enough, you must be dealt with and learn a lesson. This is not a radical concept; it is merely common decency.

Article 16

December 31, 2008
Hope

As 2008 prepared to recede into our memories, the optimism that was the hallmark of the Obama campaign was very much alive despite a continued worsening of economic indicators and performance. The true benefit of revisiting articles written in real time is to relive and remember the attitudes that shaped their construction. This piece was written on New Year's Eve and, as that time symbolically represents a passing from one year to the next, the prospect of a passage from darkness to sunshine had become a reality due to the recent election.

The possibilities seemed endless; the anticipation was breathtaking. The hopes and dreams of a majority of the nation and the active participation of a new generation of voters were positive signs that, symbolically, a torch had been passed and we were about to enter a new dawn full of promise, hope, and change.

The problem with such a scenario, in hindsight, is that you run the risk of setting the bar too high, espousing unrealistic expectations, and setting a goal that is virtually impossible to attain. Of course, we were constantly being introduced to a plethora of problems that were much, much deeper than our leaders had known or wanted us to know. The more we peeled back the layers of the onion, the more we cried. Tears were certainly ahead for us, but no pain, no gain, so hopefully we would be ready for whatever lay ahead.

Perhaps the problems and the damage done were too great to surmount without a level of pain no one was prepared to countenance. Perhaps our optimism was misplaced or unrealistic. Perhaps we subconsciously knew we were in too deep, but could not accept the fact that there were obstacles we could not overcome in the short-term. Or perhaps we were not prepared for the vehemence of obstruction and the deep polarization that had come to characterize our political system, and hence our institutions of governance. Perhaps the system was corrupted beyond repair.

Whatever the reasons, we progressives entered 2009 anxious to right the wrongs of the past eight years. After all, we are all Americans, and we believe there is no crisis we cannot overcome and come out better than before. This is the essence of American exceptionalism, and a healthy dose of swagger and self-assurance had always served us well before.

This was the prevalent attitude among many as we entered the new year. In "The Crisis Dividend: Profit and Purpose," my intent was to capture this feeling of unbounded optimism.

Posted December 31, 2008
The Crisis Dividend: Profit and Purpose

So let's take stock of where we are as we leave 2008. 1) We have a transformational figure positioned to lead the country at a time when we need solid, bold, and creative thinking in a way not seen since the 1930s; 2) We have the prospect of a fifty-nine seat majority in the US Senate to help with the transformation required; 3) We have a true mandate to do the things that are required to correct for the disastrous policies that have brought us to this historic moment; 4) We must confront crises both internationally and domestically that fall somewhere on the spectrum between daunting and catastrophic; and 5) We must dispose of a thorny issue regarding the appointment of a successor to the Illinois Senate seat that will surely test the skills of the Democratic majority.

At one and the same time, these challenges are frustrating and exhilarating. They give purpose and urgency to the need to summon the best and brightest of our citizens to engage in a renewed sense of public service. For those so disposed to take up this challenge, it represents a historic opportunity to contribute to the achievement of ideals that define who we are and what we can be. In a very real sense, we progressives are afforded a luxury few of us have ever known: namely, the ability to participate in the shaping of a world that benefits future generations and a stunning rejection of the "me first" mentality that has captured the greater part of the past half century.

In Chinese, the word "crisis" is composed of two symbols, one representing danger, and the other opportunity. In psychic and economic terms, we can profit from the crisis. If we approach the current crisis appropriately, we will effectively take what we have inherited and profit from it, profit by virtue of an enhanced physical environment and the creation of an economy that succeeds in creating millions of green collar jobs. We will also profit by having our decaying infrastructure needs addressed, thereby at one and the same time creating jobs and strengthening the bricks and mortar that sustain our society.

We profit from a world that seeks to tamp down suspicions and mistrust, and attempts to find common ground upon which to collectively address problems. Economic adversaries can be healthy; military ones are rarely so. But seeking common ground internationally will help free up scarce financial resources for non-military purposes and promote preservation of scarce natural resources.

It is a brave new world we are about to enter, and we have the right people at the helm. This should give us reason to celebrate as we enter the new year. As we enter 2009, we must strive to make hope a reality. It will not be easy; thinking and acting big never is. But it is critically necessary and we all must be up to the challenge. It is a fight which can and must be won, and the immensity of the challenge is what we Americans seemingly thrive on.

So as the ball drops this evening, share a toast that we are ready for the long trip ahead of us, that we are prepared as never before to fight the good fight, that failure is not an option. And as we approach the dawn that lies ahead, we can rest assured those future generations will indeed profit from our investments.

The Evolution of Revolution:
An Attack upon Reason, Compromise, and the Constitution

Article 17

January 4, 2009
Don't Go Away Mad, Just Go Away!

Some people just don't know when to shut up. As the sun was setting on the Bush years—although the sun had set on their tenure long before they were forced to leave—Dr. Evil, alias Dick Cheney, was dead set on wreaking as much damage as he could before he was carried, kicking and screaming, from the party. If ever there were an individual drunk on power, it was this wretched troll. A chickenhawk who had wrangled five deferments during the Vietnam War, and at one point remarked that he had better things to do than defend his country, he was quite willing and perfectly giddy about sending others to defend it.

Now he was spewing invective at the incoming president, questioning his desire and ability to defend the country and its citizens, obviously hell-bent on defending his own questionable direction and involvement in taking the country to war under false pretenses. It was a classless act in accord with a classless tenure which included his treasonous role in outing Valerie Plame, a covert CIA agent. The man has no shame, and he was determined to go out in a blaze of glory.

Of course, in hindsight, maybe we should have read into this the seeds of the toxic vitriol that would become a hallmark of the then-fledgling Tea Party, but hindsight is always twenty-twenty. The interminable transition continued to slog toward Inauguration Day, and the attempts by the outgoing administration to validate their tenure was a public relations blitz to salvage what they could from a widely acknowledged failure in leadership. As the end drew near, Cheney had amazingly little difficulty overshadowing his nominal boss—President George W. Bush. There had been no doubt about the identity of the man behind the curtain, controlling the fire and brimstone during the Bush presidency, but now it had assumed a surreal quality as the Great Oz revealed himself, unabashedly taking center stage. It was the ultimate act of disrespect for the incoming president and the outgoing president, but most of all the American people.

In "It Just Makes Me Want to Gag: Cheney," I vented my spleen over what I saw as a poorly planned, disingenuous, and pitiful exit that was as pathetic as most of the decisions that had been rendered during the previous eight years. Somehow I still believed that politicians could be gracious in defeat and, in this case, at least gracious and thankful for the opportunity to have been given the keys to the vault. Instead, this show of disrespect was a harbinger of the new politics of polarization. At the time I thought it was an isolated thing; however, it proved to be an instruction manual for the new order.

Posted January 4, 2009
It Just Makes Me Want To Gag: Cheney

Is there anyone capable of putting a gag in Dick Cheney's mouth? This is getting ridiculous. A few weeks ago he essentially called President Obama a traitor, saying that he gave aid and comfort to the enemy. This week he continues, in his venomous and vindictive way, to question the president's commitment to honor what may be the most essential and predominantly fundamental responsibility of any commander-in-chief: namely, to protect the American people.

I have neither expected nor asked former Presidents Bush, either of them, to weigh in on matters of significance, moral or political, and fully expect that it would be fruitless anyway, but at this juncture I would call on both of them to rein in their wayward comrade and in the not so gentle parlance of the Internets (sic) tell him to STFU. (For the uninitiated, it represents a phrase with the first word being "shut" and the last being "up"—I'll leave the rest to your imagination and interpretation.)

There must be someone, somewhere in the upper echelons of the conservative movement/Republican Party hierarchy who finds this distasteful and counterproductive drivel to be beyond the bounds of patriotic fervor. Will someone of significant conservative stature please stand up and demand an end to this childishness? It does not advance rational discourse on the issues facing the nation or its citizens. It does not advance the goal of making the world a safer place. It merely continues the fear mongering, cynicism, and division that have characterized our political environment for far too long.

So I implore those who may disagree with the politics and policies of the current administration to focus on ways in which we can fix problems rather than create new ones. We must restore civility in our public discourse on problems ranging from climate change to health-care reform to economic recovery and all issues in between. Irrational and inflammatory accusations such as those consistently spewed out on right-wing talk shows or out of the mouth of a former vice president merely fan the flames of discord that prevail in our society today, and further entrenches virulent pockets of distrust that render problem-solving that much more difficult.

While I had serious reservations for the policies and pronouncements of the last administration, I never could nor would have presupposed or suggested that there was a lack of concern or patriotism which motivated their misguided prescriptions. I have never doubted or questioned their love for America. We are all Americans, and we all share in the desire to live in a peaceful and prosperous society. Similarly, we all share in the profits of a world in which violence is minimized and respect for cultural, religious and other differences is maximized. And we all— yes, Dick, even Democrats and liberals—realize that there is a need for strength and, in some instances, a role for intervention in order to protect ourselves.

But the childish and juvenile belief that not believing what you do or not acting the way you want is a clear reflection of a desire to fail simply diminishes any respect your previous office may seem to afford you. Your disgusting behavior accomplishes absolutely nothing. If you are purposefully doing these things for raw political gain, then you yourself deserve all the derision and disrespect that we can muster.

A new year dawns, and there will be plenty enough political maneuvering that will buffet the American electorate in the next eleven months. You will have plenty of time and opportunity to score political points. But for God's sake, it is purely absurd to bet against your team. And for better or worse, America is your team, and Americans are your teammates. You may not like it, but it is a fact. If you choose not to be on the team, join another, move, or—here is a novel idea—just shut up. You have every right to disagree and voice your opinions, but you have no right to try to take the team down.

The Evolution of Revolution:
An Attack upon Reason, Compromise, and the Constitution

The First Year: 2009

Article 18

January 23, 2009
Finally, the Interminable Wait Is Over

Somehow, I made it until Inauguration Day. I've been attending inaugural events since 1976, and must admit that I even attended a couple of Republican ones. The coldest one for me was the Carter Inauguration, but that could have been because I did not even own an overcoat and witnessed the event on the east front of the Capitol in a denim suit—the only one I owned.

Each of the eight inaugurations I attended had its own distinctive flavor and a certain degree of excitement, but without question the historic significance of the first Obama swearing-in is one that will never be recaptured, for he will always be the first African-American president of the United States.

The crowds were unlike anything I had seen. The weather was cold, but at least I owned an overcoat and gloves this time. The energy and excitement was as breathtaking as the chill in the air. What struck me more than anything else was the diversity of the crowd. Most of those I met and saw were not there to attend the balls or to hobnob with the political glitterati; they were there to witness an historic event. When Obama took the oath, there was not a dry eye in sight. The streets surrounding the Mall were packed with buses which had arrived under cover of darkness and would depart the same way. The importance of the moment was unmistakable; it was an overwhelming moment, one where passion, excitement, and joy came together to form a magical, if not mystical, experience.

This was truly the people's event. And now the moment of truth had arrived, the long winter of discontent had ended, a new day dawned, and the hope and change that had reverberated throughout the campaign would now be given a chance to be put into action. It was a glorious event, a glorious day. And when the helicopter carrying the former president did its perfunctory buzz over the crowd, aside from many one-finger salutes, the feeling was generally good riddance, let's get to work.

In "Our Long Winter of Discontent," I tried to capture the feelings of that day. And now the hard part begins. I am sure that conservatives were overwhelmed by the specter of Ronald Reagan rescuing the nation from disaster, but because it would mean a return to prosperity on behalf of folks who had already known what prosperity felt like, I can only assume that the general feeling was one of relief. In this instance, because so many people were present who had never known prosperity or even opportunity, the feeling was one of genuine pride and salvation. Many of the buses would depart early that evening, before the balls and the galas and the parties and the fancy dinners. The main event on this Inauguration Day was the inauguration itself. For those who came to witness that event, there were no tuxedos packed away in hotel rooms; just a long night's journey and the whine of the bus engines towards home. By morning, a truly new day dawned upon America.

Posted January 23, 2009
Our Long Winter of Discontent

I have been involved in various aspects of eight different inaugurations, including the spectacular event that concluded yesterday—or, to be more exact, sometime early this morning. Inaugural events have many movements. Essentially, you have the actual swearing-in ceremony and parade, the premier daytime event, bracketed in by innumerable social events leading up to and extending beyond the more-or-less businesslike transaction signifying a peaceful transfer of power in the world's most powerful nation.

The sheer magnitude of the number of participants witnessing the Obama swearing-in event most assuredly distinguishes it from any other I have witnessed in my experiences dating back to 1976. However, the real distinguishing feature of the event was the palpable emotions exhibited by individuals who had traveled to the Capitol simply to be a part of history, to be part of, to bear witness to an historical event that can never again be achieved: namely, the ascendancy of the first African-American to hold the power and title of commander-in-chief.

The social aspects of an inauguration extend into the nighttime hours, and are confined to limited numbers of individuals with the money, power, and connections to warrant special invitations. I have and did participate in a number of these events. But the true measure of the import and significance of the inauguration is not found in these activities, but rather in the event itself.

One simply could not escape the electricity, the excitement, the exhilaration on the faces of those walking the streets in anticipation of the event. Large numbers of African-Americans, often with families in tow, bundled up, willing to forego simple pleasures like staying warm, busily rushed headstrong into inevitable bottlenecks at Metro stations [and] patiently waited to secure a spot of ground up to two miles from the Capitol. Many waited for hours simply to witness the event unfurl on large screens strategically placed on the National Mall.

And after the event, the logistical nightmare of dispersing nearly 2 million spectators once again forced individuals to bunch together like cattle as they waited to emerge from the attendant bottlenecks the large gathering necessitated. All this in freezing temperatures, with brutal winds driving the [wind]chill index down even further, with muscles tired from hours of standing and miles traveled around fenced off streets that defied the careful planning of Pierre L'Enfant centuries ago, yet all without incident.

There clearly was joy in the air; there were tears and hugs and embraces of total strangers. And as the crowds were moving back to the warmth of either hotels or buses, or elsewhere, all eyes were focused on the helicopter carrying Dubya away. The chopper made a long sweep of the District, and hearty chants of good-bye accompanied waves directed upward. Like the final official stamp closing an important deal, as the helicopter alighted and slowly disappeared into the cold gray sky, the dream that indeed a new order, a new day would soon arrive became a reality.

A few blocks from the Mall, in the southwest quadrant of the city, row upon row of idling buses filled streets that had been cordoned off to traffic. The streets were clogged with thousands of buses carrying tens or hundreds of thousands of people back to their respective communities. Many of these buses had arrived under cover of darkness that morning and would depart under cover of darkness that evening. The sheer desire to just be there, at this propitious moment in time, so overwhelmed individuals that they felt they just needed to see for themselves what to many had until only recently been unthinkable. And by this morning, the streets had cleared, the barricades were coming down, traffic was returning to the arteries, the Metro was crowded with people going to work instead of tourists. And today we begin a new chapter in our history.

It will take an enormous amount of skill, perseverance, diplomacy, jawboning, and just a dash of good luck thrown in for good measure to lift the country out of our winter of discontent. As President Obama cautioned, it will neither be easy or quick. But if it were possible to capture and bottle the hope that was evident on the Mall yesterday, there can be no doubt that together we will confront and conquer the difficulties that lie before us. Indeed, we shall overcome.

Article 19

February 3, 2009
Super Bowl

Barely two weeks after the historic transfer of power, a nation was glued to their television screens to witness an event far less momentous, but important nonetheless, to sports fans. It was time for the annual ritual that is the Super Bowl. For football and non-football fans, it has become a day for friends to gather and take in the game, the halftime entertainment, and/or the commercials. As a football fan, I have an interest in the game itself, although as a Philadelphia Eagles fan that interest is tempered by the fact that very rarely in my lifetime has my team been involved in the festivities.

What makes this particularly galling, however, is that our archrival from western Pennsylvania—the Pittsburgh Steelers—have been a player in so many of them, most recently in 2009. At the time I was working for the governor of Pennsylvania, an avid football and Eagles fan himself, being the former mayor of Philadelphia. This game featured Pittsburgh versus the Arizona Cardinals, recently transplanted from St. Louis. On this day, all focus was on the game, and we could all take a break. But politics has a way of infiltrating everything, and on this day, football would not be immune from a politics peculiar to the small northern Pennsylvania town of Pottsville.

As a Pennsylvanian, I had more than a passing interest in the outcome. But what made this particular Super Bowl so interesting to me, and maybe a couple of football aficionados, was that the Cardinals organization had been involved in a curious and little known event in 1925 which had a direct bearing on another Pennsylvania city that began with a P; Pottsville. I knew the mayor of Pottsville and had spent time with him in the small town some sixty miles north of Philadelphia. Today Pottsville is most famous as the location for the Yuengling brewery, the oldest brewery in the United States—established in 1829. And while the beer has been a staple in Pennsylvania and has branched out in recent years, it is still only available in a dozen or so states. I had the distinct pleasure of being offered a can of beer right off the assembly line, before it was even sealed. But this is not a story about beer; it is about football.

In 1925, the city was home to the Pottsville Maroons, a scrappy bunch of coal miners who also happened to play professional football. Their story is brilliantly captured in a book titled, *Breaker Boys: The NFL's Greatest Team and the Stolen 1925 Championship*, by David Fleming, a senior writer for ESPN magazine. In the book, he captures the unusual circumstances which led to the Maroons defeating the Chicago Cardinals and, through some political maneuvering, having what was then considered the national championship taken from them.

The Cardinals had moved from Chicago to St. Louis and eventually to Arizona, but had been owned by the Bidwell family since 1933. In "The Cardinal Curse," I explore the role of superstition in sports and how, until things are made right and Pottsville has the crown restored, the Cardinals organization will forever be cursed. It is an interesting bit of sports trivia as well as a fascinating story, and I thought it worth bringing to the Huffington Post readership, many of whom, like me, are sports fans. It would take a true sports fan to know the story of the 1925 Pottsville Maroons, but it was fun to write about something a tad less serious than the fate of society. Now you'll be able to wow your friends with this bit of trivia.

Posted February 3, 2009
The Cardinal Curse

Superstition can be an athlete's best friend or worst enemy. But it can get inside your head, and we humans talk freely of its power. We even devote one night in October to a ritual steeped in ghosts and goblins, and few schoolchildren are not introduced to the headless horseman and "The Legend of Sleepy Hollow." For eighty-six years, Boston Red Sox fans spoke openly of the Curse of the Bambino. Athletes and athletic organizations wrestle with superstition and, as a hedge against the probability that there just might be something to it, they pay homage to it. They grow beards during winning streaks, don't change socks or other parts of their uniforms, they refuse to clean their helmets, they wear lucky jewelry, every player has a lucky pair of shoes, and so on.

There probably is nothing to it; but then again, why take the chance? Thus, although Sunday's thrilling Super Bowl game was truly super, the Cardinals' organization was doomed from the start. It was not the Pittsburgh Steelers as much as it was the Pottsville Maroons, or rather the ghosts of the 1925 team that has, for eighty-four years, been denied its rightful claim to the NFL championship that triumphed Sunday evening. And to those who believe that the "Cardinal Curse" still prevents this organization from achieving only one championship over that period of time (1947), Sunday night was a vindication of superstitious justice.

You see, the Bidwell family, which has owned the Cardinals since 1933 and has taken the team from Chicago to Saint Louis to Arizona, has played a role in unfairly denying Pottsville its justly deserved crown. And until they relinquish their bogus claim to the 1925 championship, the curse will continue.

On December 7, 1925, the 9–2 Maroons beat the 9–1–1 Chicago Cardinals 21–7 in what was unambiguously declared by newspapers to be the NFL Championship game. The Chicago Tribune headline read, "Cardinals Play Pottsville for Pro Title Today," and wrote, "A victory for either team carried the national title." However, due to financial troubles experienced by what would certainly in today's parlance qualify as a small-market team—Pottsville—they had agreed to play the preeminent football team of the day, Notre Dame, in Philadelphia the following week. Miscommunication, confusion, and internal political intrigue all conspired to lead the NFL commissioner to suspend the Maroons because of their involvement in this game.

According to David Fleming, author of *Breaker Boys: The NFL's Greatest Team and the Stolen 1925 Championship*, while their victory legitimized the NFL, it also destroyed the team and the town that made it possible. And thus the Cardinal Curse was born.

Now this, of course, is taking nothing away from the magnificent performance by the team in Super Bowl XLIII. They distinguished themselves and but for a few unlucky breaks, particularly the 100-yard interception return to close the first half, could have and should have prevailed. But that infernal curse, it may or may not have played a role, but why chance it? If I were a Cardinals fan, I would demand that Mr. Bidwell do everything he can to lift the curse, and that means putting to rest the travesty that has haunted the rugged town of Pottsville, Pennsylvania since the Roaring Twenties. But, of course, it is only a silly superstition, right?

The Evolution of Revolution:
An Attack upon Reason, Compromise, and the Constitution

Article 20

February 12, 2009
This Is Nuts!

An incident occurred in Blakely, Georgia, where peanut butter known to be tainted with Salmonella was allowed to be shipped in order to avoid inspection. It was just another example of greed in which the bottom line obliterated morality, and just about everything else.

Osama Bin Laden was determined to expose greed in American society as a tool for recruitment of jihadists who would see a nation of hypocrisy and injustice; greed can be very destructive. And while the concept itself is repugnant to most, it was celebrated in the movie *Wall Street* when Gordon Gekko declared that "Greed…is good." When our system allows greed to exact revenge on its own citizens, is this not a form of economic terrorism? Worse, if innocent people die, is this not terrorism in its most destructive form? Unfortunately, there are examples of our own greed, both individual and collective, opening us to criticism, ridicule, and condemnation. Just such an event was captured in the glare of media spotlight in mid-February.

In "The Peanut Butter Terrorist," I attempted to equate greed with terrorism as it allows the insidious destruction of innocent individuals and erodes society as a whole. Greed, overconsumption, perverse economic incentives, and deregulation all contribute to a degraded quality of life, and can cause injury and death to innocents who rely upon their government to protect them. In a world without oversight for the public good, where special interests can wield money to influence the perverse altering of laws and regulations to boost their profit margins, we are all at risk. In short, greed kills. The event in question should force a searing introspection into the kind of society we wish to live in, and the important role government can play in ensuring that we are safeguarded from greed and self-interest.

I was inspired when I first read Upton Sinclair's *The Jungle* in college, because it led directly to the Meat Inspection Act and the Pure Food and Drug Act, both signed into law by Theodore Roosevelt in 1906. Through his exposé of the meat packing industry in Chicago,

Sinclair raised public awareness and the consciousness of a need for public health oversight. If there is a bona-fide role for government in the health and safety of the public, no clearer example exists than that uncovered here.

Posted February 12, 2009
The Peanut Butter Terrorist

While intelligence agencies are wondering where the next terrorist attack may come from, might it be shipping cargo containers, nuclear power plants, subway systems, or contaminated reservoirs, little thought, I am sure, has been given to peanut butter. Yet right there in the heart of the country red, right there in Blakely, Georgia, was hatched a plan more insidious than even bin Laden himself could have conceived.

The more I read about this fellow Stewart Parnell and his alleged plot to turn ice cream, cookies, and peanut butter sandwiches into weapons of mass destruction, all in the name of profit, the more I am convinced that greed is equally destructive as fundamentalist religious ideology. Quite simply, greed kills.

If this man is truly guilty of what has been alleged, if he knowingly gave the order to ship contaminated products because the inconvenience of inspection ultimately affected his company's bottom line, then how is this man anything short of a mass murderer? How is it that such a profound lack of morality or ethics can either go undetected or be promoted?

The repulsive nature of this crime, if in fact it is proven in a court of law, should give us all cause to stop and reflect upon our individual culpability in the excesses of conspicuous consumption that is currently manifesting itself, writ large in our economic crisis. In our seemingly inexhaustible quest to live beyond our means, we are all responsible for the tragedy that is currently afflicting millions of people both here at home and abroad.

It is our individual and collective consumption-driven activities that fuel our addiction to oil, both foreign and domestic, with devastating consequences for the climate and mankind. It is our overconsumption of food that allows for a nation to struggle with increasing obesity while millions die of starvation and malnutrition. And, in the cruelest twist, it allows for a nation to grow food to use as fuel and to have the government subsidize farmers with taxpayer monies to do such.

If we are to learn anything from the current crisis it should be to both reflect upon our ways and live within our means. Just as we know when we are abusing credit to finance things we cannot afford, so must Mr. Parnell have known that the potential costs were not worth the benefits.

But the true war on terror must be focused inward. A culture of greed, fueled by overconsumption, is a danger to us all. The sinister actions of this peanut-butter terrorist must be viewed as exactly what they are: namely, acts of murder. Similarly, we must be responsible as a society for our complicity in global climate destruction. Greed kills.

Our responsibility to act responsibly is long overdue. Because of globalization, each day, our world becomes smaller. We are increasingly bound together by a common thread: survival. Terrorism threatens to undermine that binding through fear; greed is a form of economic terrorism that erodes from the foundation upwards. Consumption feeds greed. And unfortunately, you may need to look no further than your peanut butter jar.

The Evolution of Revolution:
An Attack upon Reason, Compromise, and the Constitution

Article 21

March 27, 2009
Move or Move Aside

It had been just over two months since the new administration had taken the reins, and the initial going was rough and getting rougher. Obama was facing strong headwinds in his attempts to deal with an economic disaster that had been years in the making. It was incredible to watch him attempt to reach out to Republicans for support of what the country had elected him to do and, time after time in the short months after his election, only to be rebuffed or summarily dismissed. Yet there he was, steadfastly adhering to the notion that, in times of crisis, we all pull together—Republicans and Democrats—for the good of the country and its citizens. The man possesses the patience of Job, and some of his loyalists were getting a little edgy.

Those of us who have worked in appointed positions are all too well aware that time is fleeting. We find ourselves negotiating a steep learning curve while simultaneously facing time limitations which, in the case of a presidential administration, are four or eight years. And the political maxim that you are never as popular as you are the first day in office is true; it's all downhill from there, so you must make every minute count and make an impact early on, while still in the "honeymoon" period.

Either the Republicans did not see the crisis—which is barely plausible since it had captured attention front and center during the latter stages of the campaign and the early months of the new year—or they were unwilling to concede that their prescriptions for the widespread economic maladies did not cure the patient, but made him/her sicker. Many Democrats were becoming seriously annoyed and frustrated with the unbending intransigence of the opposition party. Yet there was the president, sticking to his guns and his conviction that post-partisanship was what the doctor ordered. It was admirable, and he was right, of course. In a system of checks and balances, and where minorities have a seat at the big boys' table, compromise and consensus are essential. It is often ugly and produces less-than-optimal results, but in our incremental-based system of policy-making, making it work is critically important. However, in the face of an opposition that will not yield, there comes a point when you need to break out the steamroller.

The first 100 days are often used as a benchmark for marking substantial progress on high-priority agenda items for an incoming administration. Whether it is an appropriate measurement or not is debatable, and we were about to enter April with little movement toward getting the economy headed in the right direction. Hell, the Obama Administration was nearly two-thirds of the way there, and the troops were restless.

What was most astounding to me, however, was the lack of creativity or ingenuity being exhibited by the opposition. It was as if the election had not occurred; it was as if their rigid ideological aversion to debt was suddenly reawakened after a period when these very same conservative zealots had knowingly participated in the greatest reversal on debt in history, taking huge surpluses built up by the Clinton Administration and turning them into huge piles of debt.

Ideological warfare is well suited to political campaigning but, once the people have spoken, the time for setting aside differences and working to solve the problems you were elected to dispose of takes precedence. Yet it was as if we were engaged in a never-ending campaign in which governance had no place. There must come a time where the willingness to cooperate has to be reciprocated, or else it is time to get out of the way.

For the new administration, that time was fast approaching. In "Get on Board or Get Outta the Way," my frustration with the pace of action and the reservoir of patience the president exhibited was driving me crazy. I supported the president without question, and admired his perseverance and the cool, calm, adult demeanor that so differentiated him from his predecessor and his campaign rival. He certainly has more patience than any two people I know. But time was passing, and I was concerned that without a little infusion of Lyndon Baines Johnson encouragement, he would appear weak to the opposition. His patience could be used against him by making him appear malleable and indecisive.

We needed to get on with the people's business, and if there were no help from the people's elected representatives, maybe it was time to go directly to the people. Surely Obama was in an unusual position, and the degree of resistance to compromise may have been unprecedented. These were uncharted waters, and things were continuing to worsen. Did the Republican Party really want America to fail under this president? Could things have reached such a low point? I am a skeptical person, but to believe this would be cynical, and I was not prepared to go there—yet. But something had to give, and soon.

Posted March 27, 2009
Get on Board or Get Outta the Way

In the political world, hypocrisy knows no bounds. As I continue to listen to these self-righteous, sanctimonious, and preposterously hypocritical conservatives (and yes, most of them are Republicans) pontificate on the horribleness, the insanity, the disastrous level of debt we are heaping upon future generations, I want to just puke. That is a technical term for abject disgust.

As I listen to New Hampshire Senator Judd Gregg lay out in great detail charts and graphs depicting the end of the world, I cannot help but think how, in any calculus, this man could have entertained the notion of serving in President Obama's cabinet. It certainly testifies either to the man's lack of judgment or disregard for principle.

I served as a professional staff member for the US Senate Budget Committee in the 1980s. I witnessed a conservative-fueled set of economic theories that came to be known as Reaganomics result in an explosion of debt. I witnessed the incredible hardships imposed on our citizens during the 1982 recession. I similarly witnessed the growing gap between rich and poor, so studiously enunciated by Kevin Phillips, a former Republican strategist, in *The Politics of Rich and Poor* (1990).

I witnessed the politically disastrous consequences of George H.W. Bush's ill-fated conservative proclamation of "read my lips, no new taxes" in 1992 in an attempt to satisfy a skeptical and intransigent conservative voter base. Had he based his campaign on a more honest and realistic assessment of the economic headwinds, who knows what might have happened, but rather adhering to a political calculus, he was forced to recant and face chastisement.

As a member of the Clinton Administration, I witnessed economic policies that carefully and methodically wiped away budget deficits and replaced them with actual surpluses. And as one who could not stand to stay in Washington during the dark ages of the Dubya regime, I watched from afar as insidiously inequitable tax and spending policies drove the national debt to stratospheric heights while pushing the economy into a deep abyss. These nonsensical prescriptions led to a historic expansion of the gap between rich and poor, while shrinking consumer confidence and ultimately resulted in a deregulation-led financial system collapse.

Yet despite these realities, there are those who participated in such developments with unrestrained ideological fervor who now decry the very actions that are necessary to both lessen the impacts upon our under- and unemployed and save the financial system from total collapse. There are individuals elected to serve this nation, who would betray that trust placed upon them in order to thwart the implementation of difficult decisions that require they place the long-term interests of the country above their short-term politics.

Where were they when deficits and debt were increased while the economy was growing? Do they not comprehend that all debt, like all taxes, is not evil? Or is the faux-fiscal-responsibility conviction merely a convenient excuse to say "no" when difficult political decisions require foresight and sacrifice? The hypocrisy is mind numbing.

One does not need to be an economist, nor even minimally educated, to understand that difficult times require difficult decisions. Any adult should be capable of understanding that living within your means over the long-term is both wise and economically sustainable. There is a time and place for debt, and there is a time and place for government intervention, and, yes, there is a time and place for matching revenues with expenditures, which require taxes. Now is not the time for political maneuvering.

Unfortunately, rigid ideological conservatives seem to have little or no appreciation for these truisms. And it is most unfortunate that the Republican Party is increasingly beholden to interests that do not conform to realities that face millions of victims of the ill-fated economic hokum that has landed us in this place.

My only hope is that you and your foolishness will fail. My wish is that you will join in helping to set the economy on the right track, put your political voodoo in a jar, and do what you were elected to do: namely, represent your country and its citizens.

Federal officials represent the United States, not your district or your state. Sure, there will be a time and place to promote all the good things you have done for your constituents, and Lord knows you will not allow that to pass unheeded, but right now it is critically important that we all pull together for the good of the nation, and the benefits will trickle down to all of our citizens. In a very real way, consider this an opportunity to actually see the benefits of trickle-down government intervention.

The stakes are too high to continue to experiment with the worn out axioms and well-validated failures of the past. We must be forward-looking and practice prudence with respect to the long-term economic health of the nation. Yes, deficit spending can be fiscally responsible. In today's economic climate, we can afford to do no less. Either get on board or get out of the way.

Article 22

March 31, 2009
Who are Our Heroes?

The news that the head of General Motors, a man responsible for leading the company into a monumental decline, would be punished by receiving a $20 million severance package prompted me to write about the skewed rewards and penalties we as a society have come to accept over the years. When thousands of workers were losing their jobs, their benefit packages, and their pensions due to the malfeasance of corporate titans who were simultaneously rewarded with large buyouts shows just how far afield we have gone on the common sense scale. It also seemed to touch upon another bottom line that had received mixed reviews over the years—athletic performance.

I recall the arguments I had with my father over the Barry Bonds performance-enhancing drug case. Incredibly, my father, a lifelong sports fan, had little problem with the fact that some of our sports icons had taken drugs which would give them a significant advantage over teammates and rivals who did not. I argued that it was cheating; he argued that, like working out, if you found a way to maximize your performance, more power to you. Sports, politics, and business are competitive enterprises, and I have found that one can easily be compared to the other. But this was cheating, it was fraud, and it was illegal. How can you reward such behavior by passing it off as though those smart enough to cheat should reap the rewards of doing so?

Cheating is cheating, and cheaters should be ostracized and punished. The GM chief had cheated his workers out of promised and deserved benefits; some athletes had tilted the playing field by competing unfairly. Those athletes guilty of cheating should have their ill-gotten awards and their places in the record books revoked. Corporate titans who drove their companies into the ground and forced their workers to absorb the brunt of their misdeeds while benefiting handsomely should have to relinquish their assets and distribute them back to the workers. Politicians who accepted bribes to vote a certain way should lose their jobs.

In "Severance Packages and Steroids," I drew attention to this inverted system of punishment and rewards in an attempt to bring sanity and common sense back to the values, ethics, and morals we as a society profess to hold dear, and question how much longer we will allow deviation from them to be tolerated.

Posted March 31, 2009
Severance Packages and Steroids

Have we all lost our minds? Collectively, as a society, we have perverted the whole system of incentives and performance-based rewards to the point where it is not wholly unreasonable to question what constitutes good and bad. Today it is reported that the individual in charge of General Motors' phenomenal collapse would be punished by losing his job and receiving a $20 million severance package.

Athletes, too, have been rewarded for misdeeds, but the difference is at least performance-enhancing drugs actually enhance performance; the same cannot be said for performance rewards granted when the only apparent performance is dismal. In both cases, a fraud is perpetrated upon the public, and in both cases fraudulent behavior is rewarded. Until we correct this farce, we as a society will pay the price.

What is good for General Motors is not good for America. This is just another blatant illustration of a system so perversely out of touch with any semblance of fairness that it defies rationalization. If ever there were a clarion call for a radical reassessment of basic values, it is the extent to which we not only tolerate but encourage irresponsible behavior in this society.

Two concepts seem to scream out for attention here: first, personal responsibility; second, fair competition. These are two of the hallmarks of our culture that have shone like beacons in a free democratic society and that have made us the envy of the world. We gamble with them at our own peril.

Athletes who cheat should be forced to forfeit their records and be banished from the game. Use of performance-enhancing drugs is cheating, plain and simple. Rewarding such behavior teaches young aspiring athletes to be clever and creative in masking their usage. Just as importantly, however, the quintessential nature of fair competition or a fair fight gets lost in the confusion.

Rewarding business executives for poor decisions that result in lost jobs, inferior products, sacrificing long-term growth for short-term profits, and ultimately putting at risk the pension and benefits plans that employees depend upon is quite simply wrong. But in a larger sense it teaches future generations a set of skewed morals and ethics that makes us all weaker as a society. It reinforces the notion that individual gain trumps collective pain, it distorts any sense of common weal; it quite simply diminishes our economy and our nation.

The general malaise and funk we now find ourselves in, I believe, is directly related to a pervasive lack of confidence in the judgment and leadership exhibited by those to whom we turn to inspire us to be something greater. The Obama Administration is attempting to reverse years of accumulated distrust in our governmental institutions and leaders, and public opinion polls evince that they are meeting with success.

But our corporate leadership is desperately in need of an inspirational figure willing to stand up and speak out against the abuses that seem to reveal themselves on a daily basis. Similarly, we need sports legends to speak out forcefully on the need to reform what is acceptable and unacceptable within the realm of athletic competition.

It is really not complicated: cheating is wrong. But more importantly, once you get caught there are negative consequences. For far too long we have allowed our kids to dismiss, with a shrug, the notion that actions can have negative consequences. Yet they will be the first to remind us when actions deserve positive consequences—say, when they feel they are deserving of an allowance.

Today, workers are being penalized for the misguided actions of their bosses. But the bosses walk away with severance packages and golden parachutes; the workers struggle with Hobson's choices such as whether or not they can afford to carry health insurance for their families, or whether or not their kids can go to college. It is patently unfair and further expands the wide divide between the haves and the have-nots. And it makes us weaker because it exposes the disparities in our society that beg for correction.

The new sense of accountability that is being advanced by the Obama Administration is a strong indication of just how far afield we have strayed from core principles such as personal responsibility and fair competition. But it is important that our corporate leaders and sports icons join in the discussion.

The Evolution of Revolution:
An Attack upon Reason, Compromise, and the Constitution

Article 23

April 24, 2009
Change Is Good

At one point in the evolution of debate over climate change, scientific evidence of its causes and impacts and the extent to which future generations will be forced to live with the decisions this generation makes seemed to be gaining bipartisan momentum. Al Gore's excellent analysis in *An Inconvenient Truth* allowed those of us not steeped in science and technology to comprehend complex and technical interactions that have subjected the survival of the human race to public policy debate. In 2006, I felt that significant progress was being made in presenting a solid case to the American public, and it seemed that bipartisan recognition of the seriousness of the issue would presage the adoption of legislative remedies to address it. Interestingly, John McCain took a prominent role in raising awareness and promoting a legislative fix on the Republican side of the aisle. Unfortunately, that spark of statesmanship has since been snuffed out because he is still angry over his failed campaign for president or, like so many of his colleagues, he is concerned about a primary challenge from the right. Either way, it is just one more example of why so many are genuinely disappointed in the guy.

Something happened along the way. We are now deep in the throes of a concerted effort on the part of those whose profit margins are threatened to convince elected officials, mostly Republicans, and the general population to disregard the science or question the motives behind scientific inquiry itself. An astounding number of each group has been converted. In the meantime, we drift ever closer to a tipping point after which we will never be able to mitigate the dramatic impact to the planet, and will be forced to adapt to ever-greater levels of devastation and change.

This effort is blatant propaganda, meant to protect unheard-of levels of profit in an industry that has a stranglehold on the resources that fuel the current economic paradigm—the fossil fuel industry. Many Democrats have also tasted the Kool-Aid, and are supporting efforts to expand exploitation of resources found underground, courtesy of the dinosaurs that preceded us. It appears as though the issue is too much for our elected representatives to deal with; it's just too difficult, and thus they make conscious decisions not to confront it. The tactic of creating a false equivalency whereby one can portray a serious debate among the scientific community as proof that not enough is known about the issue to draw a definitive conclusion has been wildly successful. It is absolutely false, however, since the scientists overwhelming state that global warming is happening, and humans are causing it.

I was trained by Mr. Gore and The Climate Reality Project to deliver presentations based on overwhelming, worldwide scientific consensus to help promote the development of renewable resources. Amazingly, youngsters at the high-school level and younger get it; it is our present generation that has dropped the ball on what many believe is the most important issue of the twenty-first century. To watch politicians question science or the scientific community would be amusing if the consequences were not so serious. So when John Boehner, Republican leader of the House of Representatives and current Speaker of the House, appeared on a Sunday talk show in April, 2009 and proceeded to completely flub the issue—at one point not appreciating the basic elemental difference between methane and carbon dioxide, not a very difficult education given the staff resources he has at his disposal—I could not contain myself.

His posture was predicated on the idea that science is complicated and, since we know about fossil fuels, why the fuss? The anti-intellectual, anti-science, anti-evolution (of science) perspective that has now become populist script in the new Republican Party has brought to mind a quote from Henry Ford: "If I'd asked people what they wanted, they would have said faster horses." Republican ideology and the polices that reflect it not only want to maintain the status quo while the world moves forward, but also seek to turn back the clock to a time that never was.

The danger of this phenomenon cannot be overstated. In 2000, I gave a speech to an assembly of the high school I had graduated from twenty-nine years prior. The thrust was to encourage students to embrace and push for change. In the talk, I outlined the changes that had taken place since I had been a student there. As I assembled the lecture, I was astounded by the vast technological advances that had taken place in just half my lifetime. Think about those that occurred between 1971 and 2000, and you too will be amazed. It is something we should embrace and appreciate and master. Technology is progressing at an exponential rate. Consider the advances in computers over the past ten to twenty years, and those in cell phones in the last five years.

Yet the deniers want to put the brakes on science and technology. At the same time they talk in grandiose terms about how concerned they are about debt, which will burden future generations. Of course, we should be concerned about that, but that does not mean that we stop everything and move backward. Our kids will never forgive us for our failure to address this issue, and are already asking "What were you thinking"?

In "Luddites Live On," I refer to the nineteenth-century British textile artisans who protested against newly developed labor-saving machinery, and find a parallel in those who wish to stop time or turn the clock back. The sad state of what passes for debate or discussion of technical issues that directly influence our well-being as a society and impact our kids and their kids even more directly is heartbreaking. We must raise our game here; we must entertain serious discussion on serious matters lest we sink into the bottomless pit of political psychobabble. We may already be there and we will not be given a pass on this one. History will treat us harshly for our cowardice.

Posted April 24, 2009
Luddites Live On

Ohio Representative John Boehner, this past weekend, did his best to resuscitate the early nineteenth-century British social movement known as the Luddites, who were steadfastly opposed to technological progress and change in the textile industry, only the modern day iteration seems to be a refusal to even attempt to confront the overwhelming scientific evidence surrounding climate change and global warming. Worse yet, he does not even seem to grasp the most basic elements of the issue.

It is difficult to tell whether the flatulence coming from a cow's rear-end is more potent than that coming out of Rep. John Boehner's mouth, but let me take a guess—the winner in this instance is the representative from Ohio; the loser, unfortunately, is the American people, who expect at least a semblance of intelligent debate from our elected representatives. After all, they are paid by the taxpayers to take advantage of the vast resources and information available to them and their staff in order to reach semiliterate and defensible policy positions.

In this instance, he did not earn his pay.

One need not have serious grounding in science to understand the difference between methane and carbon dioxide. In my extensive travels to high schools and colleges and, yes, even elementary schools discussing the climate crisis and global warming, awareness of the distinction and recognition of the difference between the two is practically universally known and understood at all grade levels. Thus, when I saw and heard the conversation with George Stephanopoulos this weekend, I was literally stunned.

The distinguished gentleman from Ohio, in his exuberance to hear himself talk and in his excitement to show the viewing public exactly which end of the cow he has studied in depth, clearly illustrated both the intellectual laziness and science-averse political demagoguery that right wing conservatives find comfort with.

At the same time that conservatives now decry the cost of government policies to future generations, despite the abysmal record of the past eight years when they held the effective power of the purse, climate change is an issue that will more deeply affect future generations' quality of life and economic prospects than any other issue I can think of, yet the science is routinely ignored in favor of pseudo-populist political babble.

You see, it is not argument or debate over differences between informed judgments or opinions that are at issue here, but rather the absence of serious discussion due to the inability of Mr. Boehner and his allies to either comprehend or to investigate the facts.

And yes, words are important. Hence, his use of the word "comical" to denigrate near-universal scientific acceptance of the relationship between carbon dioxide concentration in the atmosphere and global warming, between human-induced burning of fossil fuels and climate change, is "tragic."

C'mon, John, what is expected here is a serious discussion about a serious issue. The nonchalance of your commitment to preparation and homework and your dimwitted approach to appreciating the basics of what I will concede is a complicated and complex but not totally incomprehensible set of interrelationships is appalling. Your effort would not pass muster in a third grade classroom.

Further, it demeans all those constituents and citizens who are struggling to reestablish respect and confidence in a system of government they feel must be responsive to and interested in their posterity.

Your job is to advance policies that will make a positive difference for all Americans, not to pander to the Luddites who are fearful that new technologies and scientific development will disturb a status quo that they have prospered under and wish to hold on to. The inability to move into the future relegates one to atrophy in the past, and future generations will not look kindly upon such intransigence. Get your facts straight, and for goodness' sake, open your mind to the notion that you are capable and willing to learn.

So, to borrow a phrase from the past—be part of the solution, not the problem.

The Evolution of Revolution:
An Attack upon Reason, Compromise, and the Constitution

Article 24

May 7, 2009
Empathy Is Dangerous? Really?

In my never-ending attempt to understand the opposition so I can check myself to see if I might be missing an important point, I never cease to be amazed at how silly their arguments are. My good friend Chris Matthews hosts a show called *Hardball* and, although an unapologetic Democrat, he does try to offer an opportunity for conservative argument on his program. While watching Utah Senator Orrin Hatch on his show one evening I discovered just how far right the Republican Party was drifting when he derided the president for choosing a Supreme Court nominee who found empathy a valuable and noble emotion.

Now the senator was ranking member of the Senate Judiciary Committee, and I recalled a chance meeting I had with him about fifteen years ago as I was walking out of a conference room with Senator Ted Kennedy in the Dirksen Senate Office Building. As Senator Hatch walked past, Kennedy grabbed him and told him that he was his favorite Republican. Now I merely passed this off as a grandiose gesture of Senatorial courtesy, but as we walked down the hall he told me that he found Hatch to be a good person and someone he had no trouble working with, and he respected him although he did not always agree with him politically.

Well, that was good enough for me; I decided to look at the senator in a different and more favorable light. So you can imagine my reaction as I listened to him chastise the president for thinking that empathy was a virtue and not a vice. C'mon, really? Are you serious? Yes, he was—at least for his political survival, he was.

Now lawyers make a living with words, and long-time service on the Senate Judiciary Committee means that you must really be good with words, so I did not take his derision of the word or concept of empathy lightly. But he made the argument that it was a "code word," the real meaning of which, in this case, would be "sabotage." "Empathy" would be used to undermine morals, values, and society as currently defined. What?

I have a word for the senator, and it is "paranoia." Establishment Republicans have become afraid of their own shadows. They view things in terms of code words, as though there is a monolithic conspiracy to fool Americans so they will willingly surrender their values, morals, and society to a force that will subject them to Sharia law, socialism, or something equally distasteful. Do these people really believe that we are that gullible? No, that stupid? One look at who elects these idiots might give us an answer we do not wish to hear. The only conspiracy I ever entertained is that Lee Harvey Oswald did not act alone, and I still believe that. But conspiracy theorists flourish in our society, and once again I believe it is a symptom of fear of the future and anger at the present.

It seems that everything directed at the president by his opponents is couched in terms of his desire to socialize America, to turn us into some sort of—God forbid—European state. This struck me as the height of absurdity and from no less a person than Orrin Hatch, whom Ted Kennedy admired.

In "Empathy is a Virtue, Not a Vice," I played off Barry Goldwater's acceptance speech at the 1964 Republican National Convention in which he proclaimed that "Extremism in the defense of liberty is no vice." I wished to attempt to register the absurdity of the notion that empathy was not a desirable quality in someone who would be making decisions that directly affect large numbers of people. Hatch would encounter opposition from the right in his senate reelection bid a few years later; he had seen the political currents he would be swimming against. What a sad commentary on the state of our political discourse. John F. Kennedy wrote the book *Profiles in Courage*; today, volumes could be written of profiles in cowardice. What a pity.

Posted May 7, 2009
Empathy is a Virtue, Not a Vice

I have been struggling hard in the post-partisan world to figure out just exactly what the opposition's rationale or foundation is on any number of issues: stimulus, budget, taxes, torture, and now the Supreme Court nomination. As best as I can tell, the overriding nugget of justification seems to be "Just say no."

I sincerely doubt that this position warrants serious consideration in a world that is trying mightily to confront the deeply dysfunctional mess left by Obama's predecessors. Intellectual honesty, and intellect itself, took a beating for the first eight years of the new century. Intricately woven into the mantra of change, I believe, was a yearning by the public for decisions based upon evidence and fact, thought and deliberation, maturity and vision.

Thus, it is with great consternation that I continually witness the conservative right, which has emerged as the primary opposition to the Obama Administration, flail at the slightest mention of any suggestions that seemingly reflect the verdict rendered by the people last November.

The latest surreal moment occurred last night on *Hardball*. There was Utah Senator Orrin Hatch, generally acknowledged as one of the more thoughtful members of the conservative community and a ranking member of the Senate Judiciary Committee, scolding the president for considering empathy to be an appropriate or acceptable prerequisite for a candidate on the Supreme Court.

Empathy! Empathy! What am I missing here? What is the outrage? I decided to check my Webster's dictionary to see what on earth I should know about this "code word" that could evoke such an irrational response from such a rational person.

According to *Webster's Ninth New Collegiate Dictionary*, empathy is "the action of understanding, being aware of, being sensitive to, and vicariously experiencing the feelings, thoughts, and experience of another of either the past or present without having the feelings, thoughts, and experience fully communicated in an objectively explicit manner." Umm, how awful, could you imagine what havoc an individual might wreak upon society if s/he possessed such dangerous abilities? To interpret laws based upon the actual effects such laws might actually have upon real individuals with real problems? Outrageous!

This is the best they can do? Attack the idea that someone might actually have the ability to understand and feel for those who may be in a different position than themselves?

The good senator kept referring to empathy as a "code word," assuming in the general hysteria that has permeated the conservative community's intelligentsia, like Limbaugh, Coulter, Hannity, that what the president really means is that he might actually choose someone who, under the guise of empathy, would seek to undermine our morals, our values, our way of life, our society as we know it. The bad people will win.

This is the reality of the conservative opposition today. They attack for the sake of attacking, and then justify the attacks upon secret meanings of words and a general assumption that the real agenda here is to bring down the system, a system they have profited quite handsomely from, and has successfully winnowed out the winners and losers, the good from the bad. Why fix what ain't broken?

Well, since I have my dictionary out, I would like to try out a word on them: paranoia. Webster describes it as "a psychosis characterized by systematized delusions of persecution or grandeur, usually without hallucinations."

The <u>absurdity</u> of their arguments and the dearth of any feasible or constructive alternatives other than to "Just say no" reinforces the notion that today's conservatives simply cannot be taken seriously. Meanwhile, the people demand that thoughtfulness dictate solutions to crises that affect them and their neighbors in ways not imaginable to those who deride empathy as a vice, not a virtue.

What is equally disturbing about the apologists for the Bush Administration that are now being trotted out to protect their homespun legacy is that they seem to actually want our country to fail so as to justify their insatiable lust for validation or redemption. Some might be tempted to label them sore losers, or even traitors. I prefer to think of them as unpatriotic.

There is a meanness and vindictiveness there that is not in keeping with the current popularity of a president who enjoys widespread support for a proactive agenda seen as an honest attempt to make things better. Obama will not be sidelined or distracted from the efforts at hand and is almost dismissive of their ankle-biting tendencies. Luckily, at this point they are little more than an annoyance; we need to keep it that way.

Article 25

May 12, 2009
Dick(ing) Around

Once again, Dick Cheney cannot accept the fact that no one cares what he has to say anymore. Wouldn't it have been nice if that had always been the case?

Five months after leaving office, he is flitting here and there, trying desperately to put a happy face on the legacy of torture that he and his puppet president had foisted on an incredulous world. While Obama mightily tries to make substantive changes in our inequitable and spectacularly unequal health-care system, the Cheney distraction should be treated as little more than that—a distraction.

Let him spout and spew like the serpent he is; we have far more important things to concern us, and Obama must continue to keep his eyes fixed on the ultimate prize: health-care reform. We are so far behind the civilized world and there is such injustice in our system that it is imperative we not be distracted from this task.

In "The High Cost of Health Care," I take great pains to point out the pettiness of the Cheney validation tour in hopes that no one else has to. These people would not go away, but hopefully, in time, they would not be able to find a venue where their opinions were welcomed. Of course, given the proliferation of right-wing nuts funded by corporate entities afraid of having to pay their fair share in taxes, and a fundamentalist conservative base afraid that America is led by a socialist Black dictator born in Kenya, I fear there will always be a place for Dick and his cronies. Enough about Dick.

Posted May 12, 2009
The High Cost of Health Care

The true definition of torture is having to listen to Dick Cheney spew ad hominem about why it was proper, even necessary, to circumvent any commonly accepted interpretation civilized society has to offer of what in fact constitutes torture. By relying on the absurd argument that he was guided by the legal rationale developed by political hacks posing as jurists in the highly politicized Justice Department is an insult to any notion of morality and decency.

No one expects or demands that our political leaders be moralists, but they should be moral. No one expects or demands from our political leaders that they be paragons of virtue, but they should be decent.

Deception and distraction are hallmarks of those who advocated and pursued the pre-emptive war in Iraq; thus it should come as no surprise that these very attributes are guiding the current tour de force being conducted by the former vice president. The purpose, I am convinced, is to somehow shift the debate from the Obama Administration's successful efforts so far to deal with the recession and move on to one of the most pervasive long-term issues facing the nation: namely, reforming our system of health care.

It is tempting, deliciously so, to become ensnared in this devious trap. Anyone with a conscience and a desire to prove to not just the world but to ourselves that we still have the ability to command the moral high ground on worldly issues is repulsed that one of the primary architects of the failed Bush doctrine is afforded the stage to insult our sensibilities. However, Obama is right to keep his eye on the proverbial prize and not be sidetracked by these diabolically orchestrated detours that are designed to lead us into political quicksand.

It must scare the bejeezus out of the conservative right that moderation and purpose are the driving forces behind the current attempt to wrest control of our health-care system from an industry that has reaped enormous profits and exerted enormous influence on a political system that has allowed our nation to be laggards of the civilized world when it comes to guaranteeing access and treatment. Politically, the threat of securing a place in history where health care is no longer a privilege but a right must further haunt a conservative movement bereft of forward thinking.

Therefore, it is important for progressives to appreciate the longer-term and larger picture vision being employed here. I, for one, am absolutely perturbed and disturbed by the criminal behavior of the previous administration and would like nothing more than to hold them accountable for their crimes, but if the tradeoff is to deny and deprive millions of Americans the right to quality health care, then the cost is too high.

Unfortunately, this is not a situation that allows us to do both. Striving to advance the greater good is the morally correct choice here, regardless of the pure desire to show the world we still have a soul and are willing to stand up and atone for our misdeeds. The president has made huge strides toward restoring our image and respect internationally, and the domestic political capital he possesses at this juncture dictates that he tackles the health-care issue.

This is not nor should it be a partisan fight. Assembling a coalition of progressives and moderates requires that we reach across the aisle as well as within the Democratic Party to formulate a winning strategy. Of course, this has proved to be a daunting prospect thus far, and partisanship has prevailed.

But the long-term adverse consequences of defeating health-care reform, both substantively and politically, are far greater than the economic and budgetary fights that are largely temporal. Conversely, the benefits of bringing our nation and its citizens into the twenty-first century on health care, once again both politically and substantively, may prove to be too irresistible to those wishing a long career in the public eye. Moderates of all political stripes need to factor this into their electoral calculus.

So, Dick, continue on with your charade of indignation, your unapologetic confidence bordering on either conceit or delusion, the indescribably sour note of fear-mongering that you and your cronies raised to a political art form, and hopefully your well-deserved irrelevance will lead you back to Wyoming.

The world will move on quite nicely without you. Unfortunately, until then we will just have to put up with you, but that is the price of progress.

The Evolution of Revolution:
An Attack upon Reason, Compromise, and the Constitution

Article 26

May 20, 2009
Who Cares?

Having just returned from Nashville, where I attended a refresher course on the critically important issue of climate change given by Al Gore, I remained energized and optimistic that the corner was about to be turned after years of neglect by an administration beholden to the economic interests of the fossil fuel-dominated status quo. Over the last several years, momentum generated by *An Inconvenient Truth* and thousands of climate-change messengers who had fanned out across the globe, bringing a customized version of the film presentation to local audiences, and these had shifted public opinion on and awareness of the issue.

I'd answered the call to become a climate-change messenger nearly two-and-a-half years earlier to promote the science and the political necessity of addressing an issue that will have a profound impact on future generations. The movement was growing, and there was a feeling that progress was being made toward a policy response and a grass-roots uprising to meet the economic and environmental challenges which were worsening exponentially. What made the issue more imperative was the fact that the situation was deteriorating far faster than originally projected.

The impetus for these efforts was largely driven by Al Gore as a result of his years of study and attention to the problem. He may not have been father of the Internet, but he was the leading legislative light on global warming. And now the real-world consequences were hitting home quickly. The issue had always had the aura of being somewhere in the future, and thus it was very difficult for politicians to grapple with. However, the adverse impact was accelerating into real time; climate change was here.

It had become readily apparent that the situation was far worse than predicted only a few years earlier. The Obama Administration was dedicated to addressing the issue via legislation; Congress was taking steps to address the situation; the public, reacting to *An Inconvenient*

Truth and localized efforts to disseminate information and initiate community action, seemed ready to address the issue; and the world community was clamoring for the United States to step up and help ameliorate a problem they had played a huge role in creating.

Gore had brilliantly taken a complex, technically challenging scientific issue and made it comprehensible. I had, by this time, delivered eighty presentations worldwide, and had seen the interest among high school, college, and middle-aged populations grow. I had rediscovered my interest in the environment during the Clinton Administration, when I helped establish the first federal Office of Sustainable Development along with an old friend of mine, former New Bedford, Massachusetts Mayor John Bullard. Together we delved deeply into the issue of sustainable development relative to the worldwide collapse of key fisheries. The office was strategically placed in the National Oceanic and Atmospheric Administration, and then–Vice President Gore had used a great deal of capital to forward the issue to the upper tier of the administration's agenda that led to the creation of this office.

The United States had dropped the ball on the Kyoto Protocol agreements in the closing days of the twentieth century, and the world lost precious time in tackling the problem in the intervening decade. But now, with the Copenhagen Summit on the horizon, there was tremendous hope that we would get in the game.

Entrenched fossil-fuel interests were poised to beat back any proposed changes to their heretofore unchallenged domination of power sources for the world economy. We were all prepared for a battle, but momentum seemed to be going our way. I was particularly hopeful that change—real change—was in the offing.

In "From Nashville to Copenhagen," I outlined my continuing belief and optimism that we were on the cusp of taking great strides toward solving a problem that would have a deeply profound impact upon the human species, effects perhaps unparalleled in history. My unbounded enthusiasm was predicated on the experiences I had witnessed during my presentations and the apparent movement from both the administration and the legislature. Hope would certainly be fueled by change.

Posted May 20, 2009

From Nashville to Copenhagen

This past weekend, nearly 500 dedicated activists met in Nashville to spend two-and-a-half days reflecting on the current science and direction of the Earth's changing climate. There were truly inspiring presentations by Nobel Laureate Al Gore and an array of scientists, intended to inform and educate an assemblage of extraordinary citizens of the planet who give their time and effort to bring a simple message to their communities: namely, we are in midst of a planetary emergency, and we need to address it now.

Just over two-and-a-half years ago, I answered Gore's call to join a movement to transform a complicated and technical set of scientific issues into an understandable and practical message that would educate and inspire fellow citizens to take effective actions that would no less than ensure the survival of our planet. Since then, over 2,500 individuals have heeded the call worldwide, and over 50,000 presentations have been delivered, reaching at least 5 million people.

Surely, the catalyst for these presentations has been the documentary *An Inconvenient Truth,* and each of us has been trained to dissect the PowerPoint slides which proved to be the centerpiece of the movie. The genius of this documentary is that it molded Earth science into a comprehensive and comprehensible set of propositions that uninitiated individuals could easily get their arms around. This alone has proved to be a feat of historic proportions.

Since its release, the basic message remains as potent as ever, and an avalanche of new scientific data and statistics have effectively accelerated the urgency for the need for action. The consequences of inaction have pushed us ever closer to an inevitable tipping point where certain conditions become irreversible. Indeed, the Union of Concerned Scientists contends that we have already crossed the threshold of mitigation and must accept a degree of adaptation to climate change.

It is said that timing in life is everything. If so, with respect to this issue, we must act immediately. It is all too easy to fall into the trap of reciting dire and dour statistics to illuminate just how serious this crisis is. It is far more difficult to illustrate the interconnectivity of issues and events that are occurring in front of our very eyes.

And while in Chinese the word crisis is composed of two characters, one representing danger, the other opportunity, it is far easier to focus on the former than the latter. But I am convinced that it is critically important that we accentuate the opportunities inherent in the crisis, if for no other reason than to dampen a general fatigue among the populace that has set in [as a] reaction to a long litany of fear-mongering.

Gore opened the session with an incredibly uplifting statistic. The average age of the Houston Space Center technician when Neil Armstrong first set foot on the moon in 1969 was twenty-six, meaning that when John F. Kennedy first issued his call to safely send a man to the moon some eight years and two months earlier, their average age would have been eighteen. The call to public service, to civic activism, to expanding the reach of scientific endeavor was palpable and infectious. The inspiration elicited by this bold announcement projected upon an entire generation. We need that same resolve today.

We are turning the corner. Science and scientific method now are at the public policy table again. Congress is poised to seriously tackle this issue. Pending before the US House of Representatives is legislation sponsored by California Rep. Henry Waxman and Massachusetts Rep. Ed Markey that sets the table on carbon emissions targets on the environmental side of the equation, and a cap and trade system on the economic front. The importance of effectively integrating the economic and environmental aspects to this issue cannot be overstated.

The importance of having an aggressive national effort to limit carbon emissions here in the only industrialized nation on Earth that turned its back on the Kyoto Treaty is monumental. As we prepare for the Copenhagen Summit in December, it is critical that the United States assume the mantle of leadership on the most important global issue of the century.

In the eighty presentations I have conducted on this issue over the past thirty months, I have witnessed two distinct developments: first, the climate crisis has deteriorated much greater and much faster than scientists had predicted; second, where circumstances under the previous administration forced us to concentrate our efforts solely at the grass roots level due to a lack of political will in the executive branch, we are now witnessing a deliberate national strategy to act, and this enhances the grass roots efforts already underway.

We are now focusing on the opportunities inherent in this crisis. Waxman-Markey offers us the ability to advance the ball toward Copenhagen, and that will allow us to lead the world in the development of a new economic paradigm that will effectively lessen, if not displace, our dependence on fossil fuels to power our collective economic engines. Lest we not forget to remind those who fret over the economic consequences of such a paradigm shift, the opportunities for innovation, creativity, and economic ingenuity present a bounty that far surpasses our bankrupt addiction to oil.

We are replacing the certainty of inaction with the uncertainty of action, and much like President Kennedy's challenge nearly a half century ago, it is a clarion call to change, and after all, change is what the American people overwhelmingly support at this point in our history. We need to look forward to a future where power is derived from the sun and the wind, where electric cars and the infrastructure to support them makes the inefficient internal combustion engine obsolete, where respect for ecology and the environment combines with economic opportunity to foster a cleaner and more productive planet.

As we left Nashville, we were energized by the knowledge that we can and must do what we can to make this world a reality. Our future depends upon it.

The Evolution of Revolution:
An Attack upon Reason, Compromise, and the Constitution

Article 27

May 21, 2009
Play Ball!

In a follow-up to the previous day's article outlining the promising future I believed imminent on climate change, I focused this article on the Congressional action which was ready for a vote. The day of this writing was significant to me as it was my oldest son's seventeenth birthday and, after all, the issue of climate change was directly aimed at his generation.

In advance of the Copenhagen Climate Summit, it was imperative that Congress show resolve so our negotiators could play a productive and forceful role in the international community. The Waxman-Markey bill, named after California Congressman Henry Waxman and Massachusetts Congressman Ed Markey, was designed to impose limits on carbon emissions and create a cap-and-trade system, which would be the mechanism for enforcing those limits.

I had attended an Environmental Economics workshop at Harvard University's Center for International Development in 1997, where carefully selected individuals from over fifty countries engaged in a three-week series of seminars and workshops to address the economic dimensions of sustainable development. A pivotal component of the workshops was exploration of cap and trade. And while I had expressed my reservations at the general concept of allowing wealthy corporations to purchase carbon credits, I had come to accept the notion that cap-and-trade probably offered the most realistic and pragmatic political approach to the problem of carbon buildup in the atmosphere.

A dozen years later, the US Congress was poised to take a run at serious legislation to police this unsustainable increase in carbon. Again I was enthusiastic and optimistic that we were finally going to start, albeit belatedly, on a course correction. A perfect storm of sorts had been brewing as the fossil-fuel industry's public relations and political-action committees' efforts had been ramped up considerably to counter the move to constrain greenhouse gases.

The playbook was straight out of the tobacco industry's efforts nearly a half century earlier—to create doubt and to deny there was a problem. Just as people of my parents' generation had become enamored with cigarette smoking, my generation had become inextricably tied to the internal combustion engine. We would not abandon our automobiles unless the crisis was real. Casting doubt and infusing denial into the equation made it intellectually convenient to question whether we really had to change our habits. The battle was being waged, and the counteroffensive, although counterintuitive, would be formidable.

In "Waxman-Markey: Time to Step Up to the Plate," I expressed how important and necessary the legislation would be to moving us into a meaningful position on the international stage, and how important it would be to the survival of humans on the planet.

Posted May 21, 2009
Waxman-Markey: Time to Step Up to the Plate

Two-and-a-half years ago, I had the distinct honor of being invited, along with 200 other individuals, to Nashville, Tennessee, to participate in a three-day exercise with Al Gore and The Climate Reality Project, aimed at arming us with the facts about global warming. Since that time, over 2,500 individuals worldwide have been similarly trained, and together we have delivered over 50,000 presentations designed to educate citizens of the planet on the scientific evidence about a global planetary emergency.

This past weekend, nearly 500 climate messengers gathered in Nashville with Nobel Laureate Gore and The Climate Reality Project for a reunion of sorts. And the news is sobering, to say the least. Two things have changed dramatically since this monumental grass roots educational effort was launched: one, the situation has deteriorated far quicker and deeper than scientists has thought possible; two, a new national administration has fueled momentum from the highest levels of government down for timely and effective action to combat the climate crisis instead of reliance solely upon the grass roots.

Unfortunately, there are more negatives than positives to report at this juncture, but as Gore so smartly insists, there is a realistic opportunity to stanch the bleeding and spearhead a global healing process that is feasible in both economic and environmental terms. But we must act quickly and decisively in order to maximize the degree of mitigation necessary and minimize the inevitable amount of adaptation that is already occurring.

The United States must take hold of this issue and engage both developing and developed nations in a collective effort that essentially shifts the economic paradigm from one powered by fossil fuel consumption to one powered by renewable energy. The opportunity to do so will happen this December in Copenhagen. But in order to set the table for that to happen, Congress must enact a set of carbon emissions reductions targets and policy incentives (ie, a carbon cap-and-trade system) that will allow us to exert global leadership. Before Memorial Day, it is expected that the US House of Representatives will vote on the Waxman-Markey legislation that does just that.

Truly, a brighter future beckons. We have at our fingertips the important building blocks to begin to construct a world for our children and grandchildren that, at the very least, gives them a fighting chance to avoid the horrendous consequences of a world choking on pollution, rising sea levels, and increasingly devastating weather incidents such as floods, droughts, lightning strikes, wildfires, hurricanes, and tornadoes.

I will not recite a litany of statistics to validate the point here, but the fact that there is no meaningful scientific debate that global warming is happening, or that human-induced fossil-fuel emissions are significantly contributing to it reflects a sea change in the general public's attitudes on this issue over the past two decades.

And for those who still deny the science, ask yourself this question: do you want to wean the United States off of its oil addiction habit so we are less dependent upon finite resources and rely upon more abundant resources, such as the sun and the wind?

Of course, the answer is yes. It makes common sense, economic sense, and most certainly environmental sense. It is the right choice.

The new greening of America will offer a bountiful array of green collar jobs. It will also have positive and dynamic impacts upon our national and international security apparatus. Competition over scarce resources, whether it be fisheries depleted by an increasingly acidified ocean or lost due to the evaporation of a lake (witness the disappearance of the Aral Sea or Lake Chad), lost crops due to loss of soil moisture, warmer temperatures forcing the displacement of certain crops, loss of drinking water, or loss of corn for human consumption in favor of fuel, can lead to conflict.

Competition among rapidly industrializing economies over oil can lead to conflict. Displacement of huge populations along coastlines due to rising sea levels will contribute to mass migrations, border tensions, and huge humanitarian relief and rescue operations, all increasing the prospect for conflict.

We have the ability to collectively embark upon a new course of action. Given the nature of the season, let me liken it to a baseball analogy: it is like being in the eighth inning of a game where we are behind by three runs and the bases are loaded, there are two outs and the count is three balls and two strikes. Chances are it may be the last best time to hit the ball out of the park to win the game. We need to hit the home run. The situation may arise in the ninth, it may not. Therefore, we need to take advantage of the opportunity in front of us.

Our lawmakers are up to bat. It is their time to shine.

Article 28

May 30, 2009
What Is the Question?

The Bush-Cheney Torture Tour of 2009 was again in full view, a pathetic attempt to rationalize, justify, and validate the limp legacy that would define their reign. I have made it a hallmark of my professional life as a public servant and my personal life as a parent to encourage solid questioning. I have taught my children to question, and it has come back to haunt me on more than a few occasions. However, the courage and tenacity with which one intellectually challenges conventional beliefs and practices is a critical component of a forward-moving society. I remember the bumper stickers popular during my formative years which demanded that we Question Authority. That still resonates with me, and seems like a wise maxim and astute general principle.

I have striven to walk the walk over the years by persistently questioning not only others', but my own, decisions and actions. And, importantly, it is essential that we ask the right questions. If we do not, we cannot expect to get the right answers. The lack of intellectual curiosity, of disciplined examination, of objectivity, and the deceitful perversion of analysis practiced in the previous administration had raised disingenuousness to new heights, and yet here were these purveyors of dishonesty using valuable press coverage to attempt to validate their misjudgments. It was enough to make the most patient soul irrational and angry.

In "Questions, Anyone?" I explore the importance of raising penetrating questions to guide our decision-making, and question the motives behind not doing so. These jerks would not go away. They were lucky not to have been tried as war criminals, for Christ's sake.

Posted May 30, 2009
Questions, Anyone?

There is an enormous value to the art of questioning. For instance, public opinion as measured by polling can be construed to say one thing, when in actuality it is really expressing something totally different, depending on what and how questions are posed. To ask people whether or not they support raising taxes, in the abstract, will most likely elicit a strong negative response. However, asking them whether or not they support raising taxes to support our troops may very well elicit a totally different response.

Questioning is very important. I come from a generation that took questioning to a new level, most particularly its questioning of authority during the Vietnam War. Asking questions is a good, healthy, and emphatically democratic exercise. We should encourage it, as a government, as a society, and as parents. We should also strive to question ourselves regularly in order to keep our individual quirks and biases in check.

It seems to me that the act of questioning itself signifies an intellectual curiosity that keeps the mind sharp and our political leaders and institutions on their proverbial game. It is a sign of maturity and confidence, it is a critically necessary component of leadership, and is required for a larger vision or statesmanship.

What is so refreshing about President Obama is his willingness, and indeed, eagerness to engage in questioning of conventional wisdom and his confidence to challenge the status quo. Both of these attributes are at the core of the change agenda he fostered during the campaign and heretofore embraced in his governance and leadership style. And it is also these attributes that buoy his high approval ratings.

What is so disturbing and twisted about the insurgency of Dick Cheney and his current Torture Tour '09, and now the apparent me-too insertion of George W. Bush into this sordid debate, is not whether or not questions were asked, but rather the intellectual depth of both the questions and the questioners. It is one thing to ask minions to render a legal opinion as to whether certain "enhanced interrogation techniques" are legally defensible, and it is quite another to question whether or not the answers satisfy a much larger and important need: namely, whether they actually made the nation safer.

The act of merely asking questions is not sufficient. The art of dissecting the answers and employing an intellectual calculus as to whether or not they meet the safety test requires an examination of a much more complicated and difficult set of variables. Merely satisfying preconceived notions does not rise to the level of leadership and statesmanship that is required to actually keep us safe, and this is where I find great fault with the previous administration. At a time when intellectual curiosity, deep introspective soul-searching, and courage were at a premium, Bush/Cheney failed.

And it is irritating to see and hear the pathetic apologetic rationalizations being played out in a blatantly political way that is intended to thwart an administration that is making tremendous strides forward in correcting the misguided and dangerous mistakes that have put us at risk internationally. Dick and Dubya both seem to be staking their legacies and their justifications on the tragically laughable tenet of, "Well, we asked and they told us it was okay!" This is sophomoric and, in universally accepted political jargon, cover-your-ass logic.

Internationally, our moral turpitude, our historical democratic integrity, have been sacrificed in order to justify torture and to cover a preemptive attack on a regime we simply felt needed to be changed. And this is the real mess that Obama inherited.

So let there be no mistake, the next time you hear the ex-president or the ex–vice president stridently attempting to defend their intuitively driven decisions, question why they are doing so. And never again allow either yourself or your government to simply ask questions, but demand that the answers are sufficiently scrutinized so as to allow for further questioning.

It is natural and dangerous for us to lighten up on our questioning of authority in times of crisis. However, this is the time when enhanced questioning techniques are needed the most. The same applies to all leaders, regardless of party, regardless of ideology. Any questions?

The Evolution of Revolution:
An Attack upon Reason, Compromise, and the Constitution

Article 29

June 6, 2009
Only the Best!

I penned this article on the sixty-fourth anniversary of D-Day. The title was meant to invoke a military patriotism which defines the country as a bastion of tolerance and freedom. The right-wing-nut criticism machine was churning at full power due to Barack Hussein Obama's audacity in traveling to the Middle East to try to soothe the strains in the most tension-wracked region in the world. How dare he?

The president attempted to defuse a gnawing criticism that policies and attitudes in the United States were being driven by a growing anti-Muslim sentiment—one that equated the religion with terror and terrorism. There had been an attitude fostered through careless speech and assumingly inadvertent proclamations from the highest levels of the previous administration drawing analogies of the current conflict to the Crusades.

In his speech, the president was critical of negative stereotypes, particularly religious ones. Once again, his reasonable, rational, cool demeanor combined with an intellectually solid argument—and presentation—was driving his opponents into frenzy. There was Obama, logically explaining that we were not engaged in a war against Islam, and getting criticized for having the temerity to suggest that there was a difference between a terrorist and a Muslim.

As I look back on this chronology of events, it becomes crystal clear that the opposition was developing a deep and disturbingly illogical line of criticism that would find fault if he acknowledged a nice day. Anti-intellectualism was rising to new heights politically, and becoming a default mechanism for the far right on virtually any issue. To the extent that intellectual positions could be presented as colliding with conventional common sense, there was no question as to which side the right would land on.

The man could get no credit. It reminds me of the conundrum Jesus might have faced if he had walked on water in the current politically charged environment; he would have been accused of not knowing how to swim. And it was becoming increasingly clear that not only was the chorus consistent, it was growing louder. There was meanness and a deep, underlying hatred manifesting itself in these criticisms that made dysfunction a self-fulfilling prophesy.

A loyal opposition is one thing, but there was a time, and in my lifetime, when even the opposition was capable of doing some things right. As much as I hated Richard Nixon, I gave him credit for going to China. I will never forget the pride I felt upon watching Air Force One land in that Communist country, and the feat was accomplished by an old Commie buster at that. Those days were way behind us, and it appeared unlikely that they would return any time soon.

But this was a different day, a different era, and a different country, and the criticism was ugly. In "Be All That You Can Be," I tried to capture the idea that we as a country needed to rise above pettiness and partisan politics, and utilize our intellectual power to cool hot spots and quell and even prevent flash points like the Middle East. This may appear self-evident, but in the contemporary political environment, it was asking a lot; maybe too much?

Posted June 6, 2009
Be All That You Can Be

The nagging criticisms leveled at the president's overtures to the Muslim world this week prove once and for all that the historical maxim that "Politics stops at the water's edge" is as quaint and irrelevant as the Victrola. Politics and political considerations now know no boundaries, and it is particularly noteworthy that the attacks are being launched by those who professed just a short time ago that any criticism, constructive or not, of our national security posture was, at a minimum, unpatriotic.

There is something particularly galling to the conservative right about the prospect of resolving problems through either diplomatic means or by collective security measures. In their worldview might makes right, and unequivocally, on this issue, the right is dead wrong.

How naive, what an appeaser, how wacky is this guy? How elitist of the president to go to Egypt and suggest that there are certain ideas, ideals, and concepts that beg mutual cooperation between our nation and those in the Middle East. Why, it is downright un-Christian to suggest that Muslim-majority countries have any conception of democratic processes, freedom, or human rights. I mean, after all, don't they hate us for our freedom?

As preposterous as it may sound, there are moderately well-educated and at times rational individuals out there who are contemptuous of the eloquence with which Barack Obama delivered his worldview this week. The eloquence of his words and the smoothness of his delivery surely must mask a fundamental misunderstanding of the region, if not the world, and put at risk the hard-fought safety rendered by a preemptive war against an unacceptable regime.

And to suggest that this great nation, America, might actually have exhibited human faults and made human mistakes such as misgauging intentions of others and not appreciating cultural and religious differences, to suggest that we may have erred in our zeal to promote democracy abroad through the outmoded and outdated methods of gunboat diplomacy rather than by showcasing our collective morality and tolerance for diversity, how treasonous.

It is interesting to watch and listen to the critics of this administration scold the president on his attempts to reconcile the differences between us by appealing to the commonalities that potentially link us together. And they are predictable in their attacks: indignant about our superiority, resistant to the notion that we may not always be right, delirious over the appearance of weakness, and defensive about their complicity in constructing the current state of affairs.

But let's look at exactly what Obama was attempting to convey through his eloquence. First and foremost, he is attempting to define the enemy. For far too long we have been told that we are in a war on terror. But war itself is terror, and it is terrifying. I must admit, I never understood the concept or the terminology. But implicit in it, I fear, was the idea that Islam was a religious foundation for terrorism, thereby fueling religious intolerance and suspicion in a country essentially founded on the concept of fostering religious freedom. Remarks from the previous administration invoking the Crusades did little to dispel the notion that religious differences were essentially at the heart of the conflict.

However, as Obama made crystal clear in his speech, the enemy was not and is not Islam, but rather violent extremism and those who practice it. What we should be engaged in is a war on terrorists, or a war on terrorism, which includes those who practice it. This is not an unimportant distinction. Terrorism and terrorists have no basis in religion.

Obama pledged "To fight against negative stereotypes of Islam wherever they appear." Under the banner of defining common ground, common principles, common dreams and shared responsibility, he called upon Muslims to reject crude stereotypes of Americans as well.

The knee-jerk reactionary-right criticisms aimed at Obama for attempting to redefine the dangerous world we find ourselves in, a world preeminently less safe, more volatile, and more economically fractured than generally acknowledged, only serves to marginalize and isolate an increasingly small but intensely frustrated fringe element in our society. If nothing else, this is a plea to give this president, in the great American tradition, a fighting chance to realize the dreams he has for our nation, dreams which are common to all of us, regardless of political party, ideology, or religion: peace and prosperity for our children.

Criticism and competition are the bedrock of a free society, and should be encouraged. Rooting for failure crosses the line, and is at best poor sportsmanship; at worst, it makes us as a society something less than we can be. We owe it to ourselves, our children, and those oppressed everywhere to be the best we can be.

Article 30

July 8, 2009
Jacko No Mo'!

Because the dividing line between entertainment news and political news has grown dimmer and dimmer, there was no escaping the fact that the death of Michael Jackson, a highly controversial figure in his later years, would capture the news across the political spectrum and dominate a couple of news cycles. It was news, but the coverage went over the top. He was a great artist with eccentricities that rivaled his stardom, but did this event really necessitate round-the-clock news coverage? I didn't think so.

What bothered me the most was the inexorable pull of his controversies into the realm of politics, and politicians attempting to capitalize on his presence nationally and internationally. On the political stage, efforts arose to memorialize him as an American legend—and, of course, there was concomitant debate over the controversies that engulfed his existence. Having worked on Capitol Hill, I was familiar with the opportunities afforded representatives and senators to place into the Congressional Record statements and memorials to virtually anyone. I had, in fact, written many of them, and had them inserted in this official record of Congressional business. Most would remain hidden from public view, and served as a constituent service to the member, which s/he could use to his/her benefit.

The advent of television coverage of the House of Representatives and eventually the Senate, however, had injected an entertainment component into what should be the solemn business of the people. I had witnessed the Senate pre- and post-television coverage, and it is inarguable that the quality and caliber of debate, and even the proceedings themselves, have suffered greatly. Entertainment and politics have been engaged in a longtime love affair, but now they would become inextricably linked. The death of Michael Jackson presented an opportunity to exploit the relationship.

This was an issue better left to the world of entertainment, and despite the overwhelming temptation for politicians to immerse themselves in that world, the important business affecting the everyday lives of real people should be the business of our elected officials. I have always found voluminous testimonials to individual achievement cluttering the pages of the Congressional Record to be a self-serving waste of the taxpayers' dollars.

Michael Jackson produced memorable music—period. Films, documentaries, biographies, historical accounts, and articles will be produced which touch on every aspect of his life. He will be vilified, promoted, scorned, and adored in many ways, but the intrusion of our elected officials into the fray is unwarranted.

In "Out of this World," I thought it important to point out the absurdity through which our elected officials can be so easily distracted from the work they should be focused upon. It seems that any distraction was welcomed as the battle lines for public debate grew sharper and sharper.

Posted July 8, 2009
Out of This World

I am old enough to remember the Jackson Five and the phenomenon known as Michael Jackson. Back during the time of transistor radios and AM radio stations (growing up in Philadelphia it was WFIL 56 AM, or WIBG 99 AM, or at night we could reach Cousin Brucie on AM Channel 77 WABC out of New York City), one could not escape the inexorable cavalcade of hits from this group of youngsters from Gary, Indiana.

And when watching *Sonny and Cher*, or *The Smothers Brothers Show*, *Soul Train*, or *The Ed Sullivan Show*, you were drawn into the hottest trends in pop music on a weekly basis. Of course, growing up in Philly, it was almost required to watch American Bandstand with Dick Clark on Saturdays just for good measure, even after he abandoned the City of Brotherly Love for the West Coast.

Regardless of your musical tastes, you could not escape the reach of this magnificent band of brothers. And as the years went by, you could also not fail to at least listen to, if not appreciate, the talented efforts of Michael's singing and dancing. Of course, "Thriller" was a sensation that helped propel MTV into the public consciousness. At fifty-five, I got to witness all of this, and I am sure I am better for it.

We watched this incredible talent grow and mature, but we also watched him self-destruct. Not only did the face of Michael Jackson change, but he actually changed his face. Armchair psychologists and psychiatrists that we all are, one could not help but render diagnoses of deep-seated demons that drove the King of Pop seemingly beyond the pale of acceptability. But it did not take a genius to figure out that there were seriously disturbing trends at work here, and even in a world suspicious to public relations-inspired and album/CD-selling motivations, it was obvious that something was wrong, very wrong.

His marriages, Neverland, and brushes with the law all sat uneasily on our collective levels of tolerance and acceptability. Maybe it was our inability to understand, or maybe just his inability to understand our inability to understand. Whichever, I am sure he was as confused as we were. But he was never convicted of the crimes of which he was accused.

I don't know whether he died a sad figure; it seemed so, but he certainly died knowing he had made a stunning mark on the world of entertainment. He was the consummate entertainer, and his artistic accomplishments set a very high bar indeed for those who will follow. The testimonials rendered at his funeral service yesterday were moving, and one could not help but be touched in a deep emotional way by the aura of love that he engendered among friends and colleagues alike.

Thus, it is very unfortunate that today we find political controversy over his passing. His passing should not be politicized by either his supporters or detractors. Arguments over whether a Congressional resolution declaring him an American legend is appropriate or not are a colossal waste of time, and do damage to the images and remembrances of fans, friends, and family.

There are deep and traumatic economic circumstances affecting large swaths of the populace at this moment, there are serious political and policy debates surrounding climate change and access to health care that need to be resolved, there are two wars being waged simultaneously where many lives are at stake, there is starvation and poverty in large areas of the world, these and other issues demand our political attention.

Michael Jackson was an entertainer: let there be arguments over how good or how legendary his entertainment skills were. He should be honored as an entertainment icon, regardless of opinions of his personal life. There is a place where this can take place, there is an appropriate stage for honoring his accomplishments, and there is a time and place to acknowledge whether he truly deserves to be known forever more as the King of Pop, but that debate should not take place within the halls of Congress.

We already clutter our airwaves with entertainment news. There is a diminishing line separating hard news from tabloid journalism. We somehow find a need to view all issues through a political prism. Enough is enough.

Yes, the passing of an icon is news; yes, it should be covered as such; and yes, there is a sufficient public interest served so that significant air time should be devoted to an examination of his death. But to continue the deification versus personal destruction argument in the political arena is just plain wrong.

So in the name of love, peace, and understanding, let us commence with putting to rest any further debate over the significance of Michael Jackson's life or judgment of it from our elected representatives and leave it to the documentarians, historians, screenwriters, and analysts who populate the entertainment world. Final judgment may well rest with those who populate a different world altogether. But most certainly, his life, his career, rests in the fantasy world in which he thrived. Let it rest.

Article31

July 30, 2009
You Don't Need a Weatherman to Know Which Way the Wind Blows

It never ceases to amaze me how furiously candidates campaign to get into positions of power and leadership only to immediately abandon their responsibilities to exert power or lead when they get there. I'm also astounded by how willing they are to hide behind their constituents when convenient to avoid having to make tough decisions. They put a wet finger in the air to determine which way the populist wind is blowing, even though that is never an appropriate determiner for doing what should be or needs to be done.

My former boss, Governor Ed Rendell, has recently penned a book titled *A Nation of Wusses*, in which he decries our elected leaders' lack of intestinal fortitude. He has been remarkably consistent in this stance during his long political career, and he is absolutely right; we have become a nation of wusses. He may not have been right on every issue, and there were a couple on which he and I differed, but he never shied away from his core beliefs and convictions, and I genuinely respect him for that. He was not averse to taking tough stands on controversial questions and making tough decisions which were often politically detrimental, but once he decided, that was that. He has shown that projecting that aura can lead to political success, and that good policy can be good politics. He was willing to take the heat and move forward. If more politicians heeded his call, we might be advancing on important issues. Of course, this does not excuse them when they are wrong, but at least they are moving forward.

But, over time, a conviction has developed among politicians that if they stay on the popular side of most issues, regardless of how ill-informed or wrongheaded popular opinion may be, they will be rewarded with re-election and be seen as brilliant politicians. If we were only interested in winning popularity contests, I guess that would suffice as a brilliant strategy, but we must confront issues of enormous heft and consequence, and doing the popular thing is inadequate.

Early in my career, I recall listening to elected officials rationalize votes they knew were wrong to preserve their positions, arguing that if that's what it took to stay around, then it was an acceptable trade-off because if people with less enlightened views or intellect were elected to their seats, things would be much worse. There is some logic to this argument, but what a cowardly way to govern. Ultimately it has engendered a level of distrust among the electorate which has caused them to turn away and leave the process to extremists at both ends of the ideological spectrum.

I once worked with the mayor of a large northeastern city who said he would rather go down standing for something rather than remain standing for nothing. This attitude reflects the degree of trust we should demand from our elected officials. It is critically important to the preservation of our democratic process that we entrust individuals with the power to make decisions based on information we do not have; otherwise, we could vote for a buffoon who could take the pulse of the electorate and make weighty decisions based on that. This is where we are headed, if we're not there already, and it's why we're in the mess we are in.

I have argued elsewhere that it is important to elect individuals who go beyond leadership and exhibit vision and wisdom in their decision-making—two essential hallmarks of statesmanship. That would be ideal, but we cannot find individuals who are willing to exercise leadership, let alone statesmanship. And we are fully culpable in this scheme because we do not demand a higher level of accountability, nor do we invest the time and effort required of an informed electorate. We lament the loss of civility in political discourse, yet we have systematically ceded our processes to those at the furthest extremes.

We must right the ship of state in order to face the rough waters that lie ahead. The ballast needs to be filled with educated and informed voters willing to invest time and energy in a system that will endure the tempestuous seas, the jagged rocks, and the hidden shoals which will invariably pose problems.

If we continue to elect followers, we will continue to travel in circles, exhausting our energies and getting nowhere. When I was a wee lad, my father took great pleasure in telling me the story of the gooney bird, which would fly in ever tighter concentric circles until eventually he would fly up his own arse. He would always laugh when he told that story, and it was many years until I appreciated the moral it imparted.

In "Our Elected Followers," I described the unfortunate place in which we found ourselves in attempting to solve the political problems exacerbating a widening gap between the rich and poor, the haves and have-nots, and the growing frustration of our inability to confront a world that is rapidly changing. We are being led by people who are more comfortable following and, like the gooney bird, we may suffer the same fate, extinction.

Posted July 30, 2009
Our Elected Followers

Someone once told me you can tell a man's priorities by looking at his checkbook. Sound counsel for sure. But in the current atmosphere of budgetary chaos afflicting government at all levels—federal, state, and local—it is discouraging, disheartening, and distressing to watch so-called political leaders cower under the weight of the public policy responsibilities they so desperately campaigned to assume.

Rarely have we as a society been treated to such theatre of the absurd as we are currently witnessing in the halls of state capitols across the nation. Surely the draconian budget cuts being undertaken in California attest to the inability of the public interest to prevail over ideologically driven political hyperbole. Conservatives of all political stripes, Democratic and Republican, have foisted the well-worn and unfortunately effective bogeyman of higher taxes up the flagpole of freedom to thwart rational economic arguments for social spending that would have positive long-term benefits.

Adding insult to injury, discussion of a balanced fiscal prescription for economic growth, which by the very definition of balanced would mean a discussion of both spending and taxing options, gets drowned out in the din of the ear-shattering drumbeat of "no new taxes." Actually, it is no taxes period—old, new, or otherwise. The old refrain of eliminating wasteful spending to solve our budgetary imbalances is as loud today as it has ever been. Of course, the conservative zealots who propound such mush are armed with meat axes, not scalpels. Their butchery always hits the poorest the hardest, and inflicts the maximum amount of pain on those who are least represented in our political system.

The atrocious behavior of Congressional members on both sides of the aisle who stubbornly refuse to buck the health-care and insurance titans that profit spectacularly from the dysfunctional system of health care in this country is shameful, and in another context might be considered criminal. And these cowards hide behind cost arguments, a modern-day equivalent of human shields, to limply defend their positions. Yet these very same conservatives gamely support and encourage deficit-enhancing tax cuts regardless of cost. They also staunchly support our troops by subsidizing Blackwater and Halliburton and other war profiteers while failing in their responsibilities to protect our soldiers and families from the psychological trauma post-combat. It is all a sham. It is the perpetuation of political self-interest that triumphs over the public interest.

And what is so frustrating is the use of us, their constituents, to justify their actions. As I continually hear what it is the people want, ie, the people don't want higher taxes, it makes me want to scream. Just ask anybody, nobody wants higher taxes, hell, I don't want higher taxes. But I am willing to pay them for things I think are important. Health care, education, economic development, job training, improved infrastructure, energy independence, mass transit, research and development, science—hell, there are a lot of things I believe are worth paying for. Others may have different priorities; this is the beauty of the democratic system. But to blindly ascribe to the insane proposition that all taxes are bad, and most spending is wasteful, is a prescription for a very unhealthy society.

What is even more frustrating is this notion that if the people do not want it, it cannot be good. My kids did not like their vegetables— it does not mean they are not good for them. Besides, we do not call them our elected followers; they are supposed to be leaders, and thus have a responsibility to lead. We pay them to hire staffs that counsel them with the information we do not have either the time or inclination to assemble. They are charged with and charge us for the privilege of making decisions, yet more times than not I hear that they are dutifully reflecting the wishes of their constituents. Well, I could hire a ten-year-old to do that, and pay him or her considerably less.

And there is no consistency to their arguments in this regard anyway. While nearly three-quarters of the American people support a public option in the current health-care-reform debate, we still see many of our elected followers following the lead of the special-interest constituency and not the will of the electorate. If by some miracle of God or nature three-quarters of the electorate suddenly supported higher taxes, I have no doubt that these conservatives would figure out a way to pander to wealthy contributors who feel differently.

In the end, of course, we the people do share considerable culpability here. We refuse to hold our elected followers to any sense of accountability, we continue to turn the other cheek when rampant irrationality and self-interest holds sway over the decision-making process, and we even delude ourselves into accepting preposterous claims by advertisers and spinmeisters that defy common sense.

I heard George Will over the weekend decrying the Obama economic stimulus program because it was not being spent fast enough, and he believes that the recession is either over or ending, and to date only eight percent of the funds have been expended. Now, I believe he is a moderately intelligent man, but once again blinded by conservative orthodoxy. He is bright enough to know that even if technically the recession is coming to an end, or may have actually ended, joblessness will continue to remain a problem for many months to come. Thus, as job-enhancing stimulus funds continue to be spent, they will actually be addressing a problem that continues. To me, that sounds as though the program is working and doing exactly what it is supposed to do. Seems to me he is being held hostage to a political ideology, and he is neither elected nor incapable of intellectual thought. This is the level of polarization that has hamstrung our system.

It is endemic and thoughtless. It is devoid of rationalization. It is oblivious to practical consequences. It is divisive and counterproductive. But most of all, it endangers our ability to remedy problems through deliberation, discourse, and debate. Rigid ideology debases our democratic system, and we all have a responsibility to temper our ideological fervor in times of crisis. This does not mean we forego our principles or lessen our resolve, but it does mean that we sharpen our diplomatic skills. It also means that we sometimes sacrifice self-interest for the public interest. Who knows, you may actually be rewarded for it, but regardless it is your duty to do so.

The Evolution of Revolution:
An Attack upon Reason, Compromise, and the Constitution

Article 32

August 4, 2009
Storm Clouds

As special assistant for intergovernmental affairs to Governor Ed Rendell, I often found myself tasked with the responsibility of addressing and listening to groups in the ornate waiting room outside the governor's suite of offices, where my office was located. On many occasions, the governor was not in the office, and on others he did not want to speak with particular individuals and groups. Then I would get the call.

One day, there was a rather rambunctious group of forty or fifty senior citizens at the front desk, demanding to speak with the governor. The security officer called me and asked what I wanted to do. Rather than risk public confrontation, particularly since there was a reporter accompanying them who had regularly taken shots at our administration in a conservative Pittsburgh newspaper owned by Richard Scaife, I opted, as I usually did, to listen to them.

I had heard about the burgeoning Tea Party movement, but had not had the displeasure of engaging them until this time. We set out chairs for the group and, when they were positioned, I made my entrance from behind the locked wooden door which protected the governor's suite of offices. The officer at the desk was highly protective of us, and he cautiously called for backup security which assembled behind the group—unbeknownst to them.

I politely welcomed the group and explained that the governor was unavailable, but that I would be happy to relay their concerns to him. The group was older, white, armed with reams of paper, and champing at the bit to levy a fusillade at yours truly. I patiently and respectfully accepted their information and accompanying diatribes aimed at me, the governor, liberals, and the Democratic Party.

I confronted some of their criticisms with deferential disagreement, but was careful not to further excite what was an obviously agitated crowd. I could see the security personnel pacing behind them, and the officers gave hand signals asking if I wanted them to shepherd the petitioners out. I discreetly waved them off and continued to engage the group. They did not let up and did not want to leave. After a half hour or so, I finally reached a point at which I believed no further discussion would be fruitful, and politely adjourned the meeting. They disbanded reluctantly into the halls of the capitol without incident, undoubtedly to further discuss the useless exercise they had just participated in.

When I collapsed at my desk, I decided I needed to know more about the genesis of the group and began to do my homework. I discovered, via the Internet, the basic principles governing this movement, which would eventually become a major force driving our growing polarization. For me this was a revelation, this evolution of the Tea Party revolution. This was a well-organized group, armed with facts, talking points, position papers, and an agenda. They obviously had plenty of time on their hands, and were clearly motivated.

My first encounter left me curious and concerned. This was a movement that would have to be reckoned with. We had not been on the campaign trail for a couple of years and, speaking from a staff position, this was a new development. The political dynamic had changed considerably, and ill winds were strong.

In "Unpatridiotic," my neologism, I outline my introduction to the Tea Party and the basic principles underlining their actions—the 9–12 Project. Little did I know that the movement would become a driving force in upcoming elections. What appeared to be a fringe movement would explode onto the scene and become a major thorn in the side of both major parties.

I was caught off guard by this initial encounter and, after doing some research, believed they would remain on the sidelines. I was wrong. They would become a force to be reckoned with as we continued to cope with a significantly changing country.

Posted August 4, 2009
Unpatridiotic

I just cannot remember it always being this way. Since when did the idea of taxes become ipso facto a bad idea, no way, no how, under no circumstances. In my thirty-three years of public service, I can remember a time when balancing the fiscal equation meant negotiating a taxing and spending regimen that appreciated the need for government spending on things other than national defense, public safety, and corrections.

And then again maybe I am just daydreaming, but was there

not a time when both parties could defend the idea that certain social spending was acceptable not just from a compassionate perspective, but also because of the actual benefits that would derive from a more just, more equitable, more diversified, better educated, and yes, more democratic society?

Yet today, conservative ideologues and politically elected lemmings whose only calculus for leadership entails not wanting to offend constituents, threaten to derail evolutionary progress we as a society have slowly built over the history of the Republic. I neither believe that higher taxes just for the sake of indiscriminate spending are appropriate, nor that deficit spending during periods of economic growth is warranted.

However, I do believe that there is good economic rationale for increased spending to stimulate a stagnant economy, and that there are documented cases where social spending can render far more benefits to society than costs, in both an economic and compassionate sense. It seems to me that we are in a period of political bankruptcy where a significant minority refuses to entertain discussion of a fiscal solution that involves fully one half of the equation; namely, taxes.

And this is true at all levels of government, federal, state and local. It permeates all regions of the country, as evinced in the various budgetary impasses affecting states from California to New York, and it is paralyzing public discourse and threatens to exacerbate the serious adverse economic circumstances affecting huge numbers of American families.

An example of the intransigence of growing numbers of Americans to the idea of rational discourse is the so-called Teabag revolution. I must admit, until only recently I had paid little attention to the movement, despite the considerable press attention they have garnered over the past several months, and assumed that they were capitalizing on the conservative mantra against new taxes, a position that seemingly has become the sole remaining political issue of a political orthodoxy that was resoundingly rejected in the last national election.

But I found myself in the unenviable position recently to come face to face with a group of self-described patriots of the taxed enough already (TEA) movement. All white, seemingly ordinary, nondescript post-retirement souls looking more likely to be either loading up on buses to the casino or boarding a cruise ship than mounting a revolution, they politely recited their prepared talking points on why our idyllic democratic society was on the verge of total collapse. Always being one to accept a challenge, I respectfully listened. So let's take a closer look at exactly what this movement is all about.

They came with paper, reams of paper. One paper, with a considerable amount of bolded words, underlined phrases, and numbered points was titled "Taking America Back," leaving one with the clear implication that we may have already slipped into a tyrannical abyss. The document regularly invokes the term "patriots" and "rejects the insidious tyranny and usurpation of our rights by government at all levels."

It rants against frivolous spending and advocates spending cuts across the board, thereby treating all spending as bloated and wasteful, although I am not sure they would heartily embrace large defense cuts, but according to the document they distributed they did not distinguish between entitlement spending and discretionary spending or defense spending from non-defense spending.

Interestingly, they decry public-education spending and distinctly point out the need to eliminate funding for school sports. Now as a former athlete I sometimes have considerable heartburn over the inordinate emphasis on sports at all levels of education, but still believe it plays a vital role in our education system, particularly given the alarming levels of childhood obesity we are seeing in our society.

They also reject the progressive income tax and support a flat tax. They reject automatic withholding of taxes, the corporate income tax, and the so-called death tax. Although they refer to the flat tax as fair, there is absolutely nothing fair about a flat tax. It is regressive, it adversely affects the poorest the worst, and it rejects the notion that those who are most able should contribute more to the perpetuation of an equitable and just society. It assumes, blatantly, that most if not all people who don't work, won't work. This, of course, is patently absurd. Are there individuals who will not work under any circumstances? Yep. Are they a large majority of individuals? There is no empirical evidence to suggest this is the case.

They call for the adoption of the 9–12 principles and values. I was not aware of these principles so I looked them up on Wikipedia, and there again was the invocation of something called the Network of Principled Patriots. I will not focus on the values; they are just that, values, like honesty, courage, personal responsibility, humility, charity, etc. All things we should most assuredly be able to agree upon. The principles, on the other hand, are more problematic.

Let's take a look.

Principle 1: America is good.

Okay, in general I have little problem with the proposition. However, this does not mean that we do not have our flaws and that we do not make mistakes, and with very little respect to Sarah Palin that we never need to apologize. Even good people make mistakes, and as a nation we have made some critically disastrous ones. So we must be careful here to acknowledge when we are right and when we are wrong. Just as we teach our children to do.

Principle 2: I believe in God and He is the center of my life.

Simply put, we are not a Christian nation; we are a melting pot of races, religions, and ideologies.

Principle 3: I must always be a more honest person than I was yesterday.

Well, I don't get it. You are either honest or not, if you are honest today, you cannot be more honest tomorrow.

Principle 4: The family is sacred. My spouse and I are the ultimate authority, not the government.

The absence of organized government is anarchy and chaos.

Principle 5: If you break the law you pay the penalty. Justice is blind and no one is above it.

No problem here, does this also apply to I. Scooter Libby?

Principle 6: I have a right to life, liberty and pursuit of happiness, but there is no guarantee of equal results.

Okay, but what about a guarantee of equal opportunity?

Principle 7: I work hard for what I have and I will share it with who I want to. Government cannot force me to be charitable.

I see, I got mine, you get yours. Well, just pay your taxes or else we will put you in jail.

Principle 8: It is not un-American for me to disagree with authority or to share my personal opinion.

Full agreement here, but according to Principle 5 you must contain that disagreement within the confines of the law.

Principle 9: The government works for me. I do not answer to them, they answer to me.

Agreed.

The document continues that Oklahoma and Texas are leading the way in declaring their independence from the federal government. I have read that the governor of Texas has muttered the word secession, is that what we are spearheading here, a secessionist movement?

The document they passed out cites that Louisiana, Alabama,

Georgia, both Carolinas, Tennessee, Kentucky, Missouri, Arkansas, and West Virginia would likely follow this example. It continues that should Mississippi act, so will Florida. Notice any trend here well they spell it out.

The document states that you should "Save your confederate money; it appears the South is about to rise up once again," all this in defense of Tenth Amendment rights.

For those of you rusty on your constitutional law, the Tenth Amendment states that "The powers not delegated to the United States by the Constitution, nor prohibited by it to the States, are reserved to the States respectively, or to the people." Personally, I don't see a connection to secession here.

Finally, there is an assault on immigration, under the title of Stop Illegal Alien Invasion, it calls for the incarceration and deportation of illegal aliens and celebrates Oklahoma's adoption of a law including DNA samples from any and all illegals to the Oklahoma database, for criminal investigative purposes.

So this is what the teabag revolution is all about. Sounds unpatriotic to me, in fact sounds unpatridiotic. You can judge it for yourself.

Article 33

August 17, 2009
Got to Keep the Loonies Off the Path

The battle over health-care reform erupted during the August Congressional recess at town-hall meetings across the country, and no region or state was spared. My encounter with the Tea Party two weeks earlier had somewhat prepared me for what was driving the movement, but I was not prepared for the eruption that would confront us on the nightly news during that very hot August.

It had become clear to me and to others that this was a faction to be reckoned with, and it was fueled by fear of change. At the core of the movement was a visceral rejection of the fact that the face of America was changing irreversibly. We were now a country led by an African-American poised to adjust to a demographic shift that would redefine who and what we were.

The governing shift that summer was the administration's decision to put its considerable weight behind reforming a health-care system designed to separate winners and losers, and which was systematically draining our budget. The fact that most of the angry, elderly, white revolutionaries were protected by a government-run health-care system which had largely alleviated poverty among the elderly in the nearly half-century it had been around was, of course, interesting. The irony of signs proclaiming that the government should keep its hands off Medicare highlighted and underscored the delicious hypocrisy and ignorance propelling the movement.

Of all the issues these groups were concerned about, health care was an intriguing one. I can understand why they may have been concerned or misled into thinking their benefits would be adversely impacted—that would be pure self-interest and fair game in the political or policy advocacy business. However, it was something deeper, verging on the selfishness and greed fueling anti-immigration. It was an attitude of I got mine, you fend for yourself. But if these individuals were entitled to health-care protection, why should others not be? Similarly, if you or your ancestors were afforded an opportunity to become Americans, why deprive others? After all, we are a nation of immigrants.

In "Lunatic Fringe," I began to describe my newfound education and interest in this nascent group of geriatric warriors, and took their increasing clout seriously. Health care reform was going to be a legacy of the administration, an effort to change society to conform to the changes occurring within it. The countermovement was lunacy, but it was having an impact that could very well threaten the administration's number one domestic priority. The Tea Party had to be taken seriously, even if the construction of their arguments was not. It was another obstacle for the Obama Administration, which could not buy a break.

Posted August 17, 2009
Lunatic Fringe

In the early 1980s, Tom Cochrane, the Canadian singer/songwriter, wrote "Lunatic Fringe," in which he penned lyrics I believe to be relevant today.

> Lunatic fringe
> In the twilight's last gleaming
> This is open season
> But you won't get too far
> 'Cause you gotta blame someone
> For your own confusion
> We're on guard this time
> Against your final solution

If there were ever a situation perfectly tailored for a South Park episode it would surely be the spectacle unraveling on our television sets each night in what will surely be remembered as the summer when old white men went postal over their right to not face end of life decisions. It is a fight to the death over "death panels." It is a version of you will have to pry my medical card from my cold dead hands. It is death with indignity. Okay, you get the idea.

Somehow, the venerable institution of town-hall meetings has horrifically morphed into little more than senior extreme games, with enraged, belt-busting, bespectacled, graying health-care revolutionaries preparing to storm the barricades to reclaim capitalism from the socialists who have taken power. The participants in this geriatric version of a barroom brawl are intoxicated with rage fueled by hatred and fear, stocked with daily doses of venom dispensed by dreadful doctors of doom who pose as media pundits: Dr. Limbaugh, Dr. Beck, Dr. Coulter, an entire faculty at Fox University Hospital.

As a white male staring down the barrel of sixty, my first inclination is to chuckle and dismiss the rapid disintegration of civility led by the gray brigades as a product of senility combined with entirely too much free time. But such flippant dismissal ignores the deep underlying emotions that have been ignited here. As we have seen far too often over the past decade, fear is both an indictment and an incitement. It is an indictment of our resistance to accept change and an incitement to overreact to change.

Fear breeds hatred, hatred breeds irrationality, and irrationality breeds violence. Taken in this context, what might at first appear irritatingly amusing quickly turns into sober reflection.

Put simply, this is no laughing matter, particularly if you are one of the 46 million Americans with no health insurance, one of the 14,000 who lose their health insurance each day, or one of the 670,000 children in California who are projected to lose health coverage in the next year due to state budget cuts. It is a disgrace, and those fomenting and participating in the current uproar are disgraceful.

I have neither opposition to nor a problem with those who wish to rationally question or disagree with the direction of health-care reforms being considered by the administration and Congress. This is the nature and the beauty of democratic government and a free society. And to those who profess to be true patriots, town-hall meetings are designed to encourage rational discourse and discussion of issues, and should be utilized as the forums upon which to make their voices heard. It appears, however, that the ostensible goal of the opposition is to disrupt, not to discuss, leading one to seriously question the true intention of the health-care reform countermovement.

The subtext of the drama unfolding on the town-hall stage is not an argument between liberals and conservatives, but rather a tug-of-war over what and who represents conservatism. Currently, it appears as though the forces espousing what most consider fringe ideas bordering on lunacy are holding sway in this battle. The fringe elements, carefully nurtured by fear, hatred, mistrust, and fitful bouts of fantasy, are positioning the conservative opposition into a death spiral, a particularly apt metaphor given the current discussion. The conservative opposition today is now being maneuvered into a position where they can only be responsible for one of two options: either paralysis or irrelevance.

And if they are successful in paralyzing the system in a way that denies the health-care reform supported by an overwhelming majority of the American people, then they will become irrelevant. Adhering to the lunatic fringe prescriptions will most certainly take them straight to irrelevance, bypassing paralysis altogether.

But what exactly is driving the fear that so prominently guides the counter-reform movement? Is it a fear of universal access, a fear of cost containment, a fear of true reform? I doubt it. My guess is what is truly motivating this movement is a combination of greed, racism, and paranoia, the three primary ingredients of the Kool-Aid they have ingested.

What is genuinely guiding this movement is a campaign designed to disrupt and derail a popularly elected and still-popular president (who just happens to be an African-American) with an agenda that enjoys widespread support. These "patriots" are fearful of the reality of an ever-changing composition of our society, reject the reality that government plays a large and constructive role in both the economy and the health-care system already, and have no realistic conception of the fact that there are better models of health care already in operation in many places around the globe.

Let's hope that the current lunacy that has captured this debate will streak across the sky like a comet and burn itself out quickly, and that upon sober reflection cooler heads will prevail among the conservative opposition so that meaningful progress can be made on the health-care front. For those who choose irrelevancy, so be it, good riddance, and mercifully you will pay a steep price indeed. For those who wish to paralyze the system into inaction, one can only hope you will render yourselves irrelevant sooner rather than later.

The final verse of the song concludes,

Lunatic fringe
We all know you're out there
Can you feel the resistance?
Can you feel the thunder?

Article 34

August 19, 2009
I Am So Confused!

As the August heat inflamed public discourse over health-care reform, it was becoming increasingly apparent that we were coming face to face with a basic communication failure—the fact that our health-care system was sick and needed to be healed had not been sufficiently conveyed to the public.

The opposition to health-care reform had a very basic strategy— why do we need reform at all? Incredibly, the fact that 46 million people were uninsured was not sufficient to convince the majority that the system was ill. As in most complex and sophisticated policy issues, it is often best to frame the debate simplistically—how does it affect me? In a country experiencing a backlash so basic as to question whether or not the president was born in this country, whether or not he was a Muslim, and if he had a socialist agenda was not territory in which to take anything for granted.

In "Do the People Really Understand Health Care Reform?" I answered my own question with a resounding no. We had not adequately educated the American people of the need to engage the massive undertaking of health-care reform. At this critical juncture, it was incumbent upon the president to explain in the clearest and most convincing terms why it was important not just to our budgetary future, but to the basic needs of every American, including those who were currently covered. As incredible as it seemed, we needed to get back to the basics.

August had been the cruelest month for comprehensive health-care reform, and success on this front would be contingent upon significant rhetorical surgery—and the president was the surgeon.

Posted August 19, 2009

Do the People Really Understand Health Care Reform?

It is often difficult when one is close to a problem to step back and envision how that problem looks to those who do not perceive to be ensnared in the problem. It is similarly difficult to realize the complexity of large issues when there are competing issues that seem far more pressing and immediate and affect one directly. No one will argue that we as individuals, both consciously and subconsciously, perform triage on issues and prioritize them, dealing with the most serious first and the least serious last.

What makes the current cacophony of voices that substitutes for dialogue on health-care reform so frustrating is that in each of the instances identified above there is a disconnect among a large proportion of the population as to the seriousness of the issue as it affects them. A large number of the electorate fail to realize that the problem affects them in a very direct way regardless of how close they perceive themselves to be involved with it, and has a huge ripple effect on aspects of their lives that they feel are unconnected.

Make no mistake about it, this is a complicated and complex issue, but no more so than climate change and, to his everlasting credit, Al Gore has educated millions and millions of people worldwide about the importance of this largely scientific phenomenon to their personal lives. Sometimes we need to simplify in ways that seem elementary. Let me attempt to do so in a way that may help the public to become further engaged in an issue that is of tremendous long-term importance not only to them personally but to the society as a whole. I would like to ask a series of questions that need to be answered in the clearest way possible so as to craft a message that may strike the appropriate chord. And remember, as important as it is to ask the right questions, it is every bit as important to shape the answers in a clear, concise, and understandable form.

First, is there a need for health-care reform? Why? And specifically, what is it in the current system that needs to be reformed? Incredibly, there appears to be confusion as to whether or not the current system is indeed in need of reform. I know that, to many of us, it appears we crossed that bridge long ago, but evidently not. Hence, officials and others can begin their arguments with the premise that this is the finest health-care system in the world, so why fix what ain't broken?

Second, what are the best ways to fix our health-care system? How exactly would that affect me directly? What would change for me if we put this fix into place?

Third, can we control health-care costs that are spiraling out of control by fixing the system? How will this occur? What does it mean for me, both as an individual and as a contributing (read: tax-paying) member of society?

Fourth, what exactly are the goals of the current health-care system? Should we institute a better set of goals? What are the actual outcomes of the current system? Can we effect a better set of outcomes? How will these outcomes affect me as an individual?

Fifth, please outline everything, I mean everything, in terms of what it means to me. I need to know exactly how my life will change and why it will be better. If it is better for me, it must be better for everyone.

Now if all this sounds like it is a little me-centered, it is. And unfortunately, that is the only language we Americans seem to be able to relate to, at least those who are currently spewing the ill-informed spittle that is being voiced and covered at these town-hall meetings or that is being propagated by the conservative opposition forces.

I fear that sometimes we give the populace far too much credit for being well-versed on the issues. For instance, single-payer system, public option, co-ops—even though they may seem to be evident on their respective faces, far too many seem confused, and who among us would feel comfortable explaining the differences in ways that would not force average people's eyes to glaze over?

Keep it simple, stupid (KISS) would be well employed here. We must first show unequivocally that the patient, in this case our health-care system, is very ill. Strange thing, when people are seriously ill they care little about how they get better, only that that is the ultimate outcome. It seems to me that far too few people are either aware or accepting that the patient is ill, seriously ill. Thus, this must be our first and most prominent task.

Given the time table for action, it does not appear to be too late to employ such a simplification strategy. Given our failure to succeed in reforming the health-care system, it seems imperative that we take the time to lay the proper foundation for this debate and, in many instances, we need to fill in the cracks of the current foundation, one that is permeated with misinformation and deception.

The opposition forces are strong, but the forces for change are stronger. We must arm these forces for change with arguments and rationales that are understandable and persuasive. My guess is that if understood and conveyed correctly, they will be persuasive.

Article 35

September 4, 2009
Trust Me, I'm from the Government!

Conspiracy theories, paranoia, and general distrust of governmental organizations have helped foster a takeover in the Republican Party. Moderation has given way to extremism, not only in the opposition but in the constellation of institutions ostensibly designed to protect us at the national and international levels.

It is a disturbing trend that has enormously adverse consequences which threaten the perpetuation of a system of governance designed by the Founding Fathers to operate on consensus and compromise. In a world where a preposterously large number of people distrust our institutions of government, the ability to operate within the confines of the system becomes at best strained and at worst impossible.

When I was younger, we developed a healthy level of distrust over what we viewed as deadly wrong policy decisions, eg, the Vietnam War, and the paranoia that led an administration to spy on its own people and cover up corruption—Watergate. But that did not lead to a wholesale rejection of the system; instead, it led to changes within it to protect against subversion of the greater good. Sure, some may have abandoned the system, but a lot of us were propelled to change it as best we could and became self-described change agents within the government we were troubled by. Of course, this opens up the threat of being co-opted by the order you're trying to change. I find myself constantly defending my career selections to my kids, who accuse me of being a pawn in the system I once distrusted. My only comeback is that at least some of us tried.

I am disturbed by the institutionalization of corruption in our system, which is fostered by the inordinate influence of money in politics and policymaking. It does not lead me to reject the system, but rather to attempt to rectify the problems. The distrust inherent in our current polarization is troubling because it is corrupting what was once a moderate wing of the Republican Party. Unless the virus of extremism is exorcised, the prospect for a functional political and policy-making process is jeopardized.

In "It Is an Issue of Trust," I examine the issue of trust and the growing level of distrust, which exemplifies the difficulties we are experiencing in making progress on highly contentious and intractable issues. The current system is not functioning properly, and the civility, respect, and healthy disagreement which allows for ideological differences to be hammered out must be restored to cure the policy paralysis common today.

After many years away from the classroom, I recently had the privilege of teaching a public policy course at a local community college. It forced me to revisit theories of governance and public policy that I had not looked at for decades, which was an enlightening exercise. When combining theory with nearly four decades of practice, I became more cognizant of and convinced of our Founding Fathers' genius as they constructed a system absolutely predicated upon compromise. Cooperation requires two or more players, and in our system of governance that means two parties willing to work together to reach a position that fulfills at least a modicum of needs each party feels important to the general operation of our society. If compromise as a concept is rejected, the ability to move forward is stopped dead. If compromise is unattainable, trust is impossible.

Posted September 4, 2009
It Is an Issue of Trust

Trust is defined as "assured reliance on the character, ability, strength, or truth of someone or something; one in which confidence is placed." Unfortunately, it appears to me as though the root cause of conservative opposition to virtually any progressive policy proposal is distrust. It is reflected not only on the individuals involved, but also in the systems and institutions that are ostensibly designed to advance and protect society.

In my lifetime, one which has now spanned five-and-a-half decades, there has been a discernible shift in conservative and liberal applications of the word "trust." Indeed, liberal distrust of governmental institutions in the 1960s and 1970s has given way to conservative distrust in the '80s, '90s, and nearly a decade into the new millennium.

But what is so disconcerting is the fact that so much attention is given to harboring distrust in our governmental institutions, and so little attention is paid to restoring the social contract that is the basis for the orderly functioning of society. Indeed, political points for casting doubts on the wisdom and ability of certain political ideologies and positions and the politicians who ascribe to them is most likely as old as the Republic itself. However, as our living, breathing democratic experiment has evolved and matured over the past two plus centuries, the importance of fostering trust in our governmental apparatus should have grown and matured as well. It hasn't. In fact, today I would argue trust in our government's ability to rectify market inefficiencies or societal inequities is being sorely tested.

Mistrust and distrust are borne out of frustration with the inability of our political system to effectively deal with the pressures inherent in a system beholden to special interests. And this is exacerbated by the growing frustration with the inability to temper historical economic fluctuations in a timely and effective manner.

While a certain degree of distrust has been rightly earned—for instance, the ineptitude of our leaders during the Vietnam era and the revelation of corruption at the highest levels during Watergate—these specialized instances have been overtaken by a generic form of distrust that has found currency within conservative ideology. Over the past two decades, the fires of distrust have been stoked by political expediency. Hence, the Reagan Revolution saw the genesis of "Government as the problem, not the solution" give rise to a whole generation of conservatives bent on starving the beast of government spending by promoting reactionary fiscal policies that in every sense of the word are un-conservative.

The precipitous explosion of debt fostered by Reaganomics, a fiscal policy that defied gravity by insisting that higher spending and lower revenues would in fact balance the budget, worshipping at the altar of unfettered free-market deregulation, a policy that has bankrupted the financial engines that drive our economy, and the effective abdication of responsibility for protection of basic human rights have rendered us morally and economically suspect not only to the international community, but to our people at home. The insidious destruction of trust in our government now finds comfort in the hands and hearts of those dedicated to resist change, even when it is in their best interests.

And it is not limited to distrust of our national institutions. Suspicion of the goals and mission of the United Nations, the International Criminal Court, the World Trade Organization, even the Nobel Commission have gained currency among ultra-right-wing nuts that have come to inordinately represent and influence one of our two major political parties. My fear is that it is not only limited to the reactionary right wing, but is becoming more generally accepted in conservative dogma among those who might be inclined to be somewhat more moderate in their social views.

For instance, just this past week I brought to the attention of a friend of mine who normally possesses a more moderate political stance on social issues despite her Republican party affiliation, an issue I felt to be sure to inspire genuine bipartisan concern: namely, cautions being issued by the scientific and medical community of the expectation that swine flu will spike this fall as the new school year commences. As a concerned mother of three children, I just assumed that these cautions would be welcomed and heeded. Instead, I was confronted with a most unexpected reaction; essentially it was "Oh, I don't put much stock in precautions from the World Health Organization." It was as if that is just one more example of a corrupt organization with an obviously corrupt agenda.

What made this reaction so astonishing, to my mind, was not the assumption that this was something worth watching, but rather that it was not even worthy of consideration merely because it had to be one of those leftist alarmist organizations bent on disturbing the tranquility of free-market capitalism—sort of like Obama threatening to lead a government take-over of our sacred health-care system.

How is it that a certain segment of the population is perfectly content to resist even the notion of questioning whether or not we can make things better? How is it that prevention connotes disruption? How is it that large governmental and non-governmental organizations have nefarious agendas, while large for-profit corporations must inherently have not profits but our best interests at heart? How is it that compromise and negotiation, the fundamental building blocks of our democratically representative political system, have become so elusive and even scorned? How is it that the politics of secession is rearing its ugly head 144 years after that issue was so painfully laid to rest? Where are the voices of moderation in the conservative movement?

I would argue that true conservatism is becoming a relic of the past, cast aside by a reactionary tsunami that very well might destroy any semblance of a two-party political system. Now, I have little problem with this outcome, as long as it does not stand in the way of immediate correction of the dramatic and traumatic social inequities currently operative in our society, and the most immediate correction must be guaranteeing health care to all as a right, not a privilege. The problem, of course, is that there are individuals in both parties seemingly affected by this infectious disease.

It is a disease that is spread as rapidly as the special-interest dollars that fuel the political system. And it must be stopped. The common ground to start the discussion has always been that we have a broken health-care system that needs fixing. How is it that this can actually be in dispute? Yet it is not apparent that we have crossed the threshold of even agreeing that 46 million uninsured is unacceptable.

This is the message that needs to be forcefully delivered by the president next week. As self-evident as it may seem, that message has not been forcefully characterized and portrayed to the American public. It needs to be. And for those who cannot agree upon this simple assertion, one backed by facts, statistics, and common sense, I say too bad; we shall move forward without you. On the larger issue of restoring trust in the system, nothing succeeds like success; let this be our attempt to prove that "We are from the government, and we are here to help" is no longer a punch line but a lifeline.

The Evolution of Revolution:
An Attack upon Reason, Compromise, and the Constitution

Article 36

September 30, 2009
We Are Always Learning

I consider myself very lucky to have had such a varied and interesting career, one which has afforded me the opportunity to be continually at the forefront of current issues while allowing me to spend time studying the past. I strove to make the most of chances to learn as much as I could to broaden my perspectives when delivering judgment and advice to officials. The most valuable thing we can do in our lives is never stop learning.

I met Susan Eisenhower at the Democratic National Convention in Denver in 2008. This extraordinary individual, from a venerable family with strong Republican roots, had, after much thought, decided to support Barack Obama in 2008, and was a part of a group of two dozen generals and admirals on stage that final evening at what was then Invesco Field, All had decided to place their support and military bona fides behind this man, who was under attack from the right for perceived softness on defense policy.

I was the person in charge of ensuring that this distinguished busload of military superstars got through security, made their way backstage, and were in their stadium suite in time for the candidate to accept his party's nomination. Susan and I stayed in touch, and I was honored to receive an invitation to Gettysburg College for a weekend of workshops and discussions re-examining the historic meeting that had taken place fifty years prior between President Dwight D. Eisenhower and Soviet Premier Nikita Khrushchev. The event was sponsored by the former president's granddaughter and the former premier's son, who had accompanied his father to the United States on that trip.

Since I consider myself a student of history, I was surprised by how little I knew of the Eisenhower Presidency, aside from his advancement of the Interstate Highway System, his penchant for golf, and his warning about the adverse consequences of an unchecked military-industrial complex. The weekend was fascinating, and it prompted me to do some follow-up research on Ike's place in history.

I read the farewell speech Eisenhower delivered three days before Kennedy's inaugural speech invoking the passing of the torch to a new generation, and his famous edict to "Ask not what your country can do for you, ask what you can do for your country." As I read Eisenhower's speech, I could not help but marvel at its eloquence and his commitment to peace and to mankind. What has become clearer to me throughout my years in public service is that those who have known war are usually the strongest voices for avoiding conflict. Eisenhower talked about disarmament; the scourges of poverty, disease, and ignorance; and of peace.

It forced me to think about how far the Republican Party has drifted from the noble aspirations of a generation that had just endured a world war and was hell-bent on building a peaceful existence for their sons and daughters, and for future generations. If one were to read the speech in its entirety today and were asked who delivered it, my guess is that very few would not say a liberal Democrat. What happened? How did we, as a nation, stray so far off track?

His words were spoken with deliberate moderation, minus fiery indictment, in measured tone. Where in the world was that party today? I tried to envision the prospects for advancement if these had been our adversaries today. Surely we would be much better positioned to find a middle ground for growth—economic, societal, and spiritual.

I strongly encourage today's Republican leaders to stretch back fifty years or so and take a lesson from a leader who had had the most solemn responsibility imaginable—leading our troops and an international coalition to victory in World War II. Just a few years later, President Kennedy would exercise restraint, intellect, and resolve in refusing military advisors the opportunity to risk everything in staving off what was the most serious threat to nuclear confrontation mankind had faced namely, the Cuban Missile Crisis.

Extraordinary times demand extraordinary actions from our leaders. Do we have the same degree of confidence in our leadership today? We face different crises, but we must demand the same level of restraint, intellect, and situational awareness exhibited fifty years ago. Strict adherence to ideological rigidity can be dangerous; yet we today have one of the two major political parties toeing a line that leaves no room for discussion. So much can be learned from history, and of course we all know Santayana's admonition that "Those who cannot remember the past are condemned to repeat it." We can learn to emulate our successes as well.

We may never again see that moderation, but we must aspire to copy what worked and avoid what did not. This not only applies to Eisenhower's policies, but also to FDR's New Deal successes and failures. In "A Lesson from History," I took great pains to present moderation as a virtue in the political arena, and found myself captured by the sentiments expressed by a conservative mid-twentieth-century Republican president. We must never stop learning, especially lessons from history, and it would serve us well to incorporate those lessons into contemporary contexts.

Posted September 30, 2009
A Lesson from History

This past weekend I had the honor of participating in a series of lectures and discussions surrounding a celebration of the fiftieth anniversary of Premier Khrushchev's visit to Gettysburg, Pennsylvania, to meet with then-President Eisenhower. Of course, any visit to Gettysburg is a sobering experience, its rolling hills steeped in historical relevance almost beyond mortal description. The significance of the battle there has received, and legitimately so, a prominent place in our history, both its teaching and learning.

However, the occasion that brought us together this past weekend involved an event that has garnered much less attention, even to those of us who consider ourselves students of American history. In fact, astonishingly enough, I cannot recall any political science or history class in which attention was given to the Khrushchev-Eisenhower meeting during my academic career. Hopefully, I am the exception, not the norm.

In light of the enormity of the nuclear challenge facing the United States and the U.S.S.R. in 1959, particularly as it helped shaped the Cold War, the ability of these two military veterans, both familiar with and involved in war, to engage in personal talks in an effort to help ease tensions between the two superpowers is an abject lesson in diplomacy that I believe will hold the Obama administration in good stead. It is unfortunate that the chickenhawks who directed our defense posture during the previous eight years did not learn from this historical experience, especially given that they were of the age to witness and absorb it.

The appeal of face to face meetings, the incalculable goodwill and trust that can be generated from personal interaction and the power of personality simply cannot be overstated. Of course, it needs to be fortified with solid, substantive, and well-thought out policy objectives, but the fact that the leaders of nations that were sworn enemies such as Eisenhower and Khrushchev could meet and share ideas, thoughts, concepts, and personal stories speaks volumes to the need to reach out to the world community to solve what sometimes seem to be intractable problems. I am particularly thinking here in terms of the upcoming meeting in Copenhagen regarding a global solution to climate change, but it applies to the world's economic and financial crisis, or any other issue that threatens our ability to peaceably coexist.

The two star attractions of the weekend confab shared the same last names as the stars of the initial meeting, namely Susan Eisenhower, granddaughter of the former president, and Sergei Khrushchev, son of the former premier, who accompanied him on his two-week sojourn across America half a century ago. The stories, as told by these two relatives, showed a personal and human nature of the individuals to which so much was entrusted.

The ageless maxim that those who do not learn from their mistakes are bound to repeat them is instructive here. I was inspired enough to reach back into my own memory and reread a copy of Eisenhower's farewell address. For those who have not read it, it is seemingly timeless and contains wisdom that should help guide us today. What makes his words even more credible or incredible is the fact that they came from a professional military man.

I would like at this point to quote a few passages from the speech, delivered in January 1961, just three days before turning the keys of the White House over to his successor.

"America's leadership and prestige depend, not merely upon our unmatched material progress, riches, and military strength, but on how we use our power in the interests of world peace and human betterment." He goes on further to add that "In the councils of government, we must guard against the acquisition of unwarranted influence, whether sought or unsought, by the military industrial complex. The potential for the disastrous rise of misplaced power exists and will persist."

And finally, "Disarmament, with mutual honor and confidence, is a continuing imperative. Together we must learn how to compose differences, not with arms, but with intellect and decent purpose...that all who are insensitive to the needs of others will learn charity; that the scourges of poverty, disease, and ignorance will be made to disappear from the earth, and that, in the goodness of time, all peoples will come to live together in peace guaranteed by the binding force of mutual respect and love."

When I look around and see the venomous vitriol spewed by the conservative opposition to progressive thought and policy today, I wonder from where it derives its political justification. Certainly it is not embedded in the conservative Republican ideology of the 1950s as represented by Eisenhower. I also wonder at what point these self-described conservatives deviated from the rational model of political discourse.

When I see teabaggers proselytizing on the merits of secession or administration opponents publicly challenging the veracity of the president on policy differences or right wing pundits questioning the legitimacy of a democratically elected leader and suggesting that either his failure or demise would benefit the nation, I cannot help but think that rational discourse has abandoned our political system.

I would heartily suggest that maybe a history lesson is very much in order here. In fact, it would probably benefit us all to hark back to the wisdom of this moving address in hopes that it might help improve the state of public discourse and foster greater cooperation instead of conflagration. And in the process it just might contribute to a greater level of trust and confidence in our institutions and elected officials, further marginalizing those who have captured an inordinate share of public babble that passes for rational debate.

Article 37

October 2, 2009
Race Factor

Let me state my biases up front on this one. First, I traveled to New Hampshire from Georgia in January 1976 as part of a contingent known as the Peanut Brigade to campaign in the nation's first primary for former Governor Jimmy Carter. Second, I worked in six other primary states for Carter. Third, I was a delegate coordinator for Carter on the floor of the '76 convention in New York City. Fourth, I ran a congressional district for Carter in Pennsylvania during the general election that fall. Fifth, I was a political appointee in the Carter administration. Sixth, I have ardently defended Carter's policies, agenda, intellect, honesty, and vision since the day he left office in 1981.

This having been said, I have watched him over the past three decades and marveled at his energy and commitment to world peace. He is, in my estimation, the most effective ex-president the nation has ever seen. Therefore, I come to this issue with a strong predilection to take seriously any advice Carter has to offer on the human condition, but especially on race, an issue that Carter witnessed first-hand when growing up in a rural town in southwest Georgia, and dealt with as a progressive southern governor at a time when the region and his state clung tenaciously to the ways of the past.

I have been suspicious of the role that race has played in opposition to the first African-American president in history. That is not to say that it is the sole or the driving factor in all instances. However, if one studies closely the voting results in the Old Confederacy and conservative states throughout the middle of the country and the west, one cannot help but be suspect that race may play a role in the fervent opposition to Obama. Subsequent efforts to enact voter suppression legislation through voter identification and the challenge to The Voting Rights Act do little to quell my suspicions and show that latent racism is even more widespread than originally thought. Efforts in my home state of Pennsylvania to restrict not enable greater voter participation are shocking.

As the Tea Party ascended in importance nationally, the growing talk of secession, of the Tenth Amendment, of religious and racial intolerance, and of anti-immigration sentiment played nicely into a stacked deck against the country's inevitably changing demographics. Carter has written extensively since he left office, traveled around the world trying to facilitate justice and peace, and has taken his role as a senior statesman quite seriously, speaking in only carefully measured terms. For this man of peace to voice his suspicions is ominously disturbing, but instructive and invaluable in any public discourse about this scourge that has so stained our national identity as a nation where freedom and liberty hold center court.

In "Jimmy Carter and the Race Card," I wanted to draw close attention to the words of this wise and venerable statesman, and educate those who summarily have dismissed him and his presidency as a failure. He offers tremendously valuable insights, and his observations spring from an intellectual capacity never fully appreciated. In many ways, his logic and vision were ahead of its time—something Americans have little stomach for. Our zeitgeist is held captive by short-term thinking, conspicuous consumption, and unhealthy competition, and when Carter talked of long-term solutions like renewable energy and sacrifices for the betterment of future generations, he was effectively silenced by a public unwilling to accept what they did not want to hear. But on this issue, his message must be heard and heeded.

Posted October 2, 2009
Jimmy Carter and the Race Card

As a baby-boomer, born a year before the landmark Brown v. Board of Education Supreme Court decision, it seems like a very short time ago when overt racial segregation and both de jure and de facto racism were accepted forms of behavior in our society. In my lifetime we have seen massive changes and challenges to the status quo: Rosa Parks, lunch counter demonstrations, James Meredith, Charlayne Hunter-Gault, Martin Luther King, Jr., the Voting Rights Act, the Fair Housing Act, affirmative action, Thurgood Marshall, Malcolm X, Freedom Rides, the Pettus Bridge, the Mississippi Freedom Delegation, and the War on Poverty, just to name a few.

Yet here we are, almost a decade into the new millennium, and the echoes and ghosts of a darker chapter in race relations once again threaten to dim the sunshine of equality that so many have paid such a steep price to advance. Since the election of Barack Obama, there has been a steady and dangerous concentration of storm clouds on the horizon. Recently, the emergence of teabagger revolutionaries, fueled by secessionist fervor, given legitimacy by compliant and complicit media outlets like Fox Noise, revered by "punidiots" like Beck, Limbaugh, Hannity and others, and buttressed by a conservative ideology that abhors progress and progressive thinking, has raised the tension meter to a dangerously high level.

Former President Jimmy Carter has recently lent his considerable credibility and political/personal experience with race to a growing chorus of voices that are drawing particular attention to the ugly tone of racism that is permeating substantive discussion of issues that will define who we are and where we are headed as a nation. No one can seriously doubt the sincerity of Jimmy Carter's dedication and commitment to social justice. Regardless of how one judges the success of his presidential tenure, Jimmy Carter has set the bar very high in the nearly three decades he has been out of office with respect to advancing economic and social justice worldwide.

Carter is a product of the South; he has confronted and addressed racial injustice since his early days growing up in southwest Georgia. I attended college in south Georgia in the early 1970s and witnessed firsthand the vestiges of racism which abounded in a small, rural southern town seventeen years after *Brown v. Board*. I shall never forget the rusting sign still hanging in Statesboro in 1971 with an arrow pointing down an alley which read "Colored Motel." I can still recall the billboards along Route 301 in North and South Carolina on my way to school, touting the benefits of joining the White Citizens Council.

I shall never forget the time I spent running an athletic and educational program at the Bulloch County Correctional Institute as a college student, spending weekends with members of Georgia's famed chain gang, neatly segregated into two dorms: one white, one black. Since our county was dry, liquid refreshment required a thirteen-mile road trip to the county line, where a package store literally was perched on the county line, and inside were pool tables separated by jail like bars designating a black side and a white side.

Racism, of course, is not the sole explanation for the personal and hateful rhetoric that has been leveled at the president; it may not even be the driving rationalization, but to suggest that it plays little or no role is I believe both wishful thinking and naïve. I do not subscribe to the notion that any attack on Obama has to be racially motivated; I reject it. If the attacks were purely substantive in nature and reflected a thoughtful consideration of differing approaches to a common end goal, I would not even mention it. However, there is a venomous rant at work here that is a reflection of the geopolitical reality that is evident in our national elections: namely, a predominance and unity of opposition from states affiliated with the old Confederacy. In particular, and I have written about this in past posts, look at the teabag resolutions pending in state legislatures asserting that the Tenth Amendment to the Constitution gives a legal justification for secession. Although there are states entertaining such resolutions that are not from the Old South, every state in the Old South is in play.

Jimmy Carter knows this region and he has witnessed firsthand the changes that have occurred there. He is also aware of the renewed and lingering hatred that also is evident there. I have known and watched him over the years, and believe that his integrity and honesty are unquestioned. For him to wander into the political minefield of racial politics would require a firm and unshakeable belief that we are truly in danger of slipping backwards in our quest for a color blind society. It behooves us all not to blindly dismiss his warnings, and I say this with all due respect to those who wish to minimize these admonitions. And the latest actions by those who are now under Secret Service investigation regarding a questionnaire on the Internet asking whether or not the president should be assassinated bring special attention to this apparently clear and present danger.

This ought to be a clarion call to all those who wish to advance our society and culture to a place where all are "not…judged by the color of their skin, but by the content of their character," to quote Dr. King. This ought to involve conservatives and liberals, Republicans and Democrats, Northerners and Southerners, Christians and non-Christians, rural and urban dwellers alike. Racism has no role in either partisan or ideological politics. Now is the time for conservative and religious leaders to stand tall and reject the bigotry that has characterized the actions and activities of the birthers, teabaggers, and anti-immigration, anti-Muslim, self-described patriots who are garnering an inordinate share of attention on the stage of public discourse today.

It is important to nip this in the bud before it gets out of hand. We as a society must address and confront even the appearance of racism, if one were to assume that what we are witnessing is not racism at all but merely a political calculation to use racism as a diversion from the actual issues. Even an appearance of racism is enough to engage in a national dialogue. If President Carter is wrong then we are in better shape than many believe. If he is even remotely right we need to get on with averting a potential catastrophic development in our societal evolution.

The Evolution of Revolution:
An Attack upon Reason, Compromise, and the Constitution

Article 38

October 20, 2009
And That's the Way It Is!

In another instance of entertainment supplanting news, the nation was captivated by the story of a wayward helium balloon that had escaped its moorings and drifted aimlessly across the landscape with a six-year-old boy on board. It garnered minute-by-minute coverage, harking back to the agonizing car chase involving OJ Simpson. Did we really need the intense coverage of either journey?

In the end, it was discovered that the boy was not on board, but hiding in an upstairs attic. That should have been the end of the story, but the news stations continued their coverage.

What was so mind-numbingly troublesome about this story was that no one had any idea how to rescue the child or corral the runaway balloon. We have amazingly effective and elaborate plans to destroy things, but to peacefully retrieve them? Nope. The balloon eventually drifted harmlessly to terra firma, and all's well that ends well. But we could not figure out a way to resolve this problem? It does not bode well for our ability to solve real problems.

But, once again, we were treated to what the media organizations felt was important news. I was pulling for the safety of the young man, but the big news here is that we could not figure out what the hell to do.

In "When the Line Between News and Entertainment Blurs," my frustration with the inability of the authorities to solve the problem or the news honchos to present us with real news leads me to believe that we as a society are not prepared to tackle the large issues which affect mankind—just a pet peeve.

Posted October 20, 2009

When the Line between News and Entertainment Blurs

Last week, the nation sat, captivated, by the apparent news of a wayward helium balloon squiring a six-year-old boy towards the heavens while a helpless nation watched and officials furiously (I assume) attempted to solve this unconventional problem in a way which would ensure the safety of the young aviator. This is a noble endeavor and, to the truly compassionate among us, myself included, was eagerly observed in hopes that the boy would be saved and the problem solved.

Can there be any doubt that had it been a vehicle armed and headed towards a population center such as Washington, DC, we most assuredly would have had an effective military response just waiting for proper authorization? But what was equally as disturbing to me as the fate of the young man was the seemingly endless amount of time that passed with no apparent idea of how to respond in an effective manner. And that does not preclude a peaceful military solution; our military responds magnificently to peaceful disasters and emergencies as well as those requiring force.

But as the man-made UFO streaked across the Colorado sky, with the fear that young Falcon was being held hostage to the winds and a finite payload of helium, no solution was forthcoming. In the end, the problem solved itself as it gently drifted onto a plowed field. It was quickly discovered that indeed no child was aboard and there is no assurance that had he been aboard it might not have had a happy ending. In this instance, a child left behind was a blessing.

But, luckily, there was a happy ending. All along, the boy was safely hiding in a box in his upstairs attic. The happy ending, however, was little more than a happenstance. It was not due to ingenuity or cleverness or quick thinking. It just happened.

Now this is disturbing enough and it all too clearly reveals the incapacity of this great superpower to exercise creativity when it comes to solving problems that do not require brute force, although I would argue that our track record there is not stellar either. How in the world are we supposed to deal with the potentially catastrophic impacts of global climate change if we can't even figure out a way to coax a helium balloon safely to Earth?

But the way in which this story was treated by the entertainment-driven news media is also instructive and disturbing. The moment it was confirmed that indeed little Falcon was alive and safe it should have reverted to what it was: namely, an entertainment story. Yet there it was front and center on the evening news, prominently placed atop the news stories of the day, more prominent that the forty or so people killed in the escalating violence underway in Pakistan, a nuclear power in the throes of an internal power struggle between the military and its civilian government over how to respond to United States entreaties for assistance in neighboring Afghanistan. Which story is news and which is entertainment?

And there it was taking primacy over continuing Wall Street excesses, double-digit unemployment, a resurgent stock market, and the president's visit to New Orleans, where he tried to explain why it is that victims of Hurricane Katrina are still haggling with government agencies over relief monies.

Have we all lost our minds? What is really important here, the boy is alive and has been for hours. Michael Jackson is dead and has been for months. What is the news here?

In an Orwellian sense, we simply substitute interesting (mostly) stories for what should be reserved for new events, pure and simple. How is it that our priorities can be so deftly manipulated? Is it really because it is what we want to know? Or is it because it is what they think we want to know? Or maybe just what they want to tell us?

Why do we not demand, as a society, the right to pure, unadulterated, investigative journalism? Why do we not demand, as a society, the right to news reporting? Is this the logical consequence of the death of newspapers? Has the bumper-sticker, sound-bite mentality embodied in our political system simply taken root in our newsrooms? Has it always been this way? I don't know the answers to these questions but I do believe they ought to be topics for serious discussion.

There are so many issues with such grave long-term consequences confronting us at this juncture that it is simply inexcusable to devote the time and energy to this story that has already been expended, and can there be any doubt that this is just the beginning of an extended three-ring circus about to tour the networks and end up on the New York Times best seller list?

We must get serious soon about addressing the issues of the day, and this nonsense is just filling space. We must start considering the consequences of what we put into the air and not just what we put up in it. Carbon dioxide in the atmosphere is far more dangerous than helium in a flying saucer. Every life is important, whether it is the six-year old in Colorado or the dozens lost in Pakistan. That is news, and it is not entertaining.

The Evolution of Revolution:
An Attack upon Reason, Compromise, and the Constitution

Article 39

October 26, 2009
He's Baack!

Dick Cheney was on the warpath again. I remember, when I was a small child, watching Douglas MacArthur's resignation speech. In it he said, "Old soldiers never die; they just fade away." Well, that would be good advice for Cheney—except that, oh yeah, he never was a soldier. He has just completed what can only be described as a supreme disservice to the American people, the Constitution, the country, and the world, and yet there he is receiving awards, living a life of wealth and privilege, and steadfastly trying to snare a place in history that is not prison.

He is so intent on securing some form of recognition and redemption that he is stuck on a treadmill to exoneration that, unfortunately for him, takes him nowhere. News flash to the former vice president: a treadmill is stationary!

The man should be in prison. But he has the right to speak his mind. That is a guarantee of the Constitution he so cavalierly flaunted. But to criticize his successors in the White House is such a classless, cheap, and despicable act that it deserves at least critical condemnation. Here it is, in "Cheney: A Tortured Soul."

Posted October 26, 2009
Cheney: A Tortured Soul

Since he left office, former Vice President Dick Cheney has exhibited a non-stop barrage of baseless, classless, and utterly indefensible insults to this nation and its commander-in-chief. Not since Spiro T. Agnew have we been so publicly assaulted by an individual so bereft of integrity and decorum. But what makes these tirades so infuriating is that they are cloaked in the wrappings of faux patriotism and the flag in much the same way that those pathetic patriots, the so-called tea baggers, mask their seditious and treasonous rhetoric under the protection of the very Constitution they wish to violate.

Former President Clinton once said, "You can't say you love your country and hate your government." Cheney does not just hate Obama; he despises the Constitution and has a deep distrust of the American people. During his tenure he participated in the greatest heist of civil liberties since the internment of Japanese-Americans in World War II. He continues to defend the abandonment and rejection of the Geneva Conventions which has brought us the use of torture as a national defense policy and Guantanamo Bay.

This is a man whose chief-of-staff, a convicted felon, was found guilty on four counts in the investigation of the leaking of information to the press on the identity of CIA operative Valerie Plame. Many are convinced that he did so only to protect his boss. In fact, just the other evening he was awarded a "Service Before Self" plaque for time in the White House. Now, without going into the nefarious credibility of the presenting organization, one can deduce that he was awarded service to Dick over service to self, but surely there is no pretense that he served his country or its Constitution.

At what point does dedication to an ideology betray the sworn oath to the Constitution? If obsessive devotion to an ideology conflicts with the ideals and precepts of the Constitution, does elective office give one the luxury to disregard it without being subject to prosecution?

What is particularly odious about this man's conduct is the contemptuous disregard he has for the American people. Whether he likes it or not, whether he agrees or not, in our democratic form of government, the people have spoken on the need for change. Now I realize that democratic governance might seem a rather odd notion to an administration that assumed office under a dark cloud of suspicion and, in any case, did not secure the majority of votes from the populace, but that does not excuse ignorance of it. They didn't believe in the people because the people didn't believe in them.

Mr. Vice President, you and your president had eight full years to chart a direction for this nation. That direction was soundly rejected by the voters in the most recent national election. Common decency suggests that at this point you just quietly retire into the dark hole in which you obviously are most comfortable.

No one should ever deny your right to speak out for what you believe is right. That, my good sir is the beauty of the Constitution you so righteously despise. But, for God's sake, do so in a respectful and dignified manner. To do anything less, as you are doing, makes you look petty and vindictive, which I have no doubt you are. But you have been in politics long enough to know that it does not help to show it. You should thank your lucky stars that you are a free man; this system has given you a free pass to dismiss the laws you were sworn to uphold.

And of course it is well known that your dedication to the nation has been a very deliberate if not cowardly one, you of the class of five deferments. Yes, your generous interpretation of service may in some quarters be suspect. Your devotion to self before service predates the recent awards ceremony. I would find no quarrel whatsoever if you decided to modify your service based on either religious grounds or on grounds of conscientious objection. Somehow I do not think that was the case. It was clearly out of self-interest, that ideology that has dictated your political career, and the obsession that has blinded your discretion on numerous issues, including those involving life and death, throughout your tenure in the White House.

Once again, unlike some decisions rendered by your administration that reflected deep-seated disdain for civil liberties— oh, let's say, warrantless wiretaps or the policy of rendition just to name two, I do not deny your right to speak out; I respect it and encourage it. But do it in a tasteful way, if that is possible, and do it in a manner that respects the office of the presidency, the Constitution and, oh yes, the American people.

I sincerely doubt you will heed my advice here as you have shown no proclivity to act in anything other than a provocative way on issues involving national security for decades. But think about it, it has not made us richer as a nation, it has made us poorer. It has not made us safer; it has made us more vulnerable. It has not made us more respected around the world; it has made us more reviled. In a very real way, you and your administration are largely responsible for Obama receiving the Nobel Peace Prize. Bet that really makes your skin curl. But your ineptitude and incompetence magnify the importance of having a reasonable, rational, and respectful foreign policy.

Write a book, go fishing, shoot something other than another human, read, travel, see a shrink, or just connect with your family. But for goodness' sake, work out your demons on your own time; do not force us to agonize over your tortured conscience. Don't go away mad, just go away.

The Evolution of Revolution:
An Attack upon Reason, Compromise, and the Constitution

Article 40

November 4, 2009
We Must Do Better Than This!

As we inch precariously toward at least a modicum of health-care reform, we are confronted with a contemporary reality of politics and policymaking; we live in a supercharged political environment where there is a need to secure a supermajority to pass legislation. Sixty is the new fifty. As far as age goes, that's a good thing, but in policymaking, it is absurd. We now exist in a filibuster-obsessed political arena in which achieving cloture to move legislation requires sixty votes. How did this happen? When did this happen? It can't be right!

In a polarized environment such as exists today, the probabilities for progress are substantially diminished, and the consequences of inaction are considerably magnified. The accomplishment of even the smallest steps forward against a well-heeled industry in our money-corrupted system becomes a monumental task, demonstrated by the disappointing progress for health-care reform. That even these advancements required the investment of so much political capital at such a cost to reach the magical sixty-vote plateau is heartbreaking.

But this is the new reality, and until the processes which govern our system are changed, it is what we have to live with. In light of these rigid barriers, we are about to salvage the very best we can do. It's better than nothing, it's not quite half a loaf, and it's no one's fault but our own that we allow our representatives and the systems which govern their actions to thwart what is in the best interest of the nation.

When writing "The Best We Can Do," I struggled with whether or not I should affix a question mark to the title. In the end, I opted not to, because I am convinced that "yes," in this instance, it is the best we can do. The Obama Administration deserves great credit for getting us this far, and now we begin the process of executing and enhancing legislation that has taken far too long to reach. What makes the outcome even more frustrating is that the fight does not stop here; full-scale efforts are underway to attempt to repeal health-care reform in its entirety, or emasculate its constituent parts.

Posted November 4, 2009
The Best We Can Do

Why is it that it is easier to take the country into war without justification than it is to ensure that every American is entitled to health care? Progressives are being cautioned not to squeal too loud over the admittedly watered-down health-care proposals inching their way through Congress because they are "the best we can do," and the nature of our system is deliberate and incremental, and we need to get a foot in the door, the camel's nose under the tent, half a loaf, not sacrificing the good in search of the perfect—just pick your metaphor.

We are told there are not sixty votes for a "robust" public option, and we have watched the kabuki dance of the past nine months of trying to partner up with a Republican, any Republican, so that we can at least pretend that there is something resembling bipartisanship. And while in the end that seems to be a fruitless exercise, we have assiduously pursued a compromise that at least all Democrats can embrace. Of course there seems to be nothing short of the status quo that will satisfy the independent senator from Connecticut, even though he caucuses with the Democrats and maintains the benefits of affiliating with the majority party for purposes of committee seniority, but I am sure that will be resolved in due time. It sure is a lot of work—making historic, landmark changes that is.

Yet, we entered an unjustified war of choice, not necessity, with much less deliberation and incrementalism, and a healthy dose of bipartisanship. We put the country first, damn the costs, and we joined together against a common enemy: terror. Well, terror is the fear of not being able to cover loved ones who might need hospitalization or medical care. My point is that as bulky and inefficient as our system is, we can move with all deliberate speed if we view doing such as critically important, and I just have a hard time seeing how it is that there are some who view the price of action more politically harmful than the price of inaction.

I have been around long enough to know and accept the limitations of our systems of governance and politics. And I certainly do not envy the Obama Administration's conundrum here. Like the proverbial man with a shovel trailing the elephants down Main Street, Obama is placed in the position of having to clean up an enormous amount of detritus from the failed policies of the past eight years. It is necessary to do so not so they don't step in it, but because they don't want us to step in it. Unfortunately, it isn't just the elephants, but the horses, and the hippos, and all the other wild things that comprised the Bush policy circus whose odious remnants are cast about the boulevard of progress.

It is frustrating that we simply do not have the political will to face the future, and make no mistake, those who are having trouble bringing the nation into the family of civilized nations, which is to say the rest of the world, that do protect their citizens from the ravages of inadequate health coverage will have to wrestle with an increasingly hostile and cynical electorate.

It is frustrating that after all of these months of posturing, negotiating, courting, cajoling, and finessing, with all the customizing, modifying, and tweaking, combined with the gyrations and machinations of seemingly endless compromises, at the end of the day we are left with no opposition support, a stunningly sour policy proposal, and an enduring search for the sixtieth vote. But that is the price of democracy.

I sincerely hope, and maybe just naïvely wish, that despite the unsatisfactory nature of the product to many, we are actually witnessing a victory over the pungent influence of moneyed interests by a popular uprising that has seen serious reform of health care as a moral imperative. The entrenched status quo in Washington, DC is strong indeed. The influence of the health-care industry is vast and rapacious, and the political polarization is toxic. Against these odds, we are actually preparing to peel back at least one layer of the onion that is the current health-care system. And from here we go on to similarly contentious issues such as climate change, escalation of the war in Afghanistan, and reform of the financial system. We will need large shovels indeed.

But progressives need not despair; it is crucial that we continue to exert political influence on a political system that is fractured, if not broken. The most short-sighted thing we could do would be to simply give up. The worst we could do would be to actively reject what is at best a tenuous solution that could lead to a more effective resolution in time. We cannot allow the pace of change to affect our commitment to the ultimate goal of universal, affordable health care. But we can affect the pace.

Last weekend I spent some time with Tom Friedman at a forum on energy in which he reiterated his wish that at least for one day we could be China and proscribe solutions from the top down. This is an intriguing if not treacherous proposition. As we saw in the period following 9/11, we can operate with ruthless efficiency and speed when confronted with a bona-fide crisis, hence our invasion of Iraq. What is missing in the health-care and energy crises that are with us is the lack of political will to acknowledge and confront them in a unified way. What is dramatically problematic is that the current reality suggests that consensus within the ruling party may be "the best we can do," and even that is difficult. And while patience is a virtue, the American electorate's appetite for change seems to be more voracious than that of its elected representatives. For those Democrats still on the fence, it is crucial to remember that the political price for inaction is usually exacted from the ruling party.

Article 41

December 8, 2009
I Can See Clearly Now!

It had nagged me for some time but, finally I finally came to see the light—and it was blinding. The Republican Party had become "The Party of No." They were prepared to oppose everything the president put forward. Thank God we already have Mother's Day, because if Obama had proposed it, I am sure they would have filibustered. Now we are not talking filibuster in the traditional Jimmy Stewart/Jefferson Smith style seen in *Mr. Smith Goes to Washington*, but the contemporary senatorial-courtesy-inspired style that requires only acknowledgment that it is a possibility. That is enough to stop legislation in its tracks. This is a process begging for inaction. Is it any wonder congressional approval ratings have dipped below double digits?

Opposition obstruction is the order of the day. I could only assume that the monster they had created—the Tea-Party, wing-nut, fanatic, extremist, lunatic fringe—had taken over their minds. And fear, a tactic they had so freely and purposefully exerted on the American people during the Bush Administration had taken over their senses, and what was left of the moderates in the party were now scared shitless that they not be seen as appeasers.

I had questioned who would co-opt whom—whether the Tea Party would co-opt the Republican Party or the other way around—but at this point it was readily apparent that the Teabaggers had won. I confess that I had been wrong to think that the party of Rove would co-opt the Teabaggers; it turned out to be the opposite. The real trick now facing the president and the Democrats was whether or not they would be able to cobble together enough votes to succeed in circumnavigating both the united Party of No and the supermajority rules which had come to be a matter of course in the Senate. Talk about a daunting task. And what would be the cost to effective policy given the multiple compromises that would have to be struck? Effective policymaking had ground to a halt, and inaction was taking hold in the machinery of governance.

Obama had inherited an absolute mess— two wars, economic collapse, financial-industry chaos, recession, foreclosures, mass exodus of jobs abroad, auto industry bankruptcy, deficits, debt, the uninsured, under- and unemployment, and climate change. And at the very time these issues required a supreme effort to tackle them on behalf of a united country, he came face to face with a level of political polarization that may very well prove unprecedented. I have no doubt that Obama was confident in his ability to diagnose problems and assemble a coalition of the willing to tackle them. Unfortunately, the calculus had changed; there was no longer a coalition, let alone a coalition of the willing. It had been replaced by a stubborn opposition determined to tear down and paralyze the government. Inaction was action enough.

No one I know imagined this scenario. In fact, most of the political prognosticators I followed had only belatedly taken the Tea Party seriously. I'd not had a clue until I had come face to face with it just a few months prior. But we were now confronted with a new reality, and a disturbing one. Against this backdrop, Obama would need to adjust his tactics and strategy, and the ultimate product would fall short of expectations. No longer was half a loaf the expectation; it would now be seen as a major victory, but at what cost? At what point would inaction be better than action from the left side of the equation? Unfortunately, we were about to find out.

In "The Republican Party of Obstruction: Disturbing and Distressing," I laid out my acknowledgment of this new world, and it was difficult to take. So much for the exuberance of the Obama ascension; so much for the hope that change would come quickly. It might come, but at what cost, and how long would it take? Even under optimal circumstances, our policymaking process is a slow one. Only in times of crisis do we have the capacity to act quickly. And now we had a united party refusing to even acknowledge that some problems, eg, health care and the level of uninsured, were a problem.

Regarding the debt and the deficit, the Republicans were willing to proclaim a crisis, but their rhetoric only included a portion of the cause—non-defense spending. There was no acknowledgment of a revenue shortfall or defense overspending; in fact, they were firmly convinced that the problem was too much revenue. They were willing to cut entitlement spending, but shied away from specifics other than attacking spending for poor people. Corporate welfare was good, public welfare was bad; income inequality was a sign of healthy competition. It is against these currents that the president and his administration needed to swim, and it would prove to be brutal.

Posted December 8, 2009
The Republican Party of Obstruction:
Disturbing and Distressing

The experiment in post partisan governance has not met with much success in the realm of health-care reform. We might be in a post-post-partisan world now, given that a solid phalanx of Republican opposition to health-care reform threatens to wreck the valiant efforts of a most, most patient Democratic Senator Reid. It is disturbing, distressing, and disgusting that the Republican Party has elected to behave in such a destructive, petty, and vindictive way.

I have a problem with conservative orthodoxy in its current form, and have voiced my concerns about conservatives many times in this forum. I have never directly attacked Republicans except to state how unfortunate it is that they have increasingly aligned themselves with some of the more radical elements of the right-wing lunatic fringe. But just to be absolutely clear, the depth of my dismay rests with conservatives regardless of their political party.

The root of my consternation lies with contemporary application of conservative ideology. As the health-care-reform drama continues to unfold, it has become painfully apparent that a search for moderate Republicans, thoughtful conservatives, or pragmatic right-leaning practitioners who place the welfare of the society and its citizens above political party has become increasingly fruitless.

It is simply incomprehensible for me to fathom how, in the eyes of some, the current iteration of health-care-reform legislation has absolutely no, and I mean no, redeeming elements whatsoever. You cannot even find Republicans who are willing or brave enough to admit that there is any common ground upon which to base some agreement and move on from there. Instead there is a constant litany of reasons not to do anything. The argument, it seems to me, has morphed into whether or not to do anything at all, not whether we ought to employ a different approach. It is as if we are addressing a problem that doesn't exist.

The Party of No simply cannot bring itself to reveal any positive vision of how to proceed. Rather, the approach is one of no new taxes, no health-care reform, no energy policy, no legal hearings for terrorists, no to closing Guantanamo Bay, no gay marriage, no stimulus, and the list goes on. No has become a policy issue, and doing nothing and opposing everything is the tactic. It should not be lost on anyone that the first two letters in nothing are *n* and *o*.

I would counter that the only appropriate issue where no is acceptable would be on the issue of unemployment. I could certainly live with the concept of no unemployment. However, this position does not work either because it is conservative economic dogma that a "full employment" economy is one containing anywhere from four to seven percent unemployment. Contemporary conservative ideology certainly does smack of elitism; there simply are haves and have-nots, and whether or not it is determined by the market or a tyrant the practical effect is the same.

The Republican Party today is completely devoid of practical solutions to policy problems. They, quite simply, have become the "No, Nothing" party. One could easily deduce from this position that either there are no problems or there is no political capital in devising solutions to problems that do exist. In either case serious questions are raised as to their suitability to govern. The obvious retort of course is that this question was more than adequately answered during their one-party reign of power from 2000–2006. Surely they had ample opportunities to weigh in on health-care reform but opted to do, well, nothing.

If their opposition were irrelevant, it would not be an issue to waste ink over. However, because conservative ideology has found a room in the basement of the Democratic household, and because the majority in the Senate is so slim when considering the tactic of the filibuster, requiring that all Democratic senators support the final product in order for it to become law, lock-step opposition from the Republican Party is important and relevant. Few, I believe, appreciate the delicate balancing act that the president faces as he continues to push this crucially important reform issue.

Practical considerations dictate that we proceed deliberately and balance the needs and desires of progressive minded citizens who form a solid base of support for the president with the more moderate and yes conservative elements of this incredibly diverse coalition of elected Democrats. It is going to be a photo finish, and the potential long-term benefits of setting out on a course of rectifying outrageous inequities in the current system do outweigh the short-term psychic benefits of sticking to one's principles and letting reform either stall or die altogether.

Few among us has the Solomon-like wisdom and Job-like patience to continually readjust the balance in order to meet the larger goals of health-care reform, yet that is the high-wire act that we are currently witnessing from ground level. We must continue to trust the political matadors who have been charged with this awesome responsibility to wrest victory from the jaws of defeat, because the betting money would certainly have been on failure to achieve meaningful reform in light of the senselessly united opposition from the "No, Nothings."

Progressives ought not to despair. What is being attempted here is a gigantic step forward. The greatest fears are being manifested by those who wish only that we maintain the status quo and do nothing.

I am so outraged by those self-righteous conservatives who each night skirt what I believe to be the central issue involved here, namely: how can it be right to deny basic health-care coverage to such a large proportion of the population and how can you oppose fixing this on moral and/or ethical grounds? Who among us opposes providing health care to everyone?

It is as basic as this. And the sooner we face the basic question the sooner we will be able to shed light on the invalidity of the "No, Nothing" approach. The decision will ultimately rest with the populace on whether or not to punish those who blindly followed the obstructionist path to reform.

If we fail to advance the issue, the "No, Nothings" will be rewarded for fomenting confusion and inaction, and that will most assuredly be to the detriment of the society as a whole and any semblance of a progressive agenda. The stakes simply could not be higher.

The reward for movement on this issue will be momentum to face other issues which are awaiting serious consideration, most especially climate change. This is a dangerous time and we must maintain patience. But we must not allow our efforts at health-care reform to falter or fail. There are other issues crying out to be addressed and time relentlessly ticks away.

The Evolution of Revolution:
An Attack upon Reason, Compromise, and the Constitution

Article 42

January 20, 2010
Happy Anniversary

Exactly a year ago to the day Barack Obama was sworn in as president of the United States I found myself, in a cruel twist of fate, writing what not long ago may have seemed improbable if not impossible. The Liberal Lion of the Senate, Ted Kennedy, joined his brothers and had been replaced by the voters of Massachusetts with a Republican.

It is difficult to write those words. In the time since the historic election of Obama, his administration had been besieged by crises and an unyielding and adamant opposition that refuses to accept the responsibility to govern. The balancing act that is legislative process in a world in which a supermajority is the new majority had been upset considerably by the results in Massachusetts. New strategies, new tactics, and shifting goals were now the order of the day.

Progressives cannot despair, but must be sufficiently aware and cognizant of the changing realities that will wreak havoc on our substantive policy agenda. The people demand action, and are not really much concerned with how that action is accomplished. The internecine political battles and arcane workings of the legislative process matter little to them, and are seen as the province of the folks they elected to deal with them.

It may be unfortunate, but it is the case that an angry and frustrated nation has little patience or sympathy for failure to meet high expectations. And because the previous administration set the bar so low, it was easy to exceed them. Obama made the case for thinking big and bold, and setting a path to rectify missed opportunities on a large swath of policy issues. Now, a year later, he was being held to those goals, and patience was wearing thin, even among those most excited about his agenda—the progressive base of the Democratic Party.

Sometimes we can be our own worst enemies. If any one group was aware of the obstacles faced by the new administration, it was this one. Many had called on Obama to forego trying to work with the opposition and declare all-out war, accompanied by a strategy of circumventing Congress and going directly to the American people. It had become apparent to many in the progressive wing that the current tactics were insufficient to deal with an obstinate opposition, particularly since Senate Minority Leader Mitch McConnell had publicly and often declared that the number-one issue for his party was be to make Obama a one-term president. Now there's a hell of a patriot. What happened to governance? You would have your turn at defeating Obama and his agenda at the ballot box. What were you planning to do in the meantime?

The tactics of the first year had clearly not yielded enough progress to dampen the growing insurrection within the Republican Party, and that insurrection was commandeering the party and rendering its leaders hostage to a reactionary agenda.

In "Progressives: We Have Met the Enemy, and He Is Us," I attempted to draw attention to the cascade of political events that were changing the rules of the game. Having a new Republican senator in Massachusetts, and having him replace Ted Kennedy, was the cruelest twist of fate given that the administration had placed all of its chips on health-care reform. Senator Kennedy championed health-care reform for most of his career, which spanned nearly half a century. The goalposts had been moved, and our team had suffered a serious injury. But, by now, this was just another day at the office for Obama.

There was a general restlessness all around. Certainly the Tea-Party insurrectionists were restless, but so too were the change agents within the progressive ranks who had waited so long to effect constructive change in a society that was shifting in so many ways. Something would have to give as mid-terms approached. Kennedy's passing and the loss of the seat put a large and bold exclamation point on the dire nature of the current state of affairs.

Posted January 20, 2010
Progressives: We Have Met the Enemy and He Is Us

In the shadow of this week's disastrous electoral debacle, it is far too easy for progressives to assemble a circular firing squad. We are absolutely wrought with the shame, humiliation, and grief accompanying the premature obituaries of our own demise. However, to engage in the self-immolation that many have been advancing even before the polls closed in Massachusetts will only embolden the idiots and the idiocy of the prevailing victors. Therefore, it is critically important for us to redouble our efforts to press forward with the agenda that has led us to the point where we were prior to Tuesday's events.

It has been clear for some time now that the only guiding objective of the opposition to that agenda has been to prevent it from becoming reality. To that extent, they have been successful. Unfortunately, there are those among us who are now questioning whether or not the ultimate goals are sound, when in actuality what should be questioned are the tactics used to achieve them.

The people are angry and the people have spoken; that is what democracy is all about. We must accept that. Regardless what the polling data may or may not suggest, I would offer that instinctually folks are fed up with the inability of the powers that control the governmental machinery, which is us, to facilitate constructive progress on the agenda we promised. The enemy has become us.

Once again, we can spend an inordinate amount of time casting blame about whom or what caused this inaction, but the people really don't care about that. They care about results and, quite frankly, we have not delivered. They want jobs; we want jobs. Deliver jobs. They want health-care reform that is cost-sensitive, removes the barriers and impediments to coverage, and ensures a high degree of quality. So do we; deliver it. They want to be confident that the nation is on the right track. So do we; we must deliver the evidence to satisfy that confidence. They want an environment that is clean and sustainable. So do we; we must deliver.

What made the election of Barack Obama so exciting and revolutionary is that after a sustained period of stasis, the American people were enthralled with the prospect of a renewed vibrancy that would propel us back to a level of greatness and respect that we had grown accustomed to from our early childhoods. And to some in the younger demographic categories, it was a return to the greatness they had only read or heard about. But there was a strong belief that we could once again regain the mantle of leadership on moral and ethical issues that has eluded us for some time. And that is still the goal that is still the dream that is still the desire of those who are not mired in the anti-intellectualism of a lunatic fringe whose only objective is to thwart progress.

Therefore, despair not progressives, but recommit to the notion that in fact we can help build a better society and a better world by adhering to the common goals of the vast majority of people who cast their lot for that agenda just a little over a year ago. And let politicians of whatever political stripe who stand in the way of that goal suffer the consequences of defeat. It is too late for Massachusetts, but let us not allow the infection that follows the fever of impatience and anxiety spread.

And let this be a warning to our elected leaders that it is not the dream that died, but rather the faith that they would be able to make it come true that took a beating this week. So get to work and deliver lest you also suffer a similar fate soon.

It is often said that what is missing in the drippy, wimpy, compassionate agenda of the progressive movement is not a lack of conviction, but a lack of strength. It is now time to exhibit strength and resolve that has been unparalleled in our time. We have the right message, we have the right prescriptions, and we have what the people want and demand; now we must devise the right tactics to get the country on the right track. And not only will we be better off for it, but there will be political rewards as well.

Currently there are relatively little political costs incurred for obstruction because an angry populace does not realize any benefits from inaction. Until we change the calculus so that the angry and anxious exact a penalty for obstruction and reap the benefits from concrete actions, results like those in Massachusetts will multiply and eventually the dream will die. But we cannot allow that to happen. Right now it hurts but there is no time to lick our wounds. We must carry forth because we know it is right.

Article 43

February 3, 2010
Deficit Dummies!

To quote Ronald Reagan, "There they go again." The Republican, ideologically-driven mantra of tax cuts as a cure-all was alive and well. Deficits? Just reduce taxes. Health care reform? Just reduce taxes. Unemployment? Just reduce taxes. Foreclosure? Just reduce taxes. You get the idea. The most disquieting thing about this constant drumbeat is that there are no instances in which cutting taxes has ever worked. But let us not quibble over details.

We Keynesians are able to point to the Great Depression. That was quite a while ago, but our policies worked. The Republican no-tax drumbeat goes on unabated. Reagan tried it, and the debt trebled in a decade; Dubya tried it, and the result was the greatest economic collapse since the Great Depression, as well as an exploding debt. Have they no room for facts? Obviously not. For them, facts are in the same place as science and intellectualism—the outhouse.

In "What Kind of Thinking Is This?" I point out the contemptuous dishonesty the Republican Party foments to distract the public from the fact that it has no intent to participate in governing or solving problems. They only perpetuate, ad nauseam, well-worn pabulum that has no basis in truth, fact, or performance. Who doesn't want lower taxes?

Yet at the same time, they insist that we have to pay for what we want, then reject that we want what we want. Unfortunately, we want what we cannot afford, and politicians constantly dance around this conundrum by devising ways to temporarily give us what we cannot afford through borrowing. Borrowing is an important concept; paying back is the problem. That is where bipartisanship finds a home; there is little taste for repaying our debts. But revenues are an important component of fiscal policy, which includes taxing and spending. George W. Bush fought two wars without paying for either. Do Republicans or Tea-Party patriots reject covering these costs?

Posted February 3, 2010

What Kind of Thinking Is This?

All right, after all the posturing and the bellyaching and the phony pleas to "please listen to me," what it all comes down to is this: Republicans believe that deficits are the problem; Democrats believe that this broken down economy that we inherited needs to be fixed.

I watched Haley Barbour and John Thune on television yesterday arguing that we need deficit reduction and tax cuts. So that's what the unemployed in South Dakota and Mississippi are sitting around worrying about, eh? Nonsense! That is what people who are not as comfortable as they once were are concerned about.

Where oh where have we heard this before? It is the same trickle-down baloney that is the one-size-fits-all economic pabulum that gets rolled out every time the Republicans need a tax cut fix. The only time Republicans are concerned about deficits is when fiscal policy does not involve tax cuts that exacerbate deficits. Yet it now appears that they have upped the ante and are only concerned about deficits whenever there is even a hint of domestic spending, regardless of whether there are a healthy dose of small business tax cuts thrown in for good measure as Obama outlined in the State of the Union address last week.

Deficits declined under the last Democratic administration, deficits and debt exploded during the Reagan-George H.W. Bush Administrations, deficits hit unheard of levels during George W. Bush's Administration. Now deficit spending to stimulate economic growth is dangerous, according to these hypocritical naysayers of negativism. I mean, they advocate deficits when the economy is growing and deficit reduction when the economy is a basket case. Yet to complete the irony of the whole sorry affair known as a broken financial and economic system that the ardent disciples of deregulation have wrought, they use high unemployment to shift the debate away from health-care reform.

But, once again, the solution to high unemployment is not jobs, not a program that proved to be so effective during the Depression, but rather the worn out psychobabble of trickle-down economic theory that has never proven itself effective, ever. If we just unleash the power of the almighty capital markets by reducing taxes, the economy will bounce back and we will work our way back to a full employment economy, which I assume at this point means something in the realm of six to seven percent unemployment.

We unleashed the potential of the private marketplace during the first eight years of the new millennium and it brought us perilously close to a total unmitigated collapse. The financial meltdown that has brought us this new blast of economic misery is a direct result of the delusion of free marketers who refuse to accept that financial markets, like nature, abhor a vacuum and from time to time need serious readjustment. And yet these are the same patriots who are delirious to the point of apoplexy when they are confronted with the hard decisions of whether or not to participate in the policy-making process.

I understand the frustration on the part of Obama; he is sincerely trying to make things work, and I know he is a true believer in the rationality of man, he just cannot help but think that when confronted with the truth, with facts, with science, that the lock-step opposition mounted by the other side will give way to what is actually best for the public good.

The anger in Massachusetts was irrational. In effect, the people were so disgusted with the lack of action on behalf of the ruling party that they decided they would send them a message by making it more difficult for them to actually take action. Of course it is counterintuitive, of course it is irrational, but so was the sad story of having lower- and middle-income Americans vote against their own economic self-interest, as they certainly did during the last administration.

We must regroup and move forward, no time outs, no re-examination, no recalibrating. Just move forward. We know what needs to be done; we have a brilliant, calm, and inspiring leader. Figure out what can be done and do it. We simply cannot afford to just compartmentalize to the point where we chuck one part of the agenda in order to focus on the other. What is required is seamless and interlocking coordination. The problem is complex and the solution is therefore, well, complex.

Health care reform is an important component of job creation. Addressing climate change through an energy security strategy that focuses on shifting the economic paradigm from one dominated by fossil fuels to one dominated by alternative energy sources creates jobs. Focusing on our deteriorating infrastructure creates jobs. Getting control of our runaway financial system will foster lending that will benefit small business and create jobs.

If they do not want to play, we must take the chance to forge ahead without them, if we are wrong we will pay the price, but if we do nothing because we spend all of our time trying to accommodate the irrationality of their arguments we will pay the price anyway.

The Evolution of Revolution:
An Attack upon Reason, Compromise, and the Constitution

Article 44

February 26, 2010
Death Panels!

No less a light than the rising star in the Republican constellation, Sarah Palin, had been hammering away at the concept of death panels. She stated that government bureaucrats would have the power to determine whether or not you got certain procedures under the Obama "takeover" of health care. That means "socialized medicine."

The president tried one last time to solicit cooperation from the opposition by hosting a discussion which resembled that of a prime minister going before the House of Commons—an entertaining and fascinating process of government. It took place at Blair House, directly across the street from the White House complex, a place where few outside the international diplomatic corps have had occasion to visit.

I was once part of a cabinet meeting there in 1999 as part of the President's Commission on Year 2000 Conversion, and had been intrigued by the fact that most cabinet officers had never been to Blair House. But in this august setting sat the president with Congressional leaders, trying to hammer out a plan which would allow progress on health-care reform.

Several things quickly became apparent. First, the president's reserved demeanor, his calmness and coolness under fire, showed signs of fraying for the first time; second, the opposition was not willing to play ball under any circumstances; and third, the Republicans were the ones advocating death panels.

In order to solve a problem, you must first define what it is. Without agreement on the nature of the problem, it is impossible to reach a solution. To Obama and the Democrats, the problem was that health care in this country is not a right, and it should be. But Republicans made it very clear that health care is not a right, and besides, we can't afford it anyway. Unless there is fundamental agreement on whether or not Americans have a right to health care, no comprehensive program to guarantee universal access will be achieved, and that is where the issue stands.

It is the Republican Party that allows decisions on life and death to be placed in the invisible hand of the omniscient, omnipotent free market. This, of course, should come as little surprise given the reverence to and mystical powers bestowed upon "the market." What is revelatory, however, is the extent to which there is unanimous belief in this tenet in the Republican Party.

In "Say No to 'Death Panels,'" I intended to draw attention to the basic disconnect between the parties on the fundamental question of whether or not health care is a right. It is sometimes necessary to ask the most basic questions, because the answers often reveal the ability to proceed down what might be a fruitful path. It had taken a lot of stroking, enormous political capital, and painful and extraordinary amounts of restraint and patience, but in the end, the path was quite clear; we would need to proceed without help from the other side.

Posted February 26, 2010
Say No to "Death Panels"

Ok, for those who cared to watch the battle at Blair House yesterday, it should be patently obvious that all efforts at post-partisanship should be put to pasture. There is simply no inclination on the part of the opposition at this point to attempt to reach a consensus on this. It is an all or nothing proposition, with the political calculus on each side set in stone.

On the Republican side, they have made their calculations that defeating anything this president and a Democratic-controlled Congress offers is a political winner. On the Democratic side, they have made the calculation that passing even a scaled-back version of what at one time was a comprehensive health-care-reform initiative is a political winner. The lines are drawn, and we will see which calculation was the correct one.

But something has to give, because the defeatist calculation has two shots at prevailing: one, they can beat it back by successfully defeating a proposal through a vote; or two, they can beat it back by inaction on the part of the Democrats. The Democrats only have one course to victory, and that is to win on a positive vote since having large majorities in Congress and the White House prevents them from credibly saying "Well, we tried and they refused. In that case, they win."

So having said this, there is only one way to proceed, and that is to push it to a vote. Since the prospects of success on a sixty-vote process are nil, you must proceed on a process that guarantees that fifty-one, a majority, is good enough to secure passage. Now isn't that a novel concept; majority rules. I certainly am sympathetic to the notion that the minority has rights, but a minority of forty-nine is acceptable; a minority of forty is not.

What I found intriguing about yesterday's exercise is that it is the first time I have seen a president so engaged in a substantive debate on a very complex set of issues. For those who have on occasion witnessed the prime minister in England being pounded and heckled before his legislative body and marveled at the spectacle, as I have, yesterday was about as close as we get in this country.

And in a perverse sort of way, listen closely Sarah Palin. What you saw yesterday was the Republican opposition tipping their hand on the issue of "death panels." Yep, there they were basically insisting that health care is not a right—oh yeah, and we cannot afford it anyway, and if you take that to its logical conclusion you come to the point where what they are essentially saying is that we, the imperial Congress, will decide who gets it and who doesn't. If you can afford it, you live; if you cannot afford it, you suffer the consequences, which could be death.

I discovered, to my deepest chagrin, many months ago that if you just boil issues down to their simplest components, you can get a good feel for the tact the opposition will employ. I asked a dear friend of mine, who happens to be a Republican, this simple question: "Does everyone have a right and should everyone have the opportunity to be afforded adequate health care?" Surprisingly, she had difficulty answering the question. I was surprised because I was sure that she was a thinking person's Republican, a moderate suburbanite not captured by the teabagger set. But she was stumped and could not answer right away. Finally, after some considerable thought, she said no.

I could have stood there and argued till I was blue in the face but I simply just looked at her incredulously and as if to say, "Is that your final answer?" I just said, "Really, that is interesting."

So if that is your belief, how could you possibly expect a set of compromises to emerge from any discussion or negotiation when the basic building blocks of reform are that you must first acknowledge what needs to be reformed?

So it turns out that the real purveyors of "death panels" are those who would deny a proportion of the population the chance to live based on whether or not they could afford it. We must get on with the agenda of the people, pass health-care reform, and begin to tackle the other pressing issues that affect us on a daily basis: jobs, economic recovery, financial system sanity, and climate change, particularly with an eye on the alternative energy jobs that are the constructive byproduct of saving the planet.

The president has done all that he possibly can to engage in a constructive bipartisan discussion on this issue; he has been more patient than even his most ardent supporters, of which I count myself as one, can stomach, and the cool demeanor and serene self-confidence that defines his persona started to fray yesterday, and for good reason. Let's reject the "death panel" position of the opposition and move forward, forthwith.

Article 45

March 2, 2010
You're Out!

Jim Bunning was a fine professional baseball player before he was a senator from Kentucky. I had had the pleasure of watching him pitch a perfect game for the Philadelphia Phillies on Father's Day, 1964. A perfect game is a very rare feat in professional baseball, and he would go down in history as a fan favorite.

As a senator, however, he struck out. What piqued my interest and compelled me to write this article was emblematic of a much larger problem plaguing the Senate, a place where I had spent nearly seven years in my early career, and that was the senatorial courtesy which allows individuals to single-handedly hold up legislation and nominations with relative impunity.

In this instance, Senator Bunning held up legislation that would have extended unemployment benefits to many thousands of American workers because he was not satisfied with how that spending would be paid for. Senatorial courtesy is one thing, but having essential veto power on issues that dramatically affect the people's business is another.

Whether it was this isolated instance or the abuse of the filibuster or simply thwarting majority will by abusing minority rights, the processes for deliberation in the upper body have come under scrutiny in light of the inability to render the legislative process functional. It needs to be revisited.

In "No Hits, No Runs, Big Error," I attempted to highlight procedural issues that are being used to subvert work on behalf of the American people, and in this case have a profound impact upon those who were unemployed and reliant upon continuation of benefits. Our elected officials are often insensitive to or ignorant of the real and dramatic impact their actions have upon ordinary citizens. This was a prime example in which being out of touch has very real consequences. Our elected officials need to be reminded of this now and then.

There is a time and place for everything, and there are all sorts of ways to make your points, but the childish actions of the junior senator from Kentucky reminded me of the power and trust we place in our elected representatives. When those are abused for petty reasons, it shows how fragile our system is. And this was an egregious lack of sensitivity and character. In another profession—say, baseball— he could have vented his anger by throwing a high, hard one under the batter's chin. It may have precipitated a brawl or retaliation on a teammate, but it would have been an isolated incident confined to a very few individuals. However, messing with people's lives, especially when they are most vulnerable, is unconscionable.

Posted March 2, 2010
No Hits, No Runs, Big Error

I was ten years old the day I watched pitcher Jim Bunning toss a perfect game against the New York Mets from the luxury of my bedroom in northeast Philadelphia on a black-and-white television with rabbit ears, through occasional snow that had nothing to do with climate change and everything to do with the quality of electronic technology. It was Father's Day, June 21, 1964, and, as I always did, I kept the book while I watched the game. It was a masterpiece and has only been accomplished seventeen other times in the long history of America's pastime.

What Jim Bunning is doing, however, proves that he is now engaged in the wrong sport and should be given the showers as quickly as possible. But what it also illustrates, in stunning clarity is the extent to which petulance, vindictiveness, and outright stupidity can all conspire to hold sway in the US Senate. I worked in the Senate for over six years and witnessed pettiness on occasion and, having served those years on the Senate Budget Committee, I am very familiar with the procedural maneuver called reconciliation that has recently entered the vocabulary of many observers of our governmental process.

I am a firm believer in preserving the rights of the minority, and familiar with the history of balancing small states' influence with large states, bicameralism, and the interplay of intergovernmental forces that delicately attempt to balance the respective roles of federal, state, and local governments. I have witnessed severe ideological and political polarization over the years that would result in votes so close as to necessitate the summoning of the vice president of the United States to come to the chamber and be prepared to cast the deciding vote. I was, in fact, intimately involved in one such occasion in 1982 in which then–Vice President George H.W. Bush was rousted from his comfy bed at the Naval Observatory and forced to sit in the chair of the Senate after midnight. His vote was not needed that evening, but he was there just in case. And that would have been to break a simple tie.

Senator, playing with people's lives is not a game. And besides, this is the major leagues of politics you are in. Grabbing your ball and refusing to play just because you are in a fit of pique over something would not be acceptable in Major League Baseball, and it is not acceptable in the United States Senate. These childish antics only reinforce the cynicism and distrust that a frustrated and worried populace feels towards their government. If that is your goal, then congratulations, you are winning. But if that is your goal, you no longer deserve to be in the game.

I have been involved in public policy for over three decades now, and I am in constant amazement at the seemingly rapid transformation that has taken place in the upper chamber with respect to what determines a majority. Since when did sixty become the norm and not the exception? And what is the rationale for such a shift? If the election of officials were contingent upon their receiving sixty percent of the vote, we would have very few officials in either chamber of Congress.

Have we all just fallen asleep at the switch, or has sanity left the building? I can only imagine the shrill cries from the Republicans if Democrats had demanded a supermajority on important issues like say going to war. They would have been derided as unpatriotic. But is ensuring the health of the nation's citizens any less important a public policy goal as defending against foreign enemies? I would argue that the health and welfare of the nation is every bit as crucial a function of government as national defense.

As a matter of fairness and effectiveness, requiring a supermajority in the most optimal setting is probably not wise, but in a time of hyperinflated partisanship and ideological polarization, it renders the Republic powerless to function and fuels an already unhealthy cynicism that is distrustful and suspicious of the very processes of governance that are required to make things work. In the latest episode of senatorial inertia, the famed baseball pitcher has dropped the ball and his ineptitude will mean additional heartache for millions who are already near the ends of their collective rope. As spring training is currently upon us, the sounds of "play ball" are not far off. The same is true for the Senate. It is time to play ball.

The Evolution of Revolution:
An Attack upon Reason, Compromise, and the Constitution

Article 46

March 10, 2010
You're So Special!

Anger abounds in the country; the conventional wisdom is that the system is so rigged that only a few can play; and that the regular guy, the guy who plays by the rules, is the real schmuck—the person who always ends up holding the short end of the stick despite doing everything they were supposed to do. And in a sense, the conventional wisdom is on target.

Skepticism is healthy, but when it is ignored, it turns to cynicism, which is unhealthy. When the concerns of many are ignored, anger builds, and when the anger is dismissed by the few who benefit at the expense of the many, a revolution is born. With a shrinking middle class and the index of income inequality soaring, there is good reason that increasingly larger portions of the population are angry. This anger can manifest itself in various ways—directed at those above who are seen as pushing you down, or at those below who are seen as pulling you down.

It is always more convenient to blame those who are beneath than to blame those who are above. As a society that prides itself on the notion that everyone has the opportunity to make it to the top, it is easier to pile on those at the bottom in the hope that, eventually, the pile will help you get to be a pusher-down; after all, it takes a large base to support the pyramid.

This distinction addresses the major difference between anger from the right and anger from the left. Conservatives blame those underneath; liberals blame those at the top. But let there be little disagreement that the population's anger has been and still is broadly dispersed. Strangely, however, with the disappearance of the middle class, the slope of the pyramid has become steeper as the middle of the pyramid is hollowed out. As in grand hotel architecture, the pyramid now resembles an atrium, supported by leaner beams and an expanding foundation. Consider the current shape as one of those modern hotels that rises fifty or sixty stories, but when you walk into the lobby, you enter an atrium which hollows out the building all the way to the top.

The conservative reaction is to seek to restore a status quo where they were comfortable. In order to restore that balance, they must take more from those who, in their minds, do not deserve what they have because they have not earned it—the takers. The liberal reaction is to take from those who, in their minds, have benefited at the expense of everyone else and deserve to pay their fair share for the privilege of having so much—the haves.

The Obama Administration staked their marbles on health-care reform. Using the logic stated above, conservatives found health care to be a rationed good and, applying zero-sum theory, believed that expanding health care would diminish the amount and quality available to those who already had it. Believing that health care is not a right, it seemed unfair that they would be asked to pay more and/or receive less, and so they were quite satisfied with and protective of the status quo.

Enough had been written about the issue, and debate seemed inexhaustible by this point in 2010. Proposals had been defined, refined, redlined, headlined, and redefined, yet there was no indication that change was imminent or inevitable. Liberals, who had been expecting significant movement towards universal access because it is a right that should be guaranteed to all in their calculus, were palpably frustrated.

Conservatives had an effective battalion of ground troops— special interests—fanned out on Capitol Hill to supply ammunition, otherwise known as campaign monies, to maintain the profitable status quo. Something had to give, and soon.

In "Ode to Special Interests," I decided to try my hand at poetry to help better define where we stood at that juncture in the Obama Administration's campaign to reform health care. I took aim at the special interests which had dramatically grown in strength in the years since I had first gone to Washington, DC. The incestuous relationships and revolving-door policy of Capitol Hill staffers leaving public service and cashing in on long-held relationships with former colleagues represents a serious threat to effective policymaking, and it demeans and perverts the democratic process. It is fueled by a system of generous campaign contributions, and the master key to unlocking the process is access guaranteed by familiarity and friendship. It is no secret, and it is seemingly unstoppable.

I have witnessed the revolving-door nature of politics firsthand and at various levels over my career, and I am constantly amazed by its corrosive nature and addictive quality. Many people I have known and respected have cashed in to take advantage of the knowledge they gained while ostensibly serving the public interest. I don't know how to deal with this phenomenon, and I have never entertained the notion of switching allegiance from the public interest to special interest, but I have seen people reap tremendous financial rewards from doing so. It seems like public interest is always at the bottom of the heap.

Posted March 10, 2010
Ode to Special Interests

As the anger builds
And the disappointment spills
Into a cauldron of despair,
Frustration mounts and tempers flare
And reason rapidly disappears
As battle lines become crystal clear.

While the Republic teeters
We rob Paul to pay Peter.
It's all a grand game
But the result's the same.
While the rich thrive
The rest merely survive.

Wall Street's wealth,
Main Street's stealth,
Big bank success,
Middle class stress.
Too big to fail?
The check's in the mail.

Does anyone really care?
Does anyone really dare
Question our leaders' desire
To quell this raging fire?
I guess, to a large degree,
The problem belongs to you and me.

Because health care is not a right,

And if you have it you must fight
To deny it to all those
Too powerless to oppose
A status quo.
That, we all know.

Will steadfastly not
Expand the pot
To cover those without
No matter how loudly they shout.
Father Profit demands
That current policy stands.

So we continue to falter
While worshipping at the altar
Of a system so sleek
And a leadership so weak
That dramatic change
Is left to the long-range.

Article 47

March 27, 2010
Rising Above the Fray

After fifteen months of intense battle, political jockeying, incessant recriminations, and a well-organized insurrection within the Republican Party that effectively turned it into an obstructionist juggernaut, the administration succeeded in passing a version of health-care reform that at least made strides towards greater access. It is certainly not everything that either the White House or the progressive coalition supporting the administration hoped for, but in light of the toxic political environment in which it was birthed, it represented progress.

If not for the president's persistence, even this bill would not have become law. It required considerable political capital, and the fight had delayed action on other critically serious issues. But politics is the art of the possible, and this is what is possible in the contemporary arena.

It should not have been this hard. We wasted a tremendous amount of precious time, but the president and his administration never took its collective eyes off the prize. Now it was time to move to other pressing items.

In "The Transcendent Presidency," I took great care to highlight President Obama's steely determination in accomplishing a feat that had evaded our grasp for several generations. Kudos to you, Mr. President. Time will tell, and history will render judgment, on whether the fight was worth given some of the other pressing issues, but no one will argue that this was one of the highest-priority items on the agenda, and no one should find fault with the administration's priorities. I make no bones about where my biases lay—climate change is number one on my hit parade, but health care was a close second—so now it was time to move on.

Posted March 24, 2010

The Transcendent Presidency

You need know little more than this with respect to the battle over health-care reform: those who supported it believe that as many people as possible should have health care, those who opposed it believe that certain people should have it and others should not, plain and simple.

This was not a debate over the best way to ensure universal access; it was not even a debate over how to ensure as many people as practical. There are no proposals, absolutely none, that were advanced by opponents of the current version that suggested a better way to insure 32 million additional Americans. This was an ideological battle over people's right to health care. What is so discouraging is that not one Republican in the US Congress believes that, if votes are any reflection of beliefs.

But in this environment, votes on issues are not reflective of beliefs or values. Unfortunately, party loyalty and political calculations that having the country falter or fail is of far greater value than the bedrock of our democratic governing system, compromise. It is a tragic illustration of how dysfunctional our two-party system has become. I personally wish that a single-payer solution had been the outcome, but realizing that was not in the cards, I can only stand by in admiration of the steely determination of our president when confronted with the incredulous machinations that have characterized this long, disjointed process. The occasion is truly historic, the achievement a defining and transformative moment that the majority of Americans envisioned when they cast their votes for Obama fifteen months ago. Of course, everyone realizes that the job is not finished, and refinements to and improvement in the product are necessary. But if a journey of a thousand miles begins with the first step, we have taken a huge one.

The myriad issues that now rise to the top of the agenda are mind-boggling and significant indeed. We must turn our attention to putting people back to work, reforming our financial system, addressing the all-important issue of climate change, and getting our troops out of harm's way. These all will require the steadfast resolve exhibited by the Obama Administration during the first year and a quarter. Does anyone really have any doubt at this point that this president is up to the task? He never even considered throwing his hands up and moving on, and there was a time only several months ago when that must have been an appealing consideration. But the values inherent in this administration place the future prospects of the American people above the short-term popularity of simple fixes or half-measures.

There is a lot of talk these days about transparency; however, I feel there is another word that receives little attention and may be every bit as important, and that is transcendence. Health care is an issue that should by any calculus transcend politics. It is too important to too many people to allow for the type of demagoguery we are currently witnessing in our political discourse. Yet the politics of fear still holds sway over many of those who have practiced it for so long with such effective results that it has now become an addiction. Obama has risen above the din and with a firm hand guided us through this treacherous minefield of health-care reform. He has proven his mettle in battle and, regardless of whether he is rewarded for his valor, he has done what he promised to do and what is good for the American people. No one can ever take that away.

Of course, let's hope that indeed there is a reward for having done the right thing. Americans are hugely proud of their sense of fairness, and if that holds we will be treated to act two and act three and however many heroic demonstrations are required of this administration to address the serious problems facing us. We should all be very proud. For those actions that are required to transcend the pettiness of the politics of obstruction, we must continue to follow our leader.

The Evolution of Revolution:
An Attack upon Reason, Compromise, and the Constitution

Article 48

March 25, 2010
Don't Tread On Me

I'd enjoyed writing the first poem so much that I had to try my hand again. This time I decided to poke a stick at the Tea-Party snakes, who were gaining in strength and visibility. The rawness of the rhetoric, the vileness of the venom, the certitude of their convictions, and the power of their persuasion were only matched by the effectiveness of their electoral strategies. They had become a force in contemporary politics which would need to be dealt with.

Democrats had, for years, relied on the strength of seniors to bolster their election prospects. Seniors vote, and securing their support largely through policies which strengthened Social Security and Medicare were always seen as effective strategies. But Social Security was now under attack not from a grossly unbalanced fiscal policy that saw spending outpace revenues, but from the perception that spending for younger, less-fortunate individuals was squeezing out spending for older folks. Class warfare had been supplanted by intergenerational warfare. Seniors feel entitled to benefits, while others who did not deserve it— youngsters and the poor—were competing for the same pot of funding. It was an effective strategy to shrink the spending pot to have more competition for less money—the traditional strategy of divide and conquer. By focusing on overspending as the chief fiscal problem, the new conservatives could zero in on traditional alliances that had aided liberals and Democrats—seniors and minorities.

I would often debate my father about his Social Security benefits, trying to explain how he would exhaust what he had contributed into the system long before he would pass. He ended up living until he was nearly eighty-nine and surely had long surpassed his contributions, but he would not hear of it. He had paid into the system, he was entitled to it, and by God he would collect until the day he died, even if his check came from someone else's pocketbook. There is a general misunderstanding of Social Security that has grown stronger over the past half century. It was never structured or intended to be a sole source of retirement income; it was always intended to be supplemental income. That somehow got lost in the mix.

No one wants to deprive our elderly a comfortable retirement; however, in order to do so, we must be willing as a society to pay for the benefits we wish to bestow upon them. Similarly, we should be willing to pay for other benefits we deem important and necessary, and that means supporting spending, both on programs and debt service, in times of economic growth. When economic times are slow, we need to adjust to be able to pull ourselves out of the trough, largely through borrowing, but keep the essential safety-net programs intact or, with programs like unemployment and food stamps, expand them to meet the greater need. But it is important that we repay the debt when the economy recovers. Austerity during economic downturns only exacerbates the problem and is an economic prescription for disaster, yet that is exactly the prescription the new conservatism offers. The lack of perspective is stunning.

In "The Snake Pit," I attempt to capture the venomous nature of the movement that would continue to put roadblocks and impediments on the road to progress. I was concerned that we were losing control of our ability to effectively counter this movement, and this intensified in the ensuing months and years. I had come to both fear and loathe the Tea-Party tsunami buffeting our political landscape, feared that they were here to stay, and loathed the regressive nature and meanness of their agenda.

Posted March 25, 2010
The Snake Pit

Angry white fools
Hurl slurs and insults
Like old dull tools
With the unintended results

Of exposing so proudly
Just what they represent
Vigorously and loudly
Spewing violent dissent

From a system that struggles

To help society
Cope with its troubles
And the faux piety

Of the spoiled and coddled
Who mistakenly see
A policy modeled
To destroy their liberty

Raw hatred abounds
For those not disposed
To heed the sounds
Or drink from the hose

Connected to a well
Filled with toxic waste
Dispensing a foul smell
And numbing the taste

Of patriots who have fought
For freedom and choice
And hopefully sought
To forever give voice

To the different and unique
And those who would not
Mindlessly critique
Such a strange lot

But the loudest reject
A mosaic so bright
And forcefully protect
What they feel is right

Good sense and civility disappear
No time to think
Reason replaces fear
Which drives us to the brink

Where the snakes all gather

As if they believe
Their propagandist blather
Don't tread on me.

Article 49

May 21, 2010
What Kinda Doctor Are You?

Dr. Rand Paul was nominated by the Kentucky Republican Party to run for the US Senate, and made an appearance on *The Rachel Maddow Show* shortly after the primary vote. What transpired defied belief; however, it was reflective and instructive in that it gave insight into the thinking—and I use that term liberally here—of the Tea-Party candidates who would be vying for Congressional seats in the fall.

He voiced contempt for Congress, the very institution he was trying to become a member of, as much for its existence as for its performance. He is a libertarian who has very little use for government per se, and believes that an individual controls his personal kingdom. His defense of an individual's right to discriminate made my hair curl. He seemed a throwback to the sort of individualism that characterized discrimination in the Deep South and the belief in Manifest Destiny that justified the en masse deaths of Native Americans. It seemed as though he was out of place in the twenty-first century; his thinking was more in line with early nineteenth century intellect.

I hoped that his performance would presage a backlash—even in Kentucky—at the polls. Alas, I was to be disappointed. He was a prime example of the type of candidate being recruited for the new Republican Party, and it was more than a little scary.

In "Dr. Paul, You Should See Dr. Phil," I attempt to analyze his performance. However, I found it difficult to recount, let alone digest, his positions or governing philosophy. This was a harbinger of what was to come in the midyear elections. Of course, we didn't know it at the time, but you will be able to discern my concern that we were entering some choppy waters, at least in Kentucky. Let me be clear—I do not have a bias about Kentucky, but it did not escape me that the senator Paul would be replacing was Jim Bunning, about whom I had written earlier, and of course his senior senator was none other than the Republican Minority Leader, Mitch McConnell, who also had invoked my wrath on numerous occasions. What was in the water down there?

Posted May 21, 2010
Dr. Paul, You Should See Dr. Phil

Watching the Rand Paul interview with Rachel Maddow was extraordinarily painful to say the least. It was painful on a number of levels, not the least of which was the fact that it is apparent that this gentleman genuinely feels that the government has no role in setting parameters of acceptable behavior within society where private business is concerned. A man's business is his personal province, and he has the right to do whatever he feels is right within the confines of his kingdom. Now that is startling enough, coming from a cock-eyed conservative in libertarian's clothing. I sincerely doubt that in Paul-Paul land this extends to the notion of public safety to enforce the laws, say against murder, or robbery, or illegal immigration, and hence the inconsistency lends itself to interpretation which can only be characterized as prejudice. Whether that prejudice is controlled by race, religion, sexual orientation, color, or hair or whatever, I suppose it is left to the business tyrant to determine. But his position surely allows for personal prejudice, regardless of his personal views towards the concept.

Saying that you are not a bigot but support the rights of other people to be bigots under the guise of the sanctity of business practices is an odd, contorted, and structurally unbalanced position. Dr. Paul, and I have no idea what he is a doctor of, but obviously must have more than a minimal amount of at least exposure to intellectual thought and teachings unless one can receive a doctorate through home schooling, obviously enjoys listening to himself think out loud. And if his tortured contrivances last evening are any indication that process must be one hell of a mess inside his head. He was simply incapable or unwilling to answer the question which he himself set up with his twisted logic: namely, does the governmental process which you wish to become an integral part of have the duty to allow businessmen or women to discriminate and would you support that position if it came to a vote?

This is not a trick question, and by virtue of the fact that he parsed the Civil Rights Act of the one provision which addresses this issue, he should be required to let those who have the solemn obligation to cast a vote in the upcoming Senatorial election in Kentucky know what his views and positions on the issue are. Anything less would be a crass political dodge, which I am sure he abhors. Yet when given the opportunity to answer the question directly, he resorted to the very act of obfuscation which I am sure he is running against. Thus, Dr. Paul, you are a bona fide phony. You are a political creature incapable or unable of the kind of honesty and transparency I assume you promote on the campaign trail.

I do not know whether it is to the progressives' manifest good fortune or their disgust that this man's nomination will ultimately play out—that is for the good people of Kentucky to decide this fall—but the robust amateurism with which he has exhibited in fumbling this position, a position that he himself has constructed, will hopefully shed light not only on his disingenuousness but his outright dishonesty. He is either an idiot or a calculated political hack, and I will be kind and grant him the latter. What the election on Tuesday did more than anything else, I believe, is reveal that the people's anger is directed at those to whom they feel have not been honest with them. Somehow Dr. Paul has persuaded enough Kentuckians to believe he was more honest than Mitch McConnell's hand-picked candidate, which of course does not speak well of either McConnell or his candidate. But Rand Paul is clearly and simply a confused child on a stage that he is woefully ill equipped to perform on, at a time when the skills of honesty and integrity are yearned for by the electorate and he exhibits no competence in those skills whatsoever.

My initial instincts with his cretinism were anger and disbelief, and every fiber in my body wanted to strangle the little twerp, but on reflection, the fact that he refused to man up and answer the questions that he himself raised left me feeling disgusted and repulsed. He should be defeated on his phoniness more than anything else, and I trust that the voters will punish him for not being honest with them. That is how the anger out there should be directed. If you fail to tell the folks how you really feel, then you are a weasel and should retreat back into the hole from where you came. It is time for Dr. Paul to go underground.

The Evolution of Revolution:
An Attack upon Reason, Compromise, and the Constitution

Article 50

July 19, 2010
Needs versus Wants

The continuing dysfunction in DC necessitated a reassessment of the fundamental concept of representative democracy. In this system, we choose people to decide what is best for us. If we do not like or agree with their decisions, we have the ultimate veto power—voting them out of office. That, at least, is the theory. However, the power of incumbency in the face of ever-diminishing support for the institution of which the incumbent is a member defies practical application of the concept of voting him or her out of office. It seems that it is never your representative who is the problem—it's all the others. This phenomenon more likely attests to the populace's ignorance of what their representative is doing, and we Americans have always had a soft spot for favorite sons. Nevertheless, incumbency is a powerful inducement to longevity, and gerrymandered congressional districts reinforce the power of incumbency.

We are witnessing a political paralysis devoid of any idea of leadership. When I was in graduate school, I learned at the feet of a brilliant and distinguished political scientist named Peter Bachrach. The professor was renowned for his development of the political theory of non-decision making. Now despite what you may think, it is not a theory about not making decisions; it is a theory about making decisions not to make decisions. This is a critical distinction.

What we are currently witnessing is a legislative body making conscious decisions not to make decisions. When the Party of No weighs in on an issue, they are making a conscious decision to not allow a vote. It is not an inability to make a decision.

As I have noted earlier, I prefer statesmanship to leadership. But in the absence of the former, we at least need the latter. We are precluded from taking action on any number of issues due to decisions to thwart decisions. Our legislative institutions, the US Senate and House, contain a sufficient number of elected officials who feel they have been elected to prevent the institution from doing what it is designed to do—to move on items. In an even more elementary sense, preventing a vote is considered even better than a "no" vote. Preventing the institution from acting on issues allows doubt and contempt to be visited upon it, whereas individual votes expose an individual to criticism for action taken.

We have the seemingly incongruous situation where an historically large majority of the people have little or no confidence in Congress, yet support their legislator. Through gerrymandering of Congressional districts and the power of incumbency, which carries with it the ability to stockpile campaign contributions and favors, incumbency re-election percentages are still disproportionate to the general dissatisfaction with the institutions they populate.

This distorts the fundamental concept of representative democracy, and something needs to be done to correct it. Of course, asking a body that makes the rules which govern it to change rules that are not in their favor is like asking someone to perform surgery on his or her own body—it is a proposition few would undertake, even under the direst circumstances.

Like all humans, the American people have wants and needs. Our elected officials should address our needs, but too often bow to pressure and accede to our wants. Leadership is a duty of an elected official, and they are responsible to the needs of all of society—not just their district or state, but of the body politic.

This is another concept that has been perverted over time. These people represent the country—they are United States Senators and United States Representatives—and their duties include protecting and defending the Constitution of the United States, yet many of them have relegated those responsibilities to a secondary position because playing to the wants and needs of their constituents is conducive to longevity. I understand those who advocate term limits to put an end to the professional politician, but I have always rejected that in favor of deferring to the people's right to vote for whomever they wish for as long as they wish. Term limits tend to empower professional staff— unelected individuals who do not have to face the voters. But more importantly, term limits restrict individuals from mastering issues and processes important to the advancement of public policies. It is a dilemma that merits discussion and deliberation, but I still believe the cons outweigh the pros.

In "The Need to Lead," I again tackle the failure of our elected officials to do their jobs. As the reader can tell, this is a recurring theme in many of the pieces presented here. However, I believe it cannot be reiterated too strongly that it is the core problem facing our nation at this time.

Posted July 19, 2010
The Need to Lead

Representative democracy is a good thing; I believe we could probably even get bipartisan agreement and even a majority to support the concept. The simplicity inherent in the concept is that we as a society agree upon the processes whereby we elect individuals to represent us on matters of complexity and importance. Either we do not possess the information upon which to make weighty decisions, do not have the time to devote to an exhaustive examination of the issues because we are too busy coping with our own weighty problems, or simply prefer to delegate the chore to those whom we pay to make decisions that affect us in hopes that they will make decisions in the best interest of our society, but we place our faith and fate in those to whom we have entrusted this solemn responsibility.

In a representative democratic government, we the people make decisions about whether or not those we have elected are collectively and individually doing a good job. If we are not satisfied, we have the ultimate veto power to vote them out of office in hopes that their replacements will perform better. We expect our elected officials to protect us from harm, whether it is in the form of an unregulated private market, whose duty is to protect its stockholders and maximize its profits, or individuals who put us in danger, or overzealous governmental bureaucracies who may from time to time overstep their bounds. Regardless, we have people who are responsible for taking care of these things.

We do not elect these people to simply do what they think will improve their chances of perpetuating their careers. If the decisions were left to us, we would probably vote every time to do the impossible: namely, make decisions that produce benefits for us without costs. After all, if we all had our druthers, we would want to avoid the unpleasantness of actually having to pay for the things we want. We all realize this, some unconsciously and others more directly; hence we pay our leaders decent salaries, stock them with brilliant staffers to help them sort through the issues, and afford them a position in society that places them high on a pedestal of influence and importance.

The need to lead has rarely been more needed than currently. We are in the throes of a seriously debilitating economic situation, unemployment and underemployment are tearing the fabric of our communities and our households, and despite some truly monumental achievements over the past eighteen months to forestall an even worse economic catastrophe, reformulate an inadequate health-care system, and come to grips with a financial services industry that defies either good business practices or common sense, we find our political system hopelessly incapable of exhibiting the kind of leadership we all feel is necessary.

And although in general the Republican party has staked its hopes for retaking control of the levers of Congress on the pathetic platform of doing whatever it is the people, read: their base, wants instead of what is needed, there are also some Democrats who have resorted to the bankrupt notion that we ought to let the people decide what is best for them. This is not leadership, it is cowardice. I am fully aware that, in a strict political sense, leadership is not always rewarded and cowardice is not always punished, but it must be called what it is: cowering under pressure.

It begs the question as to why we need a representative democracy at all if we are simply to put our fingers in the air to discern which way the wind is blowing and what will make people happy. Hell, that's easy. Give the people what they want and not what they need, and if you continue to do that long enough, the very sense of entitlement that conservatives are always crowing about will most certainly become the norm instead of the exception.

People both want and need jobs. This foolishness about people remaining unemployed because they do not want to work is reminiscent of the argument that blacks really wanted to be slaves and not free. And the people who are brandishing these arguments do so not because they actually believe it; they just think it is what their political base wants to hear, shame on you, regardless of your party or ideology.

There is a need to lead in this country, regardless of your electoral prospects, and a large part of the pervasive distrust of our political institutions and elected officials reflects the continuing inability of a system to do what we need and not what we want. Decisions that are based on "no, no, no" remind me of a small child screaming at their parents, "I don't wanna." This is not leadership. For those who continue to obstruct and obfuscate for their own personal aggrandizement, I say there is a need to leave.

The Evolution of Revolution:
An Attack upon Reason, Compromise, and the Constitution

Article 51

July 20, 2010
Déjà Vu All Over Again

I had spent six years—the first six of the Reagan Administrations—on the US Senate Budget Committee fighting supply-side economics and its devotion to tax cuts regardless of the economy's condition. Though not an economist, I still cannot fathom the idea that reducing revenues and increasing spending can somehow balance the budget. Furthermore, the notion that getting our fiscal house in order during economic downturns strikes me as a fanciful money grab for those who do well in times of economic distress.

We have proof that the cockeyed fiscal blueprint offered by the Reaganistas led to an explosion of deficits and debt. It did not work. Yet here we are again, administering the same prescription, which is known to make the patient sicker. Starving the budget when it is already meager does little more than hasten its demise. We are witnessing a sequel to a movie that ended badly the first time and acting as if continuing to watch will ultimately produce a better conclusion the second time around.

What makes the situation even more maddening is the fact that there is an alternative that not only makes more sense, but has worked in the past. President Richard Nixon once proclaimed "I am now a Keynesian in economics." If only he had imparted that tendency to his Republican successors.

So here we go again, fighting battles that have already been fought. We are up against people who have no understanding of history or economics, or who refuse to acknowledge what has happened before. Surely we can do better than this; surely the people expect more from our leaders. And surely we cannot allow fear and anger to blind us to the sober realities of what must be done to combat the problems afflicting us as a society. I fear, however, that emotion, impatience, and ignorance will dictate the direction we take. I hope I am wrong, but I too have to rely on history to guide my thoughts and judgment. We seem to be falling for the same hokum that hoodwinked us just a few decades ago.

Regular folks have neither the time nor inclination to be policy experts; that is why we hire folks to represent us, and they hire staff to help them. We trust that those we elect will carry out their responsibilities in a conscientious way. But most of all, we hire them to do a job, and that job involves the formulation and implementation of polices which are in our collective best interest. They are failing.

In "Voodoo Redux," I recount the resurgence of a failed set of economic theories known as supply-side economics, which George H.W. Bush once derided as "voodoo economics," but they continue to capture the imaginations of policy wonks in a rapidly disintegrating Republican Party. Unfortunately, bereft of ideas or creativity, the opposition has once again dredged up discredited and failed policies that were the hallmark of the popular and iconic Ronald Reagan. It didn't work then and won't work now, but let's not let facts or history or experience get in the way of a popular idea, especially when it's hard work to think of something new.

Someone once remarked that there are no new ideas, just regurgitated old ideas. I do not know if that is true, although sometimes I fear it is; but if we are going to regurgitate old ideas, shouldn't we at least dredge up those we know will work?

Posted July 20, 2010
Voodoo Redux

I think I might have finally figured out modern conservative economic orthodoxy, at least dating back to the Reagan years, when we were entertained by the absurdity of supply-side economics and $200 billion deficits "as far as the eye can see," a phrase coined by his unflappable director of the Office of Management and Budget, David Stockman. In retrospect, wouldn't $200 billion annual deficits be a godsend today? But that is not the point.

I spent six years during the Reagan years on the US Senate Budget Committee trying to hold back the popular trickle-down circus that was known as Reaganomics, I am not an economist but have an intimate knowledge of the dismal science as practiced in the political arena. Quite simply, it appears conservatives today are quite enamored with the notion that during times of economic growth, deficits really don't matter, and fiscal recklessness feeds the all-powerful private market.

Liberals, on the other hand, adhering to the tried and true Keynesian models that rescued this country from the Great Depression, believe that deficits are necessary when the economy is struggling and hence should gradually be repaid once the economy is operating at full bore. I must admit that, from the layman's perspective, there is considerable logic to this argument; besides it has already worked.

On the other hand, the illogic of a restrictive fiscal policy when the economy is failing seems more fit for a period when leeching was thought to have ultimate medicinal value. Yet this is exactly the economic policy that modern-day conservatives would have us follow as the economy sputters along with a stubborn and seemingly intractable level of unemployment, underemployment, and discouraged workers. Aside from the amorality, if not outright immorality, of the argument, how in the world is it supposed to work, and has it ever worked?

Certainly not in the 1980s, as we watched a trebling of the national debt over the course of a decade. And most assuredly not in the first eight years of the new millennium, when we witnessed the vanishing surplus of the Clinton years and a massive explosion of debt that made the '80s look tame by comparison. Conservatives seek refuge in the church of fiscal responsibility only when the fiscally responsible thing to do is to stimulate a plunging economy. Yet deficit spending during boom years is religion during economic boom times.

If I were a cynic, I might conclude that there is some pretty fancy sleight-of-hand being practiced by the snake-oil salesmen masquerading as guardians of the public trough. The inherent contradiction in this line of thinking renders the term hypocrite too gentle. Yet there is a political class who are willing to stake their electoral prospects on the notion that ordinary folks—frustrated, distrustful, and angry—will not bother to scratch beneath the surface to discover the insidious deceit that bolsters the ridiculousness of their claims. And unfortunately, this may be a gamble with better than fifty-fifty odds of succeeding.

The real test will be whether or not those who ascribe to the notion that fiscal responsibility depends upon a strong economy that must be whacked into shape with a simulative jolt equal to the depth of the slump can succeed in pointing out the difference between happy talk and serious policymaking. This will be a difficult challenge indeed, but will be made easier if average folks are made aware of the basic differences between these two economic arguments. Contemporary conservatives and the fledgling tea partiers who have attached themselves to their underbelly must be made to offer up their prescriptions for solving the economic mess, and when they are pressed, they have very little if anything to offer other than the well-worn political clichés that bear no relevance to governing. There is a clear choice, and the people must be made to acknowledge such.

Article 52

July 23, 2010
Bright Rays of Hope!

I have had the wonderful opportunity to spend part of six summers with international students invited to Lehigh University yearly as part of the Iacocca Institute's Global Village program. One hundred or more students representing over fifty countries gather for six weeks of instruction and networking, and discuss and learn about business concepts and practices. As a visiting executive representing the public sector, I have devoted my talks to both climate change and the relationship between the public and private sectors in the development of a sustainable society.

Each year I am buoyed by the energy, intellect, and eagerness to learn exhibited by these students, and each year I am grateful to be part of it. Now if only our leaders could learn from our children and act accordingly, to provide them with an environment that is in a condition at least as good as we found it, if not better—the very concept of sustainability. But alas, the most powerful country in the world is a shrinking violet when it comes to facing the difficult choices that affect future generations. Most if not all of the foreign students cannot understand how we as a nation can continue to neglect our responsibilities on this issue, and they seek answers from me. I have no good ones, but I offer some that I find embarrassing to utter. I believe we are intellectually lazy as a society, and do not hold our leaders responsible for telling us things we do not want to hear. This is a sad and sorry indictment, but I have no better words to offer.

As I was talking with the students about the need to shift from a global economic paradigm powered by fossil fuels to one powered by alternative renewable energy, Congress threw up its hands and conceded that it could not reach agreement on energy policy. The students love the United States, they respect us, and they marvel at our society and its ability to create material goods. But when it comes to looking out for our children's future—and they are all our children—we are not up to the challenge.

Once again, we are looked upon worldwide as a leader among nations, and we constantly disappoint on the critical issues of environmental security, climate change, global warming, and development of alternative energy. We have failed, at every international forum, to step up to the plate—Rio, Kyoto, and Copenhagen. We have failed our citizens, but just as importantly we have failed the world community. If we are not willing to take the lead on carbon emissions reduction, there is very little incentive for others to do so given that we are the most egregious violator of common sense and the biggest impediment to securing a more livable planet.

In "A Global Village," I record my disappointment at the failure of Congress to provide even minimal protection against climate change because it is divided over the politics of the issue. It is not the science that is suspect, despite the propaganda spewed by the very industries that benefit from continued fossil fuel development; that is settled. It is the politics about science and its place and role in the policymaking arena. The science of climate change is not rejected, but science per se is being put on trial. I am not so much worried that we look silly to the rest of the world—there is nothing new in that—but I am disgusted that we allow raw politics and the overt influence of moneyed interests to dictate a course of action or lack thereof when it is so vitally important to the human species.

It is important from a semantic standpoint that we not confuse "survival of the planet" with "survival of the species." Experts readily concede that the planet will survive and adapt; however, the question about whether humans will fare as well is one that few can answer definitively. Unfortunately, we are well on our way to finding out the answer in the most spectacular and potentially disastrous way. We must first realize that we are all connected to one another, we are all connected to our physical resources, and we are all connected to the life cycles that determine our existence. And along with this realization, we must confront the immutable fact that for us, there is no Planet B. The parameters of the debate have been set in such a way that the discussion is too easily derailed, and we are distracted from the fundamental issue.

Posted July 23, 2010
A Global Village

Every summer, a hundred or so young entrepreneurs from around the world meet in Bethlehem, Pennsylvania and spend six weeks at Lehigh University learning and networking on important issues of business management, leadership, and strategic thinking as they prepare to assume careers in the international community. It is all part of the Iacocca Institute Global Village program, and I have been honored to participate as a visiting executive over the past four years.

While the bulk of the program is concentrated on the business of business, I have been afforded the opportunity to bring a public policy perspective to the discussions with a particular focus on the issue of global climate change. For the better part of yesterday, I was engaged in intensive and interactive dialogue with sixty students representing more than fifty countries from around the world about the role of political leadership and governance in general and, more specifically, about the economic opportunities inherent in a shift from a fossil-fuel global economy to one powered by alternative energy.

It is a fascinating look into a world few of us ever get to see: namely, a chance to get fresh perspectives of how we are viewed as a country from extraordinarily intelligent young minds from Palestine to Bangladesh, the former Soviet republics to Australia, and all points in between. Since my professional dedication and personal passion over the past two decades has been the environment and, more to the point, what we humans are doing to it, it is always interesting to listen to the views of those who see us through different lenses.

At the very moment I was trying to explain to them how we in the United States are attempting to confront the serious issues of climate change by enacting legislation to curb carbon emissions, it was being announced in Washington, DC that our Congress is hopelessly enmeshed in such a dysfunctional state that comprehensive energy policy would indeed be sacrificed this year. Now I am enough of a political realist to understand why this issue, as important and far-reaching in its potential consequences as it is, has found itself slipping on the must-do list of national priorities as we struggle with the multi-pronged disasters left by the misguided governance during the Bush years. I also understand that while the last administration contributed greatly to this current miasma, the inability of the controlling party in the Senate to corral sufficient votes for such an important responsibility also plays a critical role here. So there is enough blame to go around, and shame on you, all of you, who would play politics with this issue.

I saw Jane Goodall on television a couple of months ago and she made a statement that I found particularly insightful and disturbing.

With respect to climate change and the intergenerational injustice we are perpetrating, she made reference to the Native American proverb that "We do not inherit the land from our ancestors, we borrow it from our children," and added that currently we are stealing it from them.

As these international students engaged me in discussion, two things penetrated the dialogue with precise clarity: first, they are still in awe of what the United States has accomplished and stands for; second, they are deeply perplexed as to how we can continue to ignore the role we have in addressing the issue of climate change, particularly since we are looked upon as the world's most egregious contributor to greenhouse gas accumulation.

While we continue to squander the opportunities to create a better world for our children, and while we continue to ignore the most basic premise of sustainability, namely that we ought to leave this world in at least as good a shape as we found it, our inability to step up and set a standard for the world to follow, our inability to set a course upon which others will feel compelled to travel, sends a signal to all of the world's children that we simply do not care. Can there be any doubt whatsoever that signals such as these contribute mightily to the perception among our youth that our elected officials and institutions are the problem and not the solution?

Over the past several years, I have traveled widely, drawing attention to this issue as a Climate Change messenger trained by Al Gore and The Climate Reality Project to effectuate a grass roots education and advocacy campaign, delivering over ninety-two presentations mostly to college and high school aged youth, and resoundingly the message is the same: what are you guys doing?

The message from these international students is the same: what are you guys doing? And fifty years from now people are going to ask: what did you do?

Here we are facing an issue that involves no less than survival of the planet, and despite the technological capability to solve the problem, we are squabbling over the political implications of pushing this agenda. It is not that we do not either understand the problem or know how to solve it; we do. What is lacking, unfortunately, is the political will. And this is just unforgivable and we will be judged harshly by those whom we saddle with our own impotence.

To walk away from this issue at this point in time is unconscionable, and both the administration and Congress must be convinced that this is an issue which must be tackled effectively, now. It is simply unacceptable to look into the eyes of our youth, regardless from which part of the globe they come from, and tell them we are not up to the task of protecting their future. Who among us would do that to our own children? Well, they are all our children.

The Evolution of Revolution:
An Attack upon Reason, Compromise, and the Constitution

Article 53

October 12, 2010
One Step Forward, Two Steps Back

I was on my way to Lafayette University to give a speech to a political science class when I started to notice yard signs populating small cities and towns in northeastern Pennsylvania. This is a fairly conservative, Republican part of the state. They implored all who could see them to "Take America Back." I was intrigued by the idea and the phrasing. To where and to what, I wondered.

I have no argument about the need to learn from the past—as long as the lessons learned help to focus on what worked and what did not. Unfortunately, given the nature of the candidates and the governing philosophy that has infected the current Republican Party; I was suspicious of the intent of the signs' language. As is too often the case in politics, words can have devastating consequences, especially when complex issues are boiled down to a bumper sticker or a yard sign. If the words mean returning to a time which never existed, that would be problematic.

If "Take America Back" meant reclaiming it from the imposter who had stolen the election two years earlier, then there could be a racial overtone. Under any circumstance, however, why in the world would we ever want to retreat backward? Isn't it more important to take America forward?

I do not doubt that there is a time for retreat, but not as a first resort. It seemed as though the effort on behalf of the insurgents who had hijacked the Republican Party in the name of freedom and liberty— the self-proclaimed Tea-Party patriots—had amassed a powerful and effective campaign to reclaim America, at least if the number of yard signs was an accurate barometer of strength and power. I believe, from my experience in politics, that the number of yard signs is a good indicator of the strength of a candidate and/or movement, and so I was becoming increasingly concerned about the upcoming election.

Obama had certainly been put through the wringer in the first two years of his administration, but the Tea Party was going to be a real problem. I could feel it, and now I was witnessing it firsthand. They were organized, obviously well-funded, and had captured the anger and frustration of an electorate flabbergasted by the lack of action out of Washington on the kitchen-table economic matters affecting them and their neighbors.

In "Taking America Forward," I cautiously drew attention to these issues without raising undue concerns that would border on gloom and doom; but I was concerned. Sometimes we need to rely on our gut instincts, and mine told me we were up against a potent force.

Posted October 12, 2010
Take America Forward

Cruising around Pennsylvania this past weekend, I started to take notice of political yard signs promising to "Take America Back." Immediately, I asked myself from whom, and to what? Since the slogans are generated from Republican candidates, it only makes sense that they intend to wrest control back from Democrats, but the intriguing nature of the battle cry being voiced from within their own party seems to indicate that there is a burning desire to wrest control away from both Republicans and Democrats.

And there is a general anger in the electorate, a legitimate anger I might add, that speaks to the notion that special interests have hijacked the entire system of governance. In my lifetime, I cannot recall a higher level of disenchantment with the status quo since the late 1960s. Then, people were dying; today, people's dreams are dying. In times such as these, rational thought is a rare commodity indeed, and the greatest fear is that this anger will be misdirected to fringe elements that have neither an answer nor the ability to govern. In the end, the party that directly expropriates the message to deal with this anger will gain control of the apparatus to address the concerns felt and perceived by the disaffected.

But back to the slogan "Take America Back." Where are we going back to, and what are we going back to? I certainly do not want to diminish the importance of looking back, because that is a useful exercise to glean what has worked and not worked in the past so as to help us devise a genuine forward-looking set of solutions with which to attack our current problems. But I fear that the lessons learned from looking back might not yield a productive solution without some sense of historical perspective. There are fewer and fewer among us who lived through the Great Depression, and unfortunately fewer still who studied the policies of FDR.

If a look back stops with Bush or Clinton or Reagan, then I fear the phantom prosperity built upon ever-increasing mounds of debt or deregulatory zeal will lead us to the wrong conclusions. It appears to me that there are two distinct courses which need to be followed: first, we need to address the backlog of physical infrastructure neglect that has left us far behind other industrialized nations, and represents an opportunity to put people to work immediately on national public works projects—remember the WPA? The CCC? Second, we need to look forward to the jobs of the future—green jobs, and the research and development resources to garner supremacy in development of alternative energy for a world choking on the carcasses of fossil fuels.

We did not dig this hole overnight; it was the culmination of decades of political pandering and fiscal insanity. We will not rectify it overnight; it will take decades of effort and the national will to accept the realities of the twenty-first-century economy and the environmental requirements of an increasingly interdependent world. Quite simply, it will take money, and there simply is no way around it. Americans need to remember what it was like to save enough money for that first car, that first home, that dream vacation. Sacrifices were made in the process of building the resources to make those dreams become a reality. And it is not different with the challenges that we face today.

But in the meantime, there is a tremendous amount of work that needs to be done right here and right now. We can put people to work restoring the nation to a first-rate country with a first-rate infrastructure, repairing our deteriorating roads and bridges, investing in modernization of our woefully inadequate public transportation network, restoring sewer systems in our major cities, and in the process reinvigorating an economy that thrives on a populace that is employed at a living wage.

The answer is not to wall in the nation and put alligators in the moat. That is a fourteenth-century solution to a twenty-first-century problem. Middle-class expansion does not equate to socialism, reducing the vast gap between the richest and the poorest among us is the quintessential American Dream, and ironically, the vast majority of those who benefitted from this post-World War II expansion now populate the ranks of the Tea Party movement. "I got mine, now you get yours"—the same sort of philosophy that drives the anti-immigration movement here in a society built by immigration. Namely, I am in and you stay out.

The anger out there is real and it deserves attention, but pandering to the misguided notion to feed fear rather than face it does a tremendous disservice to the present and the future. We do not need to take America back; we need to take it forward, and in a sane and rational world, there would be bipartisan agreement on this basic premise. We can always argue about the particulars as to how to do it, but we would at least agree it needs to be done. On that count we still have a long way to go.

Article 54

October 23, 2010
Don't Ask, Don't Get

With the midterm elections only a week away, I was extremely nervous about the outcome. I had observed the inadequacy of opposition candidates and their inability to offer anything remotely resembling solutions to the problems they so ardently identified. But the arguments were largely devoid of substance, and the vitriol and venom was mostly targeted directly at the president. It was becoming increasingly clear that the opposition strategy was to decry the state of the union, and under no circumstances open yourself up to scrutiny by exposing what exactly you would do about it.

Emotions were running high, largely spurred on by the vociferous Tea Party, and change simply for the sake of change seemed to be the popular justification for their candidacies. The congressional elections did not have a hint of substantive flavor, but were conducted on a throw-the-bums-out, I'll-never-support-the-president, help-me-go-to-DC-and-gum-up-the-works feel to them.

Absent an agenda, except to reject the signature accomplishment of the last two years—health-care reform—there was little on which to hang a candidate's desire to assume the position except that they would shut the place down. That seemed an amateurish and nonsensical platform, but the anger and emotionalism in these campaigns was real and pronounced. It was shaping up to be a rough night for those who had, just two years ago, come into power cloaked in the mantle of hope and change, and with an energy fueled by infectious optimism.

In "Question Authority, Act Authoritatively," I attempted to validate the need to question authority, as I have always maintained, but more importantly to act forcefully to find solutions. The only fixes these imposters offered were to shy away from acting at all. There was such palpable anger and disgust at procedural paralysis that, counterintuitively, people were proposing to put other people into it who would perpetuate the paralysis. If government were the problem, then having a completely dysfunctional one was better than having one which was trying but coming up with the wrong answers. The operative policy position was to do nothing; all of the problems were manufactured, anyway. It was completely insane.

This was going to be a curious election indeed. Do-nothings were the answer, yet do-nothings were the problem. Go figure. Jimmy Buffett was right; "If we weren't all crazy, we would go insane." It was like watching a train wreck in slow motion—knowing it was going to happen and not being able to do anything about it left one with a feeling of total helplessness.

Posted October 23, 2010
Question Authority, Act Authoritatively

So the mid-term elections are only a little over a week away, and folks, it is now time to get serious. As the political hyperbole, half-truths, distortions, and personal attacks mount to a furious crescendo in advance of November 2, citizens now get their opportunity to thumb their noses at the pundits, consultants, and yes, the politicians themselves, and perform that most precious of democratic exercises: namely, vote.

Each election cycle is strange in its own way, and rarely is there an election that does not warrant bombastic boasts such as "this is a watershed year," "this is the most important election in our lifetime," or "the caliber of the candidates is worse than any time I can remember." Truly there is electricity in the air, and a level of anger that is substantial. How this translates into the wishes of the electorate manifesting themselves in a revolutionary way is unclear, and will not be known until after all the ballots are cast. But there can be little doubt that many of the contests being held offer a stark contrast of perspectives, styles, and ideologies.

What strikes me as significant in this current election year is the number of candidates who have made conscious and very public decisions to shield themselves from even a hint of scrutiny, and who blatantly avoid the slightest degree of inspection in the public arena. I have always believed that while opening one up to public inspection and scrutiny carries significant risk, it also prepares the candidate for the rather rough and tumble world they are attempting to break into. Public service is just that—public—and opens up the individual to a very high threshold of criticism. The nature of the political world is to put yourself in the position of having to make difficult decisions on matters of great importance, hence the reason why you receive the benefits and perks that accrue to these positions of power.

If these individuals are unable to withstand the pressure now, how will they be able to withstand the pressure of having to actually be accountable to the public for their actions once they are in office? Political contests do provide a public service in themselves in that they act as the proving grounds or a training program of sorts for the difficult job that lay ahead. Yet we see many candidates employing the unusual tactic of insulating themselves from the rigors of the profession, which should send a cautionary signal to the electorate that maybe they are not actually up to the task they seek.

It would be similar to having your doctor telling you surgery is required, yet not telling you what the nature of the problem or the surgery is. Under these circumstances would you rationally submit to the surgery? Certainly I would not, despite how much trust I have in the doctor, no matter how badly I felt, no matter how insistent he or she was—I would demand that certain questions be answered.

So too it should be in our electoral decisions. Here are a few questions we all must ask ourselves before we cast a vote. First, has the candidate given me every opportunity to explore their strengths and weaknesses, either through debate or public interview? Second, has the candidate effectively talked about what I perceive to be major problems and come up with effective and detailed solutions that I agree with? Third, once the emotionalism of the campaign dissolves, does the candidate exhibit an ability to govern? Lastly, if my candidate is elected, does the system benefit from he or she being a part of it?

Look, there is a significant degree of anger out there and it is wholly justified, but when all is said and done, do we run the risk of further polarizing the society and reinforcing inaction by choosing candidates based on raw emotion? Do we run the risk of exacerbating the frustration level and worsening the situation?

We have candidates spewing nonsense about cutting spending, yet refusing to identify what exactly they would cut. Some are disingenuous; others are just flat out wacky. Too often there is no discernible strategy for governing, just an eagerness to mimic frustration and play to your fears. We have seen a glimpse of the politics of paralysis, and I fear we might be about to get a larger dose of this reckless reality unless thoughtfulness and rationality take hold and a tidal wave of voters who have taken the time to ask and answer these questions honestly descend upon the voting booths.

The maxim "Be careful what you wish for" is instructive here. To my conscientious friends from all political stripes, let me offer the following: to Democrats, "Don't throw the baby out with the bathwater"; to Republicans, "Those that sleep with dogs get fleas"; to liberals, "You can't always get what you want"; and to conservatives, "Change for the sake of change may not be in your best self-interest."

This election is important, but every election is important—treat it thusly.

Article 55

October 28, 2010
If It's Broke, Fix It

The midterm elections were upon us, and I had reached the conclusion that we were going to get pummeled. There was no rhyme nor reason to this election, just the fact that the electorate had given up and was mad as hell. And just like the hothead who, when angry, strikes a concrete wall in a show of defiance and breaks his hand, then proclaims that he showed that wall who was boss. Was it worth it? No. Did it make him feel better? No. Would he do it again? Probably not—but maybe, depended upon how mad he was. No rhyme, no reason.

The defeatists were going to prevail, and what that signaled for the larger agenda was anyone's guess. What ailed the country was about to grow in intensity, which would further inflame an already angry populace. What would be important from the standpoint of governance would be how the Obama Administration and the Democrats would handle it. Would there be a pullback, a retreat from the agenda so expertly designed just two years ago? Would all decision-making come to a grinding halt? Would the paralysis be so profound as to precipitate a worldwide depression?

I was convinced that emotion had overcome sound judgment, and that the Tea Party would play a huge role in making an even bigger mess of a system which, under the best of circumstances, is messy. Policymaking has often been likened to sausage making; if you witnessed it, you would be reluctant to eat the product, but when cooked, it's edible. Unfortunately, it was our agenda that was going to get cooked. Now I was prepared to concede that the progressive agenda would be compromised beyond recognition.

In "Fix It, Don't Nix It," I took one last stab at trying to convince a hostile public to collect itself and consider whether an act of emotion was worth the adverse consequences that would accompany it. I did not suffer from any delusion that it would have an appreciable impact, but I felt I had to make an attempt to reach those I could. The revolution had evolved into a bona fide and serious threat to governance. We had been caught flat-footed, and did not fully appreciate the level of anger and frustration in the electorate, or at least how irrational it could get.

We had relied too much upon conciliation and not been sufficiently confrontational early enough to thwart the growing movement, and henceforth would be forced to deal with an emotionally-charged and more unreasonable opposition that could legitimately point to a mandate from voters. Compromise was viewed as weakness in the new governing formula; the old rules were no longer operative.

We would have health-care reform to show for our efforts, but the political cost would be steep for what had been achieved. Still, the Obama Administration had been true to its word and had accomplished something that, in light of the changing dynamic of the political system, was consequential. I hoped against hope that I was wrong and would wake up to eat crow, but I doubted that would be the case. Time was running out, and quickly.

Posted October 28, 2010
Fix It, Don't Nix It

In light of the increasingly violent nature of our politics, it is extraordinarily difficult to hold one's emotions, passions, and natural inclination to strike out in check. The bullying and intimidation that has become all too prevalent as this election season draws to a conclusion dramatizes the ugly side of human nature. To those who incite, encourage, or simply turn a blind eye to what is happening in their names or campaigns—you exemplify the very worst of what you purport to support, namely freedom.

What we are witnessing today is the hypocrisy of democracy. Fear is the favored tactic of those who feel inferior—intellectually, physically, morally. You simply cannot embrace freedom and operate under a cloud of secrecy. Yes, the country is facing daunting challenges, and yes, there may be differences of opinion as to how to address those challenges. There certainly are different ideologies, philosophies, styles, and ideas about how to confront the large issues hammering America and Americans. Bring them to the table and argue, discuss, dissect, and resolve those differences. That is the democratic system.

What should be unacceptable to the populace, however, is an unwillingness to offer up solutions. What is unconscionable, though, is to offer up gridlock and stagnation in protest of a system that is based on compromise. To do so is to question the very essence of democracy itself. Yet I hear no candidate running against democracy; in fact just the opposite. I hear these self-proclaimed patriots clinging to the Constitution in their hopes of convincing a majority of voters that they are worthy of making decisions that have far-reaching consequences for all of us.

Where are the problem-solvers? Who among this crop of dissidents has put forth a comprehensive program for actually tackling the serious issues before us? Maybe this is symptomatic of an electorate so disenchanted, disillusioned, disappointed, and disheartened by what they see as dysfunctional government that it is proverbially getting what it asks for? Still, to save a democracy by employing undemocratic means is the height of cynicism.

Democracy is messy. Surely there are governmental systems that function far more effectively and efficiently than our own, but at what cost to civil liberties? The true genius of our system is that it actually is self-correcting, but it is dependent upon the quality and caliber of the individuals and the depth of their commitment to make difficult decisions. Merely railing against the system or decrying the state of conditions may be an important step to our recovery, but it is just that—a step. It is not the solution.

Solutions in a democracy require skillful negotiation, intellectual awareness, keen instincts, and a willingness to devote considerable study to the complex issues. And in the end, like it or not, it requires compromise. That is just the way it is. That is the price we pay for this democratic experiment that we hold so dear. Yet we now stand poised to turn a blind eye to the fact that many candidates either refuse to offer or simply have not even considered how they will function after the election is over and the hard part begins: namely, the art of governance.

And sadly, I fear that a majority of citizens are willing to gamble on their fears and frustrations and let the emotionalism of the moment dictate a solution that will neither solve the problem nor strengthen the system. At this point, I am afraid that essentially the die is cast and we will deal with the cards we have been dealt. However, we must never cease our efforts to attempt to persuade those citizens to search deep into their souls and reexamine their options. While it is late, it is not too late. So I offer up a plea to those who have not yet made up their minds to carefully consider what happens in the aftermath of the anger bender we are about to go on. To those who have been on a bender of any sort, the sad reality is that the head-pounding hangover does not justify the means of attaining it.

It is time for America to man up and face the hard choices in front of us, temper its anger, readjust its sights, and act in its own best interest. And it is certainly in your own best interest not to wake up Wednesday morning with a hangover that may stay with you for several years.

Article 56

Tea Time

The midterm elections were over, and Obama and the Democrats had taken a "shellacking," to quote the president. Now came the hard part—figuring out where to go from there. As I reflect on this situation, I must admit that I thought the Tea Party would not co-opt the Republican Party, but would be absorbed by them. This, I am sure, was the original plan concocted by people like Karl Rove. I was wrong; just the opposite happened. And I'm sure it was as much a surprise to the Republican establishment as to me. We now saw the Republicans tearing each other apart in a very public display of power politics. They created this monster in a high-stakes game of win at any cost, and now they would have to pay a very high price. But more importantly, we would now be subjected to a phenomenon that offered no answers, only mischief.

In "The Tea is Tainted," I lamented what I had suspected for weeks would happen—a fairly definitive repudiation of the Obama Administration. Hopefully time will shed light on the idiocy of the insurrection and the people will tire of the resulting gridlock and paralysis from the Great Venting of 2010. But I shudder to think of the damage done in the meantime. How this will play out is anyone's guess, but I remain baffled by the degree to which emotion has strangled common sense in this sordid chapter of our history.

We as a society have squandered an opportunity to start upon a new course, one toward a brighter future. But we are human, and we make mistakes. If ever there were a lesson to be learned from the events set in motion as a result of the November 2, 2010 election, it is to do the best we can to keep emotion in check when it conflicts with common sense. This is a tall order, and we are bound to fall off the wagon again, but the stakes are so enormous, especially in a time when gerrymandered Congressional districts are not reflective of the wishes and desires of the general electorate and when six-year Senate terms cement entrenched impediments which will outlast a temporary emotional venting.

But we must play the cards we were dealt, and the Obama Administration would be faced with a continuing struggle to right the ship of state—one that was dangerously listing starboard.

Posted November 8, 2010
The Tea Is Tainted

The Tea Party patriots and the establishment Republicans were right after all. A mere three days after their historic "refudiation" (a Palinism) of Obama's socialistic jihad against capitalism, the country experienced the largest jump in new jobs statistics in the nearly two years that the occupation government has been in power. It took them two days to do what Obama was unable to accomplish in nearly two years; quite impressive indeed.

The very thought of Rand Paul, Ron Johnson, Marco Rubio, and the infantry of constitutional conservatives headed for Congress was enough to tip the scales and initiate a full-scale economic recovery. My, the true power of the private sector flexing its economic muscles certainly puts the anemic impotence of a bloated government bureaucracy to shame. For the next two years, Republicans can lay claim to resuscitating the ailing economy and producing jobs.

As absurd as this may seem on the face of it, I am convinced that the spin machine behind the rise of these self-proclaimed revolutionaries will spring into action to claim credit where credit is certainly not due. After all, in this twenty-four-hour news cycle society, immediate gratification trumps sustainability, short-term results outdistance long-term thinking, and winning the battle is more important than winning the war.

Our political system operates off a system of rewards and penalties, and politicians are rewarded for accelerating benefits and avoiding costs. They reap rewards for kicking the can down the road, and are lionized for drawing attention to problems. However, they are penalized for actually making the tough decisions required to solving problems, ridiculed for even suggesting that sacrifice may be required to address imbalances, such as debt and the deficit, and scorned for pragmatism.

This is the contemporary environment in which our policies and electoral decisions are made, and the result is a polarized and dysfunctional system of governance. No clearer a message was evident last week when, in a pique of anger, Americans signaled their dissatisfaction with the status quo by reinforcing its inability to reach consensus. The mess Obama inherited was not created overnight; it was a culmination of years of blissful neglect. It certainly was not going to be solved overnight. The economic recovery required a steady hand, and fundamental soundness was made far more difficult by the intransigence of the Republican Party, who vowed to fight the president at every turn. But the economy is recovering, albeit much slower than anyone would wish, and those who attempted to obstruct serious problem solving have now been rewarded with a misconceived "mandate" to obstruct at will.

The real ideological war about to unfold is not between capitalism and socialism; it is not between Keynesianism and Hooverism, but rather between those advocating unpopular but necessary long-term solutions, and those advocating popular and politically expedient remedies certain to appeal to a generation of individuals who have unknowingly profited handsomely from the very government-directed funding they now so vociferously attack.

Borrowing is as American as apple pie. To most Americans, those who did not earn their money the old fashion way by inheriting it, dreams are built on borrowing money we do not have to make a better life for ourselves, whether it is borrowing for a small business, for a home, a college education, or a car. We borrow today so that we will be better off tomorrow. The same applies to the government; it borrows today to resuscitate the economy in the hope that the economy will make a better life for society tomorrow.

The trick is to pay the money back once you have means to do so. Unfortunately, in both Democratic and Republican administrations and Congresses over the years, we did not pay off our debts. This was particularly true during the 1980s under the cover of the Reagan revolution, when our national debt trebled over the course of a decade. Investing in society requires investments, and revenues to the government come in the form of taxes. We didn't mind reducing taxes to enhance growth, but we then forgot to pay off our debt when we had the ability to do so.

The ill-informed or deliberately and deviously disingenuous platform advanced by the radical right is that we need only look at spending, and more specifically discretionary spending, and make cuts to start paying down the debt. It is unclear how much they want to pay down immediately, but assuming that the current-year deficit is somewhere in the range of $1.4 trillion, that would be larger than the entire discretionary budget, that is slightly less than $1.4 trillion. Half of that discretionary budget is eaten up by defense spending, which one might assume would also be off-limits to these Tea Party patriots.

Even in the new math, eliminating the entire discretionary budget and gutting most operations of the federal government simply do not add up. Of course, the mother lode of spending—over $2 trillion—involves the so-called entitlement programs, Social Security, Medicare, Medicaid, and interest on the national debt. One might also assume that these programs are off limits as well.

Now I will submit that the average individual is unaware of such detail, and there is really no reason why they should feel anything other than it is the province of the elected and candidates for election who should know such things. Unfortunately, why would you trust these folks to man up and be honest and candid with you on such things if you believe the system is not acting in your interest in the first place? Well, you probably figured that those who were running to replace the power elites had an honest-to-goodness desire to serve. You might be right, but the verdict is out on that and the evidence does not suggest that to be the case.

The argument advanced by the prophets of small government, vis-a-vis the deficit and debt, are phony. Either knowingly or otherwise, they have hoodwinked a large number of citizens into thinking they were serious advocates of fiscal responsibility. In actuality, they have become pawns in the Republican army's assault upon the Democrats and the White House. Some pretend that the Republican Party has been co-opted by the Teabaggers when it is actually the other way around.

If you cast your vote on November 2 thinking that you were protesting the status quo, which essentially was one government body with two heads, one Republican and one Democratic, are you going to be surprised when you wake up next year to find a government in perpetual gridlock? In that scenario, no one wins.

You have been duped, and have merely strengthened the very situation you are most concerned about. So where will your protest go the next time around?

Article 57

November 23, 2010
You've Lost That Lovin' Feeling

If you ever get the feeling you cannot win, put yourself in the president's shoes. There was uproar about security measures at airports, which are a direct result of 9/11. Now it is asinine that those who demand that government protect them flinch at the first inconvenience when they're asked to remove their shoes, belts, and jackets before they board what we now know, all too well, can be a guided missile.

This is symptomatic of a population so used to being free of the rigors of inspection compared to the rest of the world, and so resistant to anything that smacks of effort, that sacrifice is anathema to freedom. We want to be left alone, we want to be able to fend for ourselves, and don't like the idea of sharing—hence our national aversion to taxes. The individualism built into our society stretches back to our very roots. In a world of unbounded opportunity, based on the idea of Manifest Destiny, there are no limits to which we cannot ascend. However, in a world of constraints that is getting exponentially smaller, we must accommodate to new realities. If only we could go back in time to when life was simple and everyone knew their place.

We are all too willing to let others suffer the indignity of invasion of civil liberties far worse than the very public pat-downs at airports because, after all, we should be able to know who the bad people are. They're the other guys; they don't look or act like us. But diversity complicates things, and it is increasingly harder to tell who the bad guys are. Nevertheless, don't inconvenience me! Of course, the illogical conclusion that you should only concentrate on the bad guys implies profiling. And the bad guys are very clever—clever enough to evade simple safeguards.

It is interesting how the political elite responds to uncomfortable situations in which a majority of people want to do something the elites do not agree with; they change the game rules. For instance, it is perfectly acceptable in the current political environment to poll the people and find out what they want—if it comports with what you believe they want. However, if the people want something you do not want, you set the standard at 100 percent agreement. So unless there is perfect agreement on controversial issues, there is a controversy. This is particularly true about climate change—999 scientists aligned on the issue versus one who is not constitutes a controversy. Are you kidding me? That is not a controversy; that is a slam dunk. Or take the issue of majority rule. It's fine as long as you are on the winning side, but if not, change the winning formula from fifty plus one to sixty.

In "Cheap Thrills and National Security," I poke fun at the prospect of complaining about procedures that everyone must go through in an attempt to at least enhance safety and protection at airports. C'mon, folks, really? It is the same with taxes; we do not want, collectively, to sacrifice income for things we want or need. And then there is wonder and amazement about why we borrow so much and run up debt and deficits. For those who delight in placating such a fickle populace, the game is a no-lose proposition. For serious-minded stewards of our republic, it is both maddening and frustrating.

Posted November 23, 2010
Cheap Thrills and National Security

You have to excuse me if I laugh, but all this public consternation over Transportation Safety Administration pat-downs is silly. And it seems to me that those who scream the loudest are the very people who no one in their right mind actually wants to pat down anyway. I mean, look at Americans; they quite possibly might be the most untouched and uptight collection of overweight, out of shape curmudgeons on the planet.

My guess is that if you conducted a survey, you might find an overwhelming majority of those doing the complaining to be among the most sexually repressed, confused, intellectually and physically lazy, indignant, and hypocritical waste of human ignoramuses alive. You know, the same people who attend Tea Party rallies and consistently vote against their self-interests. They are the people who reject change and pine for the good old days when white was white and black was black and each knew their place. These are the same people who yearn for the pre–Civil Rights era when all in America was wonderful, like television and movies portrayed it.

Of course, these are also the people who yelled the loudest after

9/11 about the need to exact revenge and feed the national security apparatus so as to prevent this from ever happening again. So what is a president to do? Beef up security and the people scream. Let security lapse and the people scream.

If only you could just profile the terrorists and pat them down—that would be fine. Of course, what makes the terrorists so damn effective is their ability to adapt to changing circumstances, so once they figured out who was being profiled, they would use the system against us. Those sneaky terrorists, they just don't play fair.

Now this should come as no surprise, this attitude of indignation and entitlement. If our parents were the Greatest Generation, we most certainly are the Greediest Generation. The very same people who are never satisfied when sacrifice is required are the ones who, when asked how to curb the excesses of government spending merely snort that you just need to reduce waste, fraud, and abuse. It's very simple, you see; just eliminate the bad spending—you know, all the stuff that goes to other people.

Former Louisiana Senator Russell Long was famous for bellowing on the Senate floor, "Don't tax you, don't tax me, tax that fellow behind the tree." A highly successful political platform indeed, but as the economy crashes and burns and unemployment stubbornly remains high, the political witch-doctors and shamans babbling such nonsense will, at some point, be held to a standard of production in a very real sense, just like the private sector, whose altar they worship at.

And if you are convinced that there is some form of ideological purity that is to be lauded in their seemingly sincere amateurism, think again. The knee-jerk retort to every public policy issue is to ask the American people, consult the people, and do what they wish, despite the fact that human nature is to want things without paying a fair price. We are a consumer society, a materialist culture, mesmerized by cheap goods. We crave the bargain and ignore the true costs of goods, services, and resources. Hence, coal is good because it is cheap, natural gas is good because it is plentiful and hence cheap, Wal-Mart is great because everything is made in Bangladesh, or India, or China, and it is, well, cheap.

So while we strangle ourselves in search of short-term cheapness, the world is passing us by, and then we rail against those who have cheated, obviously, because we are the rightful heirs to the throne of world domination. And as global warming exacts a very high cost indeed it is simply convenient to ignore it, after all, because of our strategic geographical position on the planet it is and will have far more serious consequences for others before it affects us.

Incredibly, however, these very same advocates of public consensus also conveniently ignore the public when it suits their fancy. So despite an overwhelming public consensus on issues like the Don't Ask, Don't Tell repeal, two-faced warriors like Senator John McCain simply shift gears to appeal to more study, and of course the favorite recourse of spineless politicians is to demand that everyone agree, and 100 percent consensus becomes the new standard.

This has been a favorite of climate-change deniers for years now; find one scientist, or even someone who pretends to be a scientist, to disagree with the other thousand, and you have a ready-made controversy. It is the age-old shell game employed by public policy analysts and political figures when confronted with thorny legal issues; merely shop around until you find a legal opinion to justify your position.

So this is the current political environment we find ourselves in as we gear up for the next presidential election. I do not know if pat-downs and screening will make us safer when we fly, but I am willing to submit to either or both if it increases my chances. If not, what in the world have I lost—intrusion upon my privacy? Give me a break, these civil libertarians did not object when we started illegal wiretaps post 9/11, why start now? Besides, you just may make some TSA employee's day. Once again, a cheap thrill—it is the American way.

Article 58

November 26, 2010
Say What?

Exactly what had the voters said? Was this a mandate for course correction or a temper tantrum? The pundits had been at it for several weeks, and the only thing that was clear is that nothing was clear. Despite the pounding the progressive movement took, it was no time to quit. In fact, it was time to buckle down and go toe to toe with those who meant to derail the train of progress.

Too much was at stake, and too many people were dependent upon a functioning and compassionate government—even many of those who voted otherwise. We Democrats have the responsibility to protect the most vulnerable in society.

I once recall Bob Dole, the Republican Senator from Kansas, who had a wry sense of humor and a flippant demeanor that was sometimes funny and sometimes frustratingly annoying, tell the story of why he was a Republican. The story went that when he returned, seriously injured, from his service in World War II, he was asked to run for office as a war hero. When queried whether he would run as a Democrat or a Republican, he said that he did not know, and asked what the difference was. The political boss told him that a Democrat is for poor people and a Republican was for rich people. As Dole recounted, that settled it; he was a Republican.

Now I do not know if that story was true or not, but I suppose there is more than a kernel of truth to it. Democrats protect the poor, the vulnerable, and the unfortunate, those who have no voices other than their individual stories. We choose public service because of our dedication and conviction that a better society for all involves seeing that all are taken care of.

In "What Did You Say?" my message is to disparage despair, to rise above the cacophony of discontent, to stay true to our ideals, and to gird ourselves with steely resolve to face the fight that lay ahead.

Posted November 26, 2010

What Did You Say?

Our current governmental structure is precariously poised on the horns of a dilemma. Thanks to the verdict rendered November 2, the ideological and philosophical divide is wider than before. If the American electorate, or at least those who made the effort to vote, intended to reflect an exhaustive and introspective analysis of governance and the inability of one-party rule to solve problems, and in their infinite wisdom concluded that split government was the answer, then their colossal miscalculation will soon enough be evident. If, however, the verdict reflects impatience, irritability, and the quintessential quirkiness of a populace used to getting what it wants and wanting to send a loud and unmistakable message to those in power that it is intent on holding its breath until it does, then the upcoming train wreck will certainly make for interesting viewing and unfortunate consequences.

Either way, to those who are suffering the most—the poor, unemployed, underemployed, health-care deprived, and foreclosed upon—your nightmare is about to be extended. It would be very easy for the shellacked party to throw up its hands, sigh, and proclaim that you get what you deserve. After all, to anyone who either has lost or is in the process of losing their livelihood and hard-earned material rewards, their unemployment insurance, or who gaze at their children each night and worry and pray that they not get sick, you had a chance to influence the system, and the people—those who voted—have spoken.

To those who have given up on participating in the referendum on policy and direction, the lesson learned will be a hard one indeed. To those who actually registered their discontent in the form of choosing a set of policies and direction that are directly counter to your dreams, desires, and plain self-interest, well, get ready for some advanced courses in anger management, for you will need them.

We are all exhausted at this point by the endless analysis that has accompanied the sea change that has brought conservatism back into power. Whether or not the results represent a clear and definable mandate, it is clear that there is discontent and uneasiness rampant throughout our society. People are clamoring for clarity and certainty, yet our political leaders have tethered themselves to competing and diametrically opposing views of just exactly what the American people said.

Democrats are convinced that the rejection is born of dissatisfaction with respect to timing, and Republicans are certain that the rejection is reflective of dissatisfaction with the policy direction outlined by the president. Tea Partiers, having cast their lot with the Republicans, go a step further and believe that a radical and fundamental shift back to a mythical point in our evolution as a country will cure what ails us. It is against this backdrop that the legislative process must concoct a remedy, a legislative process that is sausage-making in its finest moments.

One group believes that government has a role to play in getting us out of this mess; the other believes that government is the problem. The true believers took a beating last week; the cynics prevailed. But it is important for the true believers to not merely toss their beliefs in the trash heap and succumb to the cynical proposition that those who need help do not deserve it. Human instinct is to abandon those who do not support you. But doing so here would make a mockery of those true beliefs. Progressives and liberals must continue to abide by the belief that no one else will come to the rescue of those who need help the most. And true public servants often pay a steep price indeed for those fast-held beliefs that society benefits most from a system that protects the most vulnerable among us.

It is easy for the cynics to reap political rewards for disparaging those less fortunate than the rest: they either are lazy, not motivated, or simply not worthy. It is always their fault, so they must live with the consequences of their actions. This is the truest form of personal responsibility, in the cynic's eye.

As much as many of us are shocked, amazed, and yes, angry about the consequences of this election, we must continue to be true to our belief that government can be a constructive force in society, and that as hard as it may seem, there are large numbers of people who are desperately dependent upon our efforts.

So the cynics will have their day soon, but not before one last shot in the lame duck session to do what is right. The Democrats cannot do it alone; they will need minimal help from the other side. That help has been in short supply these last several years, but maybe, just maybe some relief will come soon to those who are dreading this Christmas.

The Evolution of Revolution:
An Attack upon Reason, Compromise, and the Constitution

Article 59

December 4, 2010
Play Nice, Children!

In "Why Can't We Get Along?" I attempt to summarize the basic differences between the two parties regarding spending and tax policies. While the differences are stark, one spectacularly evident thing is that politicians of both parties have shown a penchant for spending money—albeit on different things and for different people. But the inescapable fact is that politicians love to spend money.

Politicians also are reluctant to pay for the things they spend money on; hence our expanding debt. There are exceptions, such as when the Clinton Administration racked up large surpluses, but despite the hue and cry from conservative quarters, spending money is an attractive proposition.

But real differences between the parties remain, and I wish to outline them. Maybe the reason politicians love to spend money is because it is not theirs. I am not a gambler, but I enjoy gambling with other people's money. I am being sarcastic, but the fact is that all elected officials are intrigued by the idea of spending for public programs, and for spending money they do not have by borrowing. The priorities constitute the difference between the two parties. Where you stand depends upon where you sit!

Posted December 4, 2010
Why Can't We Get Along?

Can we finally put to rest the absurd notion that one political party is more enamored with spending than the other? Both Democrats and Republicans relish the opportunity to spend taxpayer dollars with little or no regard to the consequences of overspending—deficits and debt.

The differences, however, lie in the nature of the spending. As a general rule, Democrats prefer to spend on social programs and prefer to forego revenue to the national coffers through tax breaks and incentives for the poor and working class. Republicans, more increasingly as a block and with near unanimity, prefer to spend on defense and prefer to forego revenue to the national coffers through tax breaks and incentives to the well-to-do.

A review of spending and revenue imbalances over the past half century shows that Democrats are far more likely to be sensitive to and effective in closing the gap between income and outgo than Republicans. In the 1990s, Clinton actually proposed and effectuated budget surpluses.

Both parties have shown an insatiable appetite and thirst for increasing entitlement spending. The exponential growth in health-care costs has been with us for at least the last four decades and, although Democrats have attempted on numerous occasions to contain costs through public sector constraints, Republicans are far more likely to support private sector solutions.

Democrats and Republicans, since the 1970s, have experimented with deregulation, from the airlines to financial services, but as a general proposition, Democrats are more amenable to correcting deregulatory failures through government regulation while Republicans once again prefer to rely on voluntary regulation and the private market.

The Nixon and Carter Administrations were particularly keen on environmental stewardship, but since 1980 environmental regulations have been on a roller coaster, and as a general principle I think it is fair to say that during Democratic administrations you see efforts to enhance environmental regulation, and during Republican administrations voluntary compliance is championed.

On economic issues, Republicans believe in trickle-down theory, namely that a rising tide will lift all boats. The supply-side theory trumpeted in the 1980s was a fiscal and financial disaster, and debt and deficits exploded. Tax increases in the early 1990s on high-income earners helped tame the deficits and, along with a strong economy and reforms in welfare spending programs and restraint in discretionary spending, produced budgetary balance and surpluses.

But if past is prologue, divided government produces compromises that ultimately give wins to both sides; hence the only thing that is a sure certainty is the fact that spending will prevail and debt will increase. If the currently evolving compromise is to extend unemployment compensation for extension of tax breaks for the wealthy, both cost money and will increase debt.

Now, of course, deficits and debt have a role to play in the economic cycle of booms and busts. There is good debt—for instance, when you invest and get a healthy return on investment; and there is bad debt—when you spend on things that reap no return on investment. Incurring debt when you have the ability and resolve to pay it off is wise. Incurring debt when there is little prospect of paying it off is bad debt.

Unemployment compensation at a time when we have persistently high joblessness is a wise investment in that it helps the economy by putting money into the hands of folks who otherwise would not be able to spend. Increasing debt by giving tax breaks to folks who do not need them and will not reinvest the dollars back into the economy makes little economic sense, but it is a reflection of an almost religious adherence to trickle-down economic theory, that bears little or no relation to reality.

What is so frustrating about the current state of debate on these issues, however, is the rank hypocrisy of those who righteously claim that they do and you must follow the wishes of the American people. Politicians today more resemble weather vanes than pillars of strength. I have consistently argued over the years that our elected officials must be leaders and not followers, and hence with the information and intelligence available to them, must make decisions that most folks have neither the time nor the inclination to study.

But this is one instance in which I wish the politicians would, in fact, follow the wishes of the people, because the basic instincts on whether it makes sense to give tax breaks to wealthy people when so many people are suffering reflects negatively on the position unanimously taken by the Republicans on Capitol Hill.

And while I sincerely believe that incurring debt to help us out of the current fiscal hole we are in is both economically and morally prudent, now is not the time to focus on the structural imbalances that both parties have helped in digging. Rather, we need to follow through and keep to the promise of addressing these imbalances when we can afford to: namely, when the economy recovers.

The current situation calls for audacity not austerity, conviction not cowardice, principled compromise not political expediency, compassion not condemnation, calculation not callousness, but most of all responsible governance, not campaign rhetoric. Is this possible? Most will say probably not. In the end the one true certainty such failure will bring about is the fact that we, the increasingly shrinking middle class, will pay the price for such failure.

And the widening income inequality, the ever-increasing gap between the super-rich and the rest of society, portends serious societal consequences down the road—you know, the one where the can is.

The Evolution of Revolution:
An Attack upon Reason, Compromise, and the Constitution

Article 60

December 9, 2010
Ball Is In Your Court, Mr. President!

In "Mr. President, It's Up to You," I fervently put forth the need for the president to grab the bull by the horns, get out of Washington, DC, take the message to the people, and use his bully pulpit to reveal the opposition for what it is—an obstructionist parasite sapping the life out of effective governance. The piece includes a memo to the president, stating strongly the discontent rampant within the progressive base of the Democratic Party and the need to step up his game. I argue that he had proved to be a fearless campaigner, but placed too much emphasis on a strategy of cooperation that was not reciprocated by the opposition.

It was time to take the message to the hinterlands and call out those who had no interest in moving the country forward. This was probably the lowest point in his administration, and there were signs that the base was fraying. It was important for Obama to show resilience and the fighting spirit that had been evident on the campaign trail, but not in his governing style. He had not lost us, but there were rumblings in the ranks.

At issue was a negotiated deal with Republican leaders to extend the Bush tax cuts, which included cuts to wealthy individuals and estates. While appreciating the predicament the president was in, many thought the issue of not extending tax cuts to wealthy individuals was a winner for the Democrats and, if explained properly to the public, the Republicans could be forced to concede and made to look like the apologists for the rich they are.

This was the first salvo in the new post-midterm political world, and of course there was considerable pressure to deal with the lame-duck Congress, which was seen as being more amenable to compromise than the incoming class, which would include a large contingent of Tea Party freshmen. Morale was low in the ranks, and there was a near-revolt by House Democrats.

This would presage battles that would surely be waged as the new

Congress settled in next month.

Posted December 9, 2010
Mr. President, It's Up to You

Politics being the art of the possible, the recurring question on nearly every important announcement, decision, negotiation, and contentious issue remains, "Is this the best we can do?" And invariably the consensus, after much hand wringing, soul searching, and sober reflection, is "yes." More often than not this reality is unsatisfactory, and leaves one or both sides feeling unfulfilled. To use a sports metaphor, in ice hockey it is often said that a tie is like kissing your sister.

As a liberal and a progressive, I am angry about the current state of affairs, which leaves us with what I can only describe as a disingenuously ineffective non-solution to the dramatic state of economic affairs that tens of millions of Americans now find themselves in: namely, chronically high un- or under-employment. The demands of those who cling to the notion that millionaires and billionaires constitute the sole source of job creation in this economy and the disproven theoretical construct of trickle-down economics amount to little more than criminal shake-downs and extortion, and will do little to further either growth or competitiveness, two rather important private sector business precepts.

The president is obviously distressed at having to choose between two unacceptable alternatives. No one should ever have to face such a lose-lose proposition. Truly, the president, a decent family man, was faced with a Sophie's Choice. No one would ever want to be faced with such a Hobbesian decision. I respect the president because of his character, integrity, demeanor, intelligence, and foresight, all refreshing traits in great demand after eight years of treacherous anti-intellectualism.

This does not mean that he gets unqualified support on every decision. My heart aches as a dedicated public servant over the seeming inability of the ruling party to rally the nation around policies and legislation that truly reflect the very best aspects of a free democratic society. I am confounded, frustrated, and at times downright despondent at our inability to clearly present our case to the American people in a way that seems genuine and commonsensical on its face.

How can we consistently end up on the wrong side of policy and political arguments when, upon reflection, we hold the moral high ground and are serving the best interests of the largest swath of society? Why is it that we are unable to persuade the public of the seriousness and effectiveness of positions that are designed to benefit them and their progeny?

We are portrayed as effete intellectual snobs, as we portray the opposition as mean-spirited, greedy opportunists. Neither one is an appealing option, yet someone has to win, and they have proved to be more nimble on that score. Why? How can you lose the argument over tax cuts to the wealthy when the overwhelming multitudes are not wealthy? The silliness of the Republican argument in this most recent debacle defies public sentiment and economic rationale.

What is deeply frustrating, however, is how strategically and tactically the Democrats allowed themselves to get boxed into a totally irreconcilable predicament. It does not serve much purpose at this point to resurrect the missteps that led to this point; there is plenty enough blame to go around.

Let it serve as an example, a painful one to say the least, of how to avoid it in the future. The most important lesson, I believe, for liberals, progressives, Democrats, and independent-minded individuals is that the American people admire and respect strength. We Americans have little regard or use for wimps and wusses; you can exhibit strength and intellect, a rare combination in contemporary politics. Strength does not mean inflexibility, however, and the keen political mind is always cognizant of the inescapable fact that compromise is a critical ingredient in our system of governance. But the current debate ripping apart the liberal left is a nagging perception that this administration, this president, does not exhibit the fighting spirit that was so evident in his remarkable ascendancy to the job.

So here is my memo to the president.

Mr. President, I will continue to support you and have faith in your desire to change our country for the better, but you must do a better job of convincing us, and all Americans, that you have the stomach for defending your convictions. To be honest, despite your remarkable achievements to date, you have failed to instill that degree of pride and commitment in your troops that will carry you into and out of battle.

We do not expect you to win every battle, particularly against the odds you will be facing now. You cannot deal rationally with irrational actors. Accept that and adjust accordingly. Show us that you have our backs. Use that bully pulpit of yours to engage the American people in a discussion of understandable and sensible principles when they are under siege by the irrational opposition. You missed that opportunity here; you cannot afford to muff the next one. Although it is a slim consolation the current angst within the ranks of liberals has given rise to a thorough public examination of the issues involved in this tax extension debate. Unfortunately, for this round, the public discussion has come too late. We cannot allow this to happen again, and this is where the president must utilize the power of his position to the utmost.

You have the ability to transcend the rough and tumble of Washington politics; do it. If you mobilize the people, the politicians will follow; you must have faith in this proposition or else you will get sucked into the meat grinder that is Washington politics. Get out of Washington, take your message to the masses, and lead the Congress into battle rather than relying on your field lieutenants. Do what you have proven to be able to do best: inspire.

For goodness' sake, do not lash out against those who look up to you and have placed their faith and trust in your leadership. Those folks, the so-called base, are very upset with you right now. They are not the enemy. Sometimes those of us who are parents get exasperated with our kids and consider saying and doing things that later seem silly, and we realize we love them and all is forgotten.

Show us the way; we desperately need it. Tensions are high, frustration is rampant, many are discouraged, but only you have the ability to grab the mantle of leadership and take us forward. We will not always get as far as we wish, but people will respect you taking us as far as we can go as long as you exhibit the resolve and backbone to face down the opposition.

Few know how discouraged you must feel, but you wanted this job and we wanted you there, so buckle up and lead the charge.

The Third Year-2011

Article 61

January 8, 2011
Back to the Future

I have stated my case elsewhere about the silliness of pining for a return to the past, which is, in many instances, a past that never existed. But let me offer one thing we should go back to, and that is a strong, vibrant, and expanding middle class.

One of the greatest tragedies of the new millennium is the ravaging of what is left of the middle class, an American triumph of the twentieth century. Politicians of all ideologies talk of American exceptionalism. Well, I argue that what made America so exceptional was the emergence of the middle class, and if we intend to return to a time when we excel among nations, it will be when we rebuild this economic juggernaut.

There is a perverse fallacy in the conservative argument that any jobs are the answer to our economic problems. We do not need to create any jobs; we need to create decent jobs that pay decent wages and provide decent benefits. The jobs of the past are not what are needed; the jobs of the future are what we need to concentrate on. So rather than investing in dirty technologies that have profound adverse effects upon workers' health and the health of the environment, we need to invest in clean technologies which will profoundly enhance the health of workers and their environment.

We must invest in rebuilding a decaying and crumbling public infrastructure, from the sewers and subways underneath our cities to the bridges that carry our citizens across vast waterways, great rivers, and small creeks. Our public transportation system needs to be modernized so we can reduce our reliance on automobiles. We need to improve our rail systems and develop high-speed passenger rail systems like those operative in dozens of countries around the world. During a brief stint as communications director for the California High-Speed Rail Authority, we received a visit from a Japanese delegation offering to help us through the difficulties of funding such an ambitious project. In their most humble diplomatic way, they reminded us that they have had a bullet train since 1962. Talk about putting things in perspective; that was more than a half-century ago, yet we are still in the planning stage and construction has not yet begun.

There is plenty of work to be done that is not make-work, but necessary work. There are plenty of skilled and industrious workers to carry out the tasks. What is required is the political will to invest public funds in spearheading works programs that are in the nation's interest, both economically and in the interest of national security. Imagine the development of a smart-energy grid that will transport wind energy from the western United States to cities east of the Mississippi River. These are the projects and jobs of the future. Yet we still clamor for jobs, any jobs, including those that perpetuate our reliance on oil and coal, as well as natural gas, which is also a fossil fuel—it is finite and emits greenhouse gases.

We are an exceptional nation, and we can and should lead by example. Other countries and citizens marvel at our accomplishments. We have the know-how and the tools to become exceptional once again, but we must focus our sights on a long-term plan which will require short-term sacrifices. This is a thorny concept for our politicians because it is so difficult to convince the public of needs rather than wants. But that is the role of the people we elect to lead us—lead us into the future, not back in time.

In "Restoring the Middle Class Will Restore American Exceptionalism," I attempt to lay out the case for a long-term program that will once again create a great and vibrant middle class. But it cannot come about by just talking about jobs, any jobs; they must be quality jobs working on quality projects which will benefit us in the long run. We must focus on the future today.

Posted January 8, 2011
Restoring the Middle Class Will
Restore American Exceptionalism

If you want to restore "American exceptionalism," you need to restore the middle class. The mantra of politicians at all levels of government this election cycle will be jobs, jobs, jobs, and appropriately so. The economy is slowly recovering from the massive hangover of misguided, ill-conceived, and flawed economic policies and deregulation of the financial markets that have effectively widened the gap between the richest and the rest.

And while restoration of jobs is priority one, two, and three on the political agenda, what I find especially troubling is the shameless rhetoric that suggests that we need to quickly restore the jobs and skill sets of the past rather than the jobs of either the present or, God forbid, the future. So while we focus on the immediacy of restoring a twentieth-century, and, more appropriately, an early twentieth-century construct that relies on the economy of a bygone era, we have completely forfeited our competitiveness to those economies that are gearing up for the technologies and job opportunities that will sustain economic growth for the medium and longer-term future.

Our steady slide away from investing in alternative energy sources is vividly playing out in states like Pennsylvania, which sits above the abundant Marcellus shale natural gas play. By pinning our hopes on the short-term prospects for profit by plumbing the depths of our planet and draining every last ounce and cubic foot of oil and gas, we will continue to feed a fossil-fuel driven economic paradigm whose days are most assuredly numbered. We will continue to focus on dirty fuels and the dirty jobs that are needed to exploit them. We will concentrate our technological development and capital investment in mining what Thomas Friedman has so eloquently called "fuels from hell"—that is, underground, exhaustible, carbon-emitting energy sources—and put a hold on developing and utilizing "fuels from heaven," such as solar and wind, that are inexhaustible and do not emit greenhouse gases.

In the shuffle for creation of jobs, any jobs at any cost, we are postponing the development of a new economic paradigm aimed at reducing dependence upon fossil fuels and making us energy independent. It is not that the development of alternative energy sources does not create new jobs, it does, but clearly the inordinate influence of big oil and gas money fuels the political short-sightedness that will delay creating clean jobs that are critical to our success in an increasingly competitive globalized economy.

And the cost, my goodness the costs incurred in terms of environmental, ecological, and, yes, the dreaded impact upon climate change that is occurring and will continue to occur at exponential rates despite the best public-relations efforts of a growing community of deniers is heartbreaking. Our collective and long-term slide into anti-science and anti-intellectualism is, by any measure, breathtaking. We are pursuing a course that is ultimately self-destructive, but the cruel genius of this blind strategy is the fact that we will not pay the ultimate price, but our children and grandchildren will.

I am, sadly, a political realist, and completely understand what is possible and what is probable. I can see the writing on the wall and, while I realize that it does not have to be this way, it is. This is an indictment of the system not of a political brand or party or ideology. The best that we can wish for at this point is willingness on the part of some to continue to voice their objections and inject their scientifically validated positions into the political system and our governing structures until, eventually, rationality will prevail.

But in reality, the longer we delay making policy decisions and investments in the future, the further we fall behind. We are losing the most important ingredient in the mix that has made this the greatest country in the world: namely, a collective vision and boldness to excel. I often hear the term "American exceptionalism," but it is in reference to returning to the past and not the future.

It is always astounding to me that those who scream the loudest about the need to take a trip down memory lane and return to a simpler time when our preeminence was undisputed conveniently forget the sacrifices that were entailed in reaching that point. So it is no surprise that they also conveniently omit the need for sacrifices that are required to reach the next level.

But those sacrifices are not solely the responsibility of the American workers; what is required is collective sacrifice. The current attack on the American workforce is premised on the false notion that they are strangling creativity, innovation, and growth, and therefore must make sacrifices in order for management to create economic growth. It is as if the shrinking middle class's collective overindulgence is holding us back. The only logical conclusion derived from such a philosophy is to assume that optimally, a cheaper workforce is good for business, and hence the ideal workforce would be one that costs as little as possible or nothing at all. Slave and child labor, under this scenario, would be the economically optimal choice. Is this the economic paradigm that is nostalgically yearned for?

Cheap labor, like cheap energy, will exact tremendous costs on the society and ultimately will render a society that is neither sustainable nor desirable. Our politics are completely untracked at this juncture, and the key to restoring the economy and jobs is to balance the costs and share the sacrifices. This means that the captains of industry and the lieutenants of small business must be at the table when it comes time to put Humpty Dumpty back together, not with their hands out, but their sleeves rolled up and willing to take America into the future, not the past. But when the only talk of sacrifice centers around spending that benefits the middle class and the most vulnerable in society, it is hard to envision an environment of shared sacrifice. The current debate has effectively harnessed public dissatisfaction and anger against the wrong culprits. Just because workers are willing to work cheaper in other places does not automatically mean that our workers are to blame for the economic mess we find ourselves in. Follow the money. Look at where the tax breaks and corporate welfare and war contracts have been going over the past decade, and you will get a good idea of the bankruptcy of our economic policies. No, it is not the American workers that are the problem, but it is they and the poor that always seem to pay the highest price.

What made this country exceptional in the twentieth century was the emergence of a vibrant and expansive middle class, and what will make this country exceptional in the twenty-first century will be the re-emergence of a vibrant and expansive middle class. To ignore such a reality is exceptionally short-sighted and unproductive.

The Evolution of Revolution:
An Attack upon Reason, Compromise, and the Constitution

Article 62

January 30, 2011
Denial Is Not a River in Egypt

It is mind boggling for me to think that the momentum gathered on climate change after the release of *An Inconvenient Truth* would slow down, stop, or even start sliding backwards. Over the years, there has been a concerted effort on the part of the fossil fuel industry that dwarfs even the tobacco industry's mid-twentieth-century campaign to promote smoking, and I shudder when I say it has been terribly effective.

I have often lamented that as the economy collapsed and the Great Recession took hold, the seeds of frustration and dismissal of reason were cultivated by the fossil fuel industry. They have created a perfect storm of sorts to deny what overwhelming scientific consensus is trying to warn us about. When you add a political system captive to special interests and fueled by their large campaign war chests filled with dollars, the corruption of our policy-making processes and our politicians rival any on earth.

A senator from Louisiana once proclaimed publicly that his vote could not be bought, but it could be rented. This, unfortunately, has become the stark reality of our current political system. Of course, politicians will be quick to deny that campaign contributions influence their votes on particular issues, but this is just another manifestation of denial. They may believe what they say when they say it, but human nature does not work that way. At the very least, campaign donations guarantee access to important policymakers, and that clearly goes a long way toward getting what you ask for.

We are now confronted with denial of scientific fact and theory. At one point, it was reasonable not to expect average persons to fully comprehend complex and technical explanations which require some basic understanding of science. That, however, was punctured by Al Gore's treatment of the issue in his documentary.

Every bit as important is the fact that our kids can more easily grasp the concepts of climate change and the need to protect the planet than their parents. I was astounded by the thoughtfulness of the questions and the quality of the discussions that followed when I delivered PowerPoint presentations to high school and college students. I came away from my discourses with a feeling of assurance and comfort that the issue was being taken seriously, and that we would make headway on the issue when Obama was elected.

Several years ago, I met Thomas Friedman at a luncheon in New York City. He had just finished writing *Hot, Flat, and Crowded,* and we talked at length about where we saw the issue going. We both concluded that momentum had slowed if not stopped, and when he took the stage he called on me as one who was out in the field on this issue to give my perspective on where I thought we were. I told him and the audience that, unfortunately, I thought the momentum had stopped and that the deniers were gaining ground. He sighed and said that was his opinion as well.

I recall a presentation I did at Cheney State University, the oldest historically Black college in the United States. I worried about how I would address climate change before an audience of mostly urban students when, in a lot of instances, they were concerned with basic issues of life and death in their neighborhoods. I decided to focus on the economic issues of new and developing technologies and industries, and how they needed to be prepared for jobs of the future.

Climate change is upon us and is worsening each day. It is a dramatically serious issue, and yet it is still treated as something far off in the future which can be tabled until later. It is here today, it is happening, and the longer we wait, the more difficult it will be to mitigate the drastic impact it will continue to visit upon Earth and its inhabitants. The incidence and intensity of severe weather events should be a clear signal that changes in the eco-cycle of life are here now. Continuing record heat and drought, a year-round wildfire season, floods, tornadoes, hurricanes, tsunamis, and melting ice caps are constant reminders that our world is screaming for attention. Yet we merrily roll along, devising new methods for fossil-fuel extraction, like fracking, which has had devastating impacts upon formerly pristine areas in Pennsylvania, a state with more miles of streams than any state but Alaska. The impact upon communities and citizens, their health and environment, is heartbreaking, and I have witnessed this devastation first hand.

There is a war on the climate that is being fueled by humans and their insatiable thirst for fossil fuels, but there is also a war on the science of climate change that is being waged by humans who have a financial stake in continuing a fossil-fuel–driven world economy. This two-front war is successfully delaying actions that are needed now. We are on a collision course with nature, and if we insist on that course we will not win.

In "The War on the Climate," I continue to raise concerns over the incredibly short-sighted mindset among our policy makers and politicians who take aim on generations that will follow. We are visiting such a profoundly destructive force upon our kids that it verges on criminality. I am not being overly dramatic when I say that we are committing genocide on a massive scale by refusing to come to grips with this issue. I use these terms cautiously but purposefully. There is no greater threat to the future of the human species.

Posted January 30, 2011
The War on the Climate

A particularly troublesome and frustrating development in the contemporary political arena is the increasing acceptance of those questioning and denying either that climate change is occurring or the indisputable fact that it carries dramatic adverse consequences for the human species. This, of course, is compounded with the takeover of key congressional committees by individuals who simply ignore the overwhelming scientific evidence that rightly should guide our policy-making bodies in their roles and responsibilities as guardians of the public trust. And now that the GOP is mounting a war against the Environmental Protection Agency's regulatory approach to the principal culprit in the climate change battle, namely the insatiable appetite of humans for the creation of greenhouse gasses, the need to combat the deniers becomes that much more critical. These foot soldiers of fortune have declared war on our children, and we must redouble our efforts to protect future generations from the genocide of anti-intellectualism and anti-science.

Several years ago, former Vice President Al Gore embarked on mission to educate citizens of the world on what had been fairly technical and complex scientific information by distilling what few were familiar with into a comprehensive presentation through the documentary *An Inconvenient Truth*. His valiant efforts on this front eventually earned him a Nobel Peace Prize.

But he took it further. In the fall of 2006, he started assembling a cadre of conscientious citizens from all walks of life to trek to Nashville and spend a weekend being trained to present the science and theory along with the practical potential consequences of a rapidly warming planet. Eventually he would train over 3,000 individuals worldwide to take the message via PowerPoint presentations, to classrooms, boardrooms, living rooms, and anywhere else where those willing to listen and learn could share with their families and friends in an effort to better educate ourselves on this unfolding phenomena.

Through the intervening years, individuals were free to augment their presentations with the most recent data, and were encouraged to taper their presentations to the audiences. As a member of one of the initial sessions held in Nashville in December, 2006, I have since delivered ninety-four presentations and, much like a Grateful Dead concert, no two have been the same. But the enthusiasm and willingness to entertain an education on these issues has definitely waned. We must not let this flame die out.

Whether it is the more pressing immediate struggles with a plunging economy, the loss of jobs, and the uncertainty of our individual and collective financial futures or the ascendency of an audacious denier movement armed with a well-publicized but fabricated scandal over East Anglican e-mails is immaterial. As is usually the case, it may be a blend of both, or maybe the people are just too overwhelmed by what they know will require a major transformation in how we live.

Although those e-mails demonstrated a lack of professional and political judgment but had no effect upon the validity of the scientific research that continues to substantiate serious concerns over our ability to mitigate and adapt to the changes that are occurring all around us, there continues to be a relentless campaign fueled by the oil and gas industry to exploit what is a public relations nightmare. Obfuscation, distraction, distortion, and confusion are well-established tactics in the art of warfare, and make no mistake about it, the powerful interests that profit handsomely from our addiction to an economic paradigm sustained by fossil fuels will invest heavily in such tactics to maintain their power.

But like Nero, we proverbially continue to fiddle while the Earth burns. There seems to be two salient tactics in the deniers arsenal of talking points: first, since not every scientist in the world agrees on the issue, the deniers contend that we must wait until there is 100 percent consensus before we act; second, those predicting gloom and doom are merely doing so for political purposes, since by nearly every measure the issue nearly splits down the middle with conservatives denying and liberals decrying; hence it has taken on a political dimension.

On the first point, there will never be 100 percent acceptance, ever, so we most certainly should not be held to that standard. The only thing we know for certain is that we need to replace the certainty of inaction with the uncertainty of action.

We would do well to follow something called the precautionary principle. This principle was outlined in the 1992 United Nations Conference on Environment and Development and offers that "where there are threats of serious or irreversible environmental damage, lack of full scientific certainty should not be used as a reason for postponing measures to prevent environmental degradation." There is little or no debate that carbon dioxide in the atmosphere is increasing at an exponentially dangerous rate, and we are entering a period where humans have never been before. That in itself is indisputable scientifically, and should command action on our behalf.

On the second point, I have never quite understood the political agenda of those demanding action to wean us off the fossil fuels other than to actually benefit the species. The only rationale for the deniers would be that it is an international scientific conspiracy to destroy free-market economies. In a politically polarized environment such as the contemporary one, the easiest way to drive a wedge into an issue is to tout its politicization. And to those who worship at the altar of the free market, any challenge to its infallibility is enough to squelch reasoned debate. But to those zealots I would offer the following from Henry Ford, whose wealth was certainly premised and dependent upon fossil fuels and who intoned that "If I'd asked people what they wanted, they would have said faster horses." The clarion call for vision and wisdom in how we progress in the twenty-first century is palpable.

No, climate change is neither a conspiracy of mad scientists who wish to take over the world nor a bunch of silly boys crying wolf; it is a sensible and rational reaction to an accumulation of knowledge that our God-given brains have yielded (this should be particularly appealing to those deniers who also question evolution, but that is another story). We have the ability to build a new economic paradigm, one that will yield profits and protection from the ravages of excessive carbon buildup.

Somehow we need to recapture the momentum that was building just a short while ago, and refocus our efforts on the sustainable development of our world. We have proven that we can explain it in a way in which the public can grasp what is behind the theoretical concepts and scientific research. It is as vital to our economic future as it is to our environmental future. So we must deny the deniers a free pass on what poses as a political strategy to confuse an already apprehensive and angry electorate.

Now while I continue to believe that statesmanship is an important ingredient that supersedes leadership as a concept, on the scale of importance I believe listening occupies the lowest rung on the ladder of important skills for advancing society. It is important to listen, but listening alone is not good enough for leading.

John Adams said that "facts are stubborn things," and the facts are on our side, and the fiddler's bow is fraying. Can we reengage the public in a national discourse on this issue? I, like others, had thought that with the election of Obama and a Democratic Congress we would make substantial progress at the national level on this issue, but with divided government it appears as though we may need to rely on the states, those laboratories of experimentation, to lead the way. California will continue to lead the way; let's just hope that others will follow.

Article 63

February 13, 2011
People Talking Without Speaking/People Hearing Without Listening

In "Listening Is Not Leading," I take to task those leaders at all levels of government who profess that they were elected to listen. Well, okay, that's part of it, but if you only listen to the things and the people you want to hear, is that really listening? Further, listening does not substitute for leading. If you only listen to the points that validate your position, you will learn nothing.

It seems that many contemporary politicians will go to any lengths to avoid the thoughtful deliberation, discussion, and analysis of difficult issues. By hiding behind orchestrated events, only being available to pundits and news organs that validate their positions, and substituting listening for leadership, they can safely avoid employing their minds.

Posted February 13, 2011
Listening Is Not Leading

Listening and leading are not the same. Every time I hear elected leaders talk about how they were sent to city hall, or the state capitol, or Washington, DC to listen, it makes me want to scream. Well, listen to this; you are wrong. You were not sent to listen, you were sent to lead. Listening is a part of your responsibilities, but it is not the sole purpose of your elevation to a position where you have the power to make decisions that affect untold numbers of people.

Every bit as important as listening is hearing, but if you only listen to those who are responsible for putting you in that position in the first place, and in a society that is as polarized on the major issues of the time as ours, that effectively means that you do not listen to, let alone hear, a large portion of your constituency. Hence, it is virtually impossible to fulfill your primary duty: namely, to reach the compromises necessary to move society forward. Listening, even if done properly and with all good intentions, is simply not the same as leading.

If you are truly interested in serving all of the people, a rather critical ingredient to leading, then you would listen to all the people and make decisions based upon the best judgment you can muster to responsibly address the myriad concerns of a diversified society. What is consistently and ominously missing from any discussions coming from too many politicians at all levels of government is a commitment to leadership, that is, making the tough decisions that folks either care not to hear or do not want to accept. The essence of leadership is the ability to convince people that, whether they see it or not, it is in their best long-term interest and the best long-term interest of the country as a whole to do unpopular things, to make sacrifices, to actually make hard decisions.

Unfortunately, there is scant evidence that our so-called leaders are either interested in or capable of stepping beyond the comfort zones of their own electoral prospects to do what is necessary and needed. I do not believe in or favor term limits, but I do subscribe to the notion that serious leaders should act as though they never intend to run for re-election, thereby strengthening their resolve to make decisions based upon the best information available and not upon whether or not it enhances their ability to remain in positions of power.

Power is the ultimate aphrodisiac, and the corrupt nature of a political system that is shaped by, led, and sustained through an endless bounty of special interest influences and financial contributions makes it increasingly susceptible to impotence. The inability to make hard decisions hurts the democratic process because the public's faith and trust in either the institutions of power or the powerful diminishes. The resulting cynicism and desperation corrupts the ability of normally rational minds to render rational thoughts, so in the end what we are listening to is of questionable value, even if they are being heard.

Listening only has value when one's mind is open to an assortment of ideas and proposals that may illuminate or educate the listener. If we only listen for the sake of hearing what we want to hear, the art of listening loses its value. Listening is important to the process of leadership, but it does not constitute leadership. So the next time you hear one of your leaders say that he or she was elected to listen, make sure they hear you loud and clear as you take them to task on the foolishness of the proposition. And make sure they listen when you tell them in no uncertain terms to do the job they were elected to do, which is to lead. If they do, then their listening skills will have been put to good use; otherwise they may be listening without hearing, and my dog is good at that.

The Evolution of Revolution:
An Attack upon Reason, Compromise, and the Constitution

Article 64

February 14, 2011
Civil Defense

Politics has always been a rough business, but several episodes at this time made it uglier than most who have been analyzing it for decades can recall. The rhetoric has escalated to levels that might be referred to as fightin' words. Though duels no longer are considered acceptable ways of settling disputes, the verbal jousting in recent campaigns and in the halls of Congress are verging on a complete breakdown of civility within the highest levels of government.

The US Senate, a place I called home for many years, has been described as the world's most deliberative body, and yet it has experienced its share of unacceptable behavior as this new political warfare has unfolded. There needs to be a return to civility, and it should be led by the president in a highly public forum.

We can disagree; that is an accepted condition of political life. But we can also respectfully agree to disagree—a favorite way of quelling overheated debate and discussion. But the personal recriminations and the heated nature of discussions that have been exhibited in this brave new world of polarization makes it that much tougher to accomplish anything. Now that may be the point, and if so it may be a conscious effort to derail any threat of compromise.

I remember chatting with Vermont Senator Pat Leahy on the tarmac in Cleveland the night of the 2004 vice-presidential debate, and we shared a laugh over a recent incident in which then–Vice President Dick Cheney said to the senator, on the Senate floor, "Go f*** yourself." One must laugh at these things; otherwise, they can spin out of control. One incident that was no laughing matter, however, occurred during the president's 2010 State of the Union address when South Carolina Congressman Joe Wilson shouted "You lie" while the president was speaking. Congressional historians like the late Senator Robert Byrd from West Virginia must have turned over in his grave.

We all need to settle down and put as much effort into public policy as we do public relations. The media's predilection for sensationalism contributes to this level of behavior, but I am convinced that raw emotionalism has corrupted common civility. Like the character in the movie *The Curious Life of Benjamin Button,* we seem to be regressing as the nation matures. It must stop.

In "A Call for Civility," I request a time-out during which we can gather our senses, regroup, and take a good, long, and serious look at how we wish to conduct the people's business. It was time to see if we could not recommit ourselves collectively to the rational discussion of difficult issues, and return to a semblance of sober deliberation on important issues.

Posted February 14, 2011
A Call for Civility

The volatility of the electorate, borne of a frustration and anger over high unemployment and persistent uncertainty of what the future may hold, is especially vulnerable to heated diatribe and flashes of white hot rhetoric. But let's take the recent events in Egypt and learn an important lesson: namely, democratic reform can be non-violent. And let's hope that whatever the future holds for the plight of that country that civility will prevail.

Increasingly, over the last several election cycles, but particularly during the most recent, many politicians in this country have resorted to fiery incitement through their choice of metaphors and a literal call to arms. While trite refrains like "don't retreat, reload," and "man up," and "put on your man pants," and resorting to "Second Amendment remedies" may seem like clever or maybe even cutesy projections of strength, the imbecilic nature of these proclamations can have both intended and unintended consequences, but consequences nonetheless.

Lack of civility, comity, respect, and faith in our institutions and leaders has been brewing for some time now, and is clearly reflected in poll after poll. Society's collective enchantment with vilifying those who even try to bring reason and sanity to the decision-making table has provided a convenient rationale for avoiding tough decisions and encouraged institutionalized cowardice on politicians at all levels of government. When doing the right thing equates to political suicide is there any reason to expect we will get anything less than candor and statesmanship from our so-called leaders?

Arizona has become the poster child for half-baked ideas and half-cocked politicians, but the nationalization of intolerance finds comfort from the wilds of Wasilla to the Deep South and plenty of places in between. It finds enough comfort that a peckerwood from South Carolina finds it somehow plausible to call the president of the United States a liar during a State of the Union address, and the former vice president of the United States can cavalierly tell a United States senator "Go f*** yourself" on the floor of the Senate. Is it any wonder that honorable men and women might shy away from subjecting themselves to such indignities?

There is a critical need for a national conversation on the restoration of civility in our governmental system. The call must be bipartisan, and should involve leaders from all walks of society, all political stripes, and must reach a unanimous consensus on the need to reinvigorate our system of governance with the tolerance and forbearance required to lead a pluralistic democratic nation.

The Republican Party has a very large role to play in tempering this bubbling cauldron. There will be plenty of time to exercise your electoral might during the next election year, but right now you need to play a constructive role in managing differences. That is your job.

There will be a time for fighting, but it is simply not a 24/7 job, and to invoke another remnant from a recent campaign, it is truly time to put "country first." You must rid yourselves of the notion that politics is more important than governing; otherwise, we will continue to see episodes where individuals take symbolism to heart and act upon it. Words matter. You must temper your penchant for illusory optics and pyrrhic victories and actually do the work of the people. Put away the Gadsden flag and unfurl the Stars and Stripes that truly represents the entire nation, not a loose confederation of states.

The president should endorse the call for a national conversation to restore civility to our discourse and lead it. The people are tired of the backbiting, name calling, divisiveness, and discord that prevent our system from functioning at anything resembling an efficient and effective level. And to those who feel the need to exploit anger and fear for their own personal or political purposes, let a renewed call for civility expose them for what they are, and let the consequences of their actions be a reaction at the ballot box. It is the only way to salvage a system that has gotten way off track. Taking these actions just might render reactions that are best for the country, and that is really all that matters.

The Evolution of Revolution:
An Attack upon Reason, Compromise, and the Constitution

Article 65

February 21, 2011
The Job Is Never Finished

As we celebrated Presidents' Day, I wanted to bring attention to the exhaustive and dedicated work that two of our living ex-Presidents have been involved in since they left office. A disclaimer is that I had the distinct honor and privilege of having worked for each, but any objective analysis and observation will bear out the accolades I accord these two giants.

Each man has used his considerable knowledge and experience to promote peace, and each has worked tirelessly to better the world and improve conditions for millions around the world. In "Two Great Ex-Presidents," I take the opportunity to boast about their accomplishments and achievements after leaving office. And while I have nothing but the utmost respect for both, I think that the conditions under which Jimmy Carter left office, after only one term, warrant considerable attention. He and Rosalynn have traveled to all parts of the world, working on health issues and free elections for people unfamiliar with either.

Both Carter and Clinton are humanitarians of the highest order, and on the day on which we honor presidents, it is important to acknowledge and praise their efforts after the proverbial thrill was gone. For them, there are always new thrills.

Posted February 21, 2011
Two Great Ex-Presidents

As we reflect on our country's history with the celebration of Presidents' Day, we do so in a tumultuous world witnessing vast and rapid transformation on a scale not seen in our lifetimes. Not only is the quest for more open democratic processes sweeping across the Middle East, but in our own country we are witnessing a challenge to unionization, a movement that rightfully can lay claim to the creation of what we know to be middle-class America and the accompanying wages and working conditions' protections that helped propel this nation to greatness. It is an exciting and challenging time.

It is a period in history that will surely test the bounds of democracy and freedom. But as we survey our nation's leaders and devise untold lists of rankings, placing those in some order of greatness, I would offer that rather than limiting criteria to simply accomplishments in office, we ought to consider a broader view of achievements throughout a lifetime. I have had the distinct honor to have served under two presidents (Carter and Clinton), and regardless of how one gauges their time in office, for surely that pendulum will swing wildly, it must be noted how they have capitalized on their unfathomable energies and collective intellectual curiosity for the betterment of mankind.

While Jimmy Carter may have left office in 1980 under the cloud of the Iranian hostage debacle, the lingering effects of an oil crisis, and staggering inflationary pressures, he never left the international stage, and in the ensuing three decades has used his personal charm, vast intellect, and the power of his presidency to achieve what few can begin to imagine. In addition to authoring twenty-three books, building homes for Habitat for Humanity, and receiving the Nobel Peace Prize, he has worked tirelessly to promote peace throughout the world through monitoring elections, led the fight to reduce the stigma of mental illness, and spearheaded the campaign to eradicate diseases, such as guinea worm disease, in Africa. Through The Carter Center in Atlanta, he and his wife Rosalynn have become peace and health ambassadors to the world. The range and extent of their efforts could fill volumes and are far too numerous to recount here.

Bill Clinton, on the other hand, left office in 2000 under the cloud of impeachment, yet he too has never left the international arena and quite likely remains the most recognizable and admired political leader in the world today. Through the Clinton Global Initiative, he has managed to leverage his charisma, intelligence, and indefatigable energy into a catalyst for improving the human condition that has affected nearly 300 million people in more than 170 countries. By employing commitments from former heads of state, business leaders, Nobel Prize laureates, and other prominent figures, he has expanded access to financial services, information technology, educational programs, clean water and energy, and maternal and child health and survival programs worldwide. Again, the scope and breadth of his accomplishments simply cannot be featured in the space allotted here.

In totality, the achievements and accomplishments of these two ex-presidents, when combined with the policy and programmatic successes of their years in office, surely must rank them in the upper echelon of our greatest humanitarians—a most noble accolade indeed. The vitriol and venom within our political system often hides notable deeds. But if time heals all wounds, then eventually these two giants will be recognized and appreciated for the positive contributions they have made to foster a better world.

So during this week in which we celebrate the birthdays of two heavyweights in the pantheon of our elected leaders (Washington and Lincoln), let us not forget the efforts of those who continue to serve the nation and the world once they no longer hold the office. We as a nation should be proud of their tireless efforts to improve the lot of mankind, regardless of our political or ideological convictions. I, for one, celebrate and salute them as American ambassadors for peace, and above that there can be no higher accomplishment. Can there be any doubt that they represent the very best of what we as a society should strive to be: namely, enablers for the progressive advancement of people everywhere?

Let us all acknowledge the strength of our democratic experiment, from the land of La Follette to the land of the Pharaohs, and rejoice in lifting the plight of peoples everywhere, for that is what makes us a greater and stronger nation. The works of these two ex-presidents exemplify what makes us proud to be Americans.

The Evolution of Revolution:
An Attack upon Reason, Compromise, and the Constitution

Article 66

March 14, 2011
Man's Limits

In the aftermath of a devastating earthquake and tsunami in Japan, which reawakened our curiosity and concern about nuclear power and why it is so potentially dangerous, it is incumbent upon us to put to rest the absurd notion that we can manipulate Mother Nature and her tremendous powers. Instead, we must figure out a way to work in cooperation with the awesome forces of nature, harness the energy contained therein, and change the ways in which we power the economy of the future.

Human creativity in seeking to cooperate with the forces of nature is truly a gift that is begging to be offered. Rather than punishing leaders who dare to think big, act big, and solve big problems, we need to reward their efforts and create incentives to capture the future today. Too often we are comforted by what we know and are fearful of those things we do not. The resulting stagnation forces us to rely on the destructive exploitation of what we know instead of fruitful exploration of what we don't. This is the case today with our continued reliance on fossil fuels and our tepid examination of renewable energy sources.

If we were true free-market advocates, we would immediately scale back our continuing subsidies to the fossil fuel industry and allow the price of carbon to arouse public consciousness and clean out individual wallets. The resulting shock would precipitate an abrupt change in attitude about reliance upon energy sources which are quickly advancing our demise.

Distinguished scientists have often remarked that the Earth will survive, and talking about the survival of the planet is not the correct assessment of what we are looking at. The real question is not whether the planet will survive, but whether humans will. I once scoffed at the distinction as academic gobbledygook, but I scoff no longer. The distinction is important, and I have little doubt that the scientists are right; the planet will survive, but we may not.

In "It's Not Nice to Fool Mother Nature," I explore the need to work in cooperation with her powers and the futility of trying to ignore her might. The confluence of the destructive powers that man has wrought, eg, nuclear power, and Mother Nature again proved that we can cooperate in enormous destruction or make monumental contributions for the good of the planet. I choose the latter. We can continue to ignore nature at our peril, or cooperate to advance the condition of mankind.

Posted March 14, 2011
It's Not Nice to Fool Mother Nature

The force unleashed by Mother Nature this past week is a stark and somber reminder of the limits of human power. The earthquake and subsequent tsunami were neither caused by nor could be corralled by the most monumental of human efforts. And if there is a singular lesson to be gleaned from the disaster it should be this: namely, it behooves us to work in tandem with the incredible strength and power in her vast arsenal. Specifically, I refer to our efforts to create enough energy to feed the ongoing population explosion that will rock this planet Earth over the next half century by capturing what it has to offer, namely wind and sunshine.

Regardless of mankind's Herculean efforts to plumb the depths of the Earth to root out every conceivable fossil fuel source, those efforts will simply be fool's gold, short-term, and ultimately destructive of the environment that is supposed to sustain populations of the future. Rather than spending and expending significant amounts of resources, both capital and natural, on tapping finite pockets of profit, we must begin in earnest to harness what is infinite, inexhaustible, and far more sustainable. Unless we accept and embark on a large-scale program to shift the economic paradigm that governs our global society from one dependent on fossil fuels to one that relies upon "fuels from heaven," our efforts will prove costly more in terms of survival than anything else.

Also, the current disaster in Japan should give pause to those who may be teetering on the verge of accepting nuclear energy as a panacea. The lengthy hiatus that has prevailed on development of nuclear energy in this country may prove to have been far-sighted and prudent, but at the very least the human costs of a nuclear meltdown, despite man's best efforts to protect against such, should cause us to soberly reflect upon any desires to pursue this path.

There is currently a healthy debate brewing in states all across the nation on the potential costs and benefits of unbridled natural gas development. Unfortunately, the forces of restraint and evaluation are heavily overmatched by corporate profiteers who can spend outrageous amounts of financial resources on a disingenuous and fallacious public relations campaign designed to capitalize on pure greed and the hopelessness spawned by an economy based upon a level of income inequality unseen since the days of the robber barons.

There are glaring gaps in the evidence over the extent to which hydraulic fracturing, the process of extracting natural gas, impacts the environment. The process of drilling for natural gas requires boundless amounts of water removal from natural streams and rivers; the pressure with which this water, mixed with an assortment of toxic chemicals, is injected a mile into the Earth, calls into question the collateral damage of contamination to both private and public water systems; the disposal of returning water, "produced water," raises serious questions over safety to drinking water for large population centers; and the resulting methane release into the atmosphere, a greenhouse gas twenty-five to thirty times more powerful than carbon dioxide, begs for further examination into the potentially adverse impacts upon climate change and global warming.

There is no consensus in the scientific community on the relative merits of the argument that natural gas extraction is significantly cleaner than coal. In other words, the avalanche of public advertising on behalf of the oil and gas lobby is carrying the day, and once again the regulators, both at the federal and state levels, have to play catch-up at the same time they are experiencing the threats of significant cutbacks in funding. We should have some reasonable degree of confidence that before we turn to natural gas as a transitional bridge fuel, it is a better alternative to coal; at this point that is not the case.

Imagine if we sunk as much energy into development of a nationwide solar grid to capture and disseminate power generated from the sun, or conducted a full-scale assault on capturing energy generated from wind. It would be profitable from the standpoint of jobs creation and sustainability.

We need to think big, we need to act big, because the energy needs are, well, big. And if the unfolding developments in the Middle East are not cause enough, we need to seriously reassess our dependence upon an energy source that is pushing prices at the pump to levels that are unmanageable to a larger and larger portion of our population—you know, the eighty percent who have not participated in the great wealth heist of the past thirty years.

Thirty-four years ago, Jimmy Carter called out the American public to face up to the growing inability of our nation to withstand a growing dependence on foreign oil. He talked turkey to the American people, declaring the "moral equivalent of war," was roundly and soundly rejected by politicians of both parties and ultimately by the power of the voters, who preferred to fantasize a return to a time that never existed, except in the movies. The solar panels were removed from the roof of the White House, and we embarked upon the realm of unreality. And here we are.

We need to divert our attention away from blaming the teachers, the public employees, the unions, and the poor; we only have to look into the mirror. We have ourselves to blame, and now we must face the music. But don't be fooled by the promises of a magic solution; it does not exist. It is not the Marcellus Shale play, or the Utica Shale, or whatever source we find hidden in the Earth. We must turn our heads to the heavens and realize what it is that hits us directly in the face, the answer lies there, right in front of us, and it is not surprisingly a gift from Mother Nature. The answer lies in working with her majesty, not in trying to fool her. And for those who find the need to look back in time for a clue, remember the 1970s margarine commercial whose tag line was, "It's not nice to fool Mother Nature."

Article 67

March 30, 2011
Home Sweet Home

The continuing inequality in American society is a foreboding signal that the train has gone off the rails. In a country that has prided itself on an expanding middle class and economic opportunity for all, we are failing to honor either of those two venerable precepts.

An economic report stating the stark realities of income consolidation and a shrinking middle class that are so obvious to even the casual observer reveals that the numbers are sobering and alarming. And the recent housing bust, accentuated by record numbers of foreclosures, continues to eat away at most Americans' single most prized lifetime investment—their homes.

While the recession may have officially ended sometime in 2009, the economic recovery at this point can only be described as anemic. What makes it even more astounding is the realization that without the leadership of the Obama Administration in securing passage of the stimulus bill, the situation would have reached unfathomable levels. Of course, he will never receive praise for having kept the country out of a full-blown depression, and it is exceedingly difficult if not impossible to convincingly talk about how much worse things might have been had the simulative actions not be undertaken, but history will take care of that.

We may never know the depth of the economic catastrophe inherited by this administration, and it will never receive the credit they deserve for avoiding a cataclysmic economic collapse. Yet this does not register even a mention by an opposition determined to impose an austerity program upon an already exhausted populace which, by all accounts, would be counterproductive and disastrous.

In "There's No Place Like Home," I attempted to draw attention to the stark statistics underlying the beating most Americans have taken during these perilous economic times, while during that same period, consolidation of wealth at the top of the income scales reached unheard of dimensions. The fracturing of income equality and the massive redistribution that has taken place may have given rise to massive protests and demonstrations in the streets in another time and place. But instead, Americans are hanging on for dear life, hoping things improve soon, or that they are not impacted more than they already have been. Of course the nascent Occupy movement, which is a manifestation of anger from the left, has drawn some attention, but a lack of a coherent or consolidated message has opened the door to its marginalization.

Posted March 30, 2011
There's No Place like Home

It is truly difficult to imagine a comparable period of time where a president has had to face so many momentous decisions on such a broad array of disasters under such withering cynicism from an opposition that seemingly questions his very existence. On alternating days questions arise as to whether he is an American, an alien, an agnostic, or an amoeba.

Surely the coolness and steady demeanor he exhibited during his successful campaign for the White House has, to a large degree, helped insulate him from the constant criticism leveled at his every decision. And incredibly, the divisiveness permeating the opposition has actually helped steady his resolve while facing down the cataclysmic events that avail themselves on a daily basis.

This is not to say that I have been totally supportive of his every decision; in fact, as a progressive, I have often been frustrated by what appears to be a hair-trigger need to reach consensus, even in advance of the kabuki dance of negotiations which forms the framework for their discussion. But that frustration pales in comparison to the consternation that accompanies the idiocy of the propositions that pass for proposed solutions emanating from the opposition.

The funeral procession of ideas that have so captured political discourse in this country is a long one indeed, and unfortunately, to continue with this metaphor, they are leading us to the grave. This is not an indictment of the current hypocrisy that grips our nation as much as it is the long-running parade of horribles foisted upon the American people at least dating back to the early 1980s, and each political party has exhibited its share of hypocrisy along the way.

Objective analysis depends upon looking at long-term trends instead of short-term fluctuations. When examining the changing complexion of our economic well-being, one of the most excruciating and damning indictments of what has happened in my lifetime is the relentlessly widening income gap that has insidiously restructured our society. Income inequality and the subsequent disintegration of the middle class are destroying this country's ability to legitimately lay claim to our self-professed mantra of exceptionalism. The numbers are quite simply mind-numbing.

A report released by the Economic Policy Institute this week titled "The State of Working America's Wealth, 2011," authored by Sylvia Allegretto, paints a vividly depressing picture of what we already know, suspect, and indeed are experiencing on a daily basis: namely, that the harder we work, the further we fall behind. And while the report documents the large-scale and debilitating impact of the financial and housing industry collapses of the Great Recession, it explores the longer-term implications of the generational slide that has largely afflicted the baby boom generation.

Technically, the report places a beginning and end point to the longest span of recession since the Great Depression as spanning December 2007–June 2009. I am sure this is little comfort to the millions of American workers who have seen their former jobs permanently exported overseas, or who are currently underemployed, or have given up searching for a job, or who tenuously cling to extended unemployment compensation benefits that are currently under attack at both the federal and state levels, or facing foreclosure, or carrying "upside down" mortgages that are greater than the value of their houses.

While the report offers a treasure trove of statistics, let me outline a few that I believe warrant an exhaustive and thorough discussion by policy makers, even though they are currently intent on slashing spending and resistant to an adequate infusion of revenues, and certainly opposed to further economic stimulation via a substantial public-works program aimed at restoring our crumbling physical infrastructure. But nevertheless, the facts are sobering.

For instance, the percentage of wealth held by the top fifth of households in 2009 was 87.2 percent, and this percentage has been steadily climbing since 1962. At the same time, the bottom four-fifths of the population hold a mere 12.8 percent of wealth, a number that has steadily decreased since 1962. These twin trends typify both wealth consolidation at the top and a growing gulf between the few and the many.

The report also offers that "the wealthiest one percent of US households had net worth that was 225 times greater than the median or typical household's net worth in 2009, the highest ratio on record...and for the first time on record, the percent of home value that homeowners own outright dropped below fifty percent—meaning that banks now own more of the nation's housing stock than people do."

The old adage, "The rich get richer and the poor get poorer," is being played out on the contemporary economic stage each and every day, and it is chipping away at the foundation of an equitable society. If we fail to seriously address the widening chasm between income classes and, more spectacularly, the shrinking middle class, our collective sense of justice, fairness, equity and opportunity will continue to fray.

We do not need statistics to validate what we see going on around us, but they are there to bolster the claims that are heard around dinner tables and in barrooms and wherever working and unemployed Americans congregate. Exacerbating this trend towards income consolidation by slashing spending programs designed to help the most vulnerable among us, attacking unions, denigrating public education and teachers, and promoting extension of revenue-depleting tax cuts, whether to billionaires or large corporations, is insane.

Homeownership has been a cherished goal of administrations of all stripes for many decades, for in this society it is believed that a man's home is his castle. Investment in one's home is, frighteningly, the largest source of savings for ever larger portions of our workers. Yet it is exactly this source of wealth that is under attack during the housing bust. Certainly there is a lot on the plate right now, but this one really hits home. It is absolutely critical that we halt the trends of wealth consolidation and income inequality and fashion a set of effective policies that restore faith and confidence in the value of work, workers, and the middle class. If we fail to address this societal schism, we will forfeit our ability to address deeper problems abroad and find ourselves home alone.

Article 68

May 16, 2011
Fossil Futility

During this week, representatives of the big five oil companies testified before Congress in a show of pomposity and arrogance that defied description. The Senate Finance Committee was the latest venue to feature fossil fools who resemble the dinosaurs that provide them with their royal profits. We continue to be enmeshed in a fantasy that suggests there are painless and easy solutions to deep-seated problems, and pander to the public's wants, not their needs.

What I find stunning about the sordid episode that has us clamoring to plumb the depths of the Earth for every last ounce of fossil fuel is the lack of policy makers' interest in taking an exhaustive look at the potential costs of the latest fad—hydraulic fracturing, better known as "fracking."

In "Dinosaurs and Fossil Fools," I made an impassioned plea to examine, through empirical study and with scientific rigor, the potential pitfalls of exploiting shale plays for more oil and natural gas. Then, policy makers and the public will be able to decide, armed with precise information, the sacrifices they will be willing to impose on future generations for the pleasure of maintaining the existing economic paradigm. And the fact that our government continues to subsidize what is the most profitable enterprise in the history of mankind makes a mockery of fair competition.

Posted May 16, 2011
Dinosaurs and Fossil Fools

Dinosaurs live. I have seen them. One need not travel to Jurassic Park; a herd was sighted in Washington, DC last week. And while physically they may have evolved into human forms, the size of their brains is unnaturally small in relation to the size of their skulls. They are still vicious predators of weaker species, they have razor-sharp teeth capable of gnawing through anything that gets in their way, and they destroy with absolute impunity and have no regard for their surroundings.

I saw them with my own eyes and could not help but marvel at the sight unfolding before the Senate Finance Committee last week as the heads of the so-called big five oil companies paraded their arrogance once again before an array of incredulous senators, vociferously refusing to even consider placing need ahead of greed. As I stared wide-eyed at the spectacle, my wonderment quickly turned to anger and disgust at the vile and despicable pomposity which governed the actions of these creatures.

The word "dinosaur" derived from the English paleontologist Richard Owen in 1842, and in essence it means "terrible lizard." One could not devise a more perfect definition of the fossil fools who ambled before Congress to argue for the continuation of unconscionable federal government spending (federal tax subsidies) while oil tops $100 per barrel, gasoline at the pump tops $4 per gallon, and their profits top $35 billion in the first quarter of this year alone, and over $900 billion over the first decade of the new millennium.

Yet the description offered by West Virginia Senator Jay Rockefeller, whose family is quite familiar with oil, was as profoundly apt as it was disturbing. He proceeded to detail the power and influence of these pernicious profiteers and the seemingly untouchable status they currently enjoy with Congress. Utah Senator Orrin Hatch, fighting for his political life by turning his solidly conservative credentials inside out in order to appease his Tea Party constituents, characterized it quite differently, labeling the exercise as a classic dog and pony show, complete with a drawing that I have no doubt will fetch a pretty penny at an upcoming fundraiser. These conservatives just have never seen corporate welfare they did not like and will defend to the death.

First we had "too big to fail"; now we have "too big to nail." The dinosaur mentality of these corporate titans was on full display on Capitol Hill, and the dinosaurs may ultimately exact their revenge upon the human race unless we exhibit an appropriate mix of intestinal fortitude and intellectual prowess. In public policy, as in life itself, it is virtually impossible to come up with the right answers unless you ask the right questions. It may seem to be an exercise in semantic gymnastics but, bluntly, we are not asking the right questions. For instance, while we spend our time devising schemes to wean ourselves off our dependency upon foreign oil, we should rather be spending our efforts on the far more important question of how to wean ourselves off fossil fuels.

Similarly, while we spend our time cleverly convincing ourselves that we must concede to the inevitability of fossil fuels to meet ever-growing energy demands, we should spend as much time figuring out how to reduce those energy demands. Leading environmental organizations seem to have fallen into this trap all too willingly as they devote considerable energies and efforts towards defending the position that natural gas development is inevitable, so we need to develop the appropriate regulatory framework to lessen its adverse environmental impacts. They are absolutely right on regulation, but what about the underlying issue of whether there is a right way of doing the wrong thing, to paraphrase Dr. Anthony Ingraffea, whose work at Cornell University on puncturing the myth of shale gas as a vastly superior alternative to coal is encountering criticism from the industry and environmentalists alike.

In the past several months, there have been groundbreaking studies on the impact of hydraulic fracturing and natural gas as a replacement for coal as an energy source. The Environmental Protection Agency is involved in an exhaustive multiyear study to assess exactly what relationships exist between extraction methods and water contamination. A study released last month by scientists at Cornell University raises the specter that natural gas may indeed be worse for the climate than coal. A Duke University study last week linked natural gas drilling and hydraulic fracturing with a pattern of drinking water contamination.

This week, a study by the Post Carbon Institute concludes that "the notion that natural gas is a panacea that can substantially offset oil imports as a transportation fuel or replace coal-fired electricity generation in business-as-usual growth scenarios is wishful thinking at best." And the Academy-Award-nominated documentary *Gasland* has raised serious questions about the environmental consequences of drilling activities from Texas to New York and everywhere in between.

In our exasperation and desperation, we have fallen prey to the hype and relentless propaganda that fantasizes an easy solution not to our needs, but to our wants. It ignores the commonsense admonition that if it seems too good to be true, it is. The point is that it is absolutely imperative that we start asking the right questions. If natural gas development is indeed inevitable, we must exhaustively explore the consequences before we pin our hopes on this latest miracle cure. Right now, there are serious questions being raised which suggest that the folks that brought us Halliburton, BP and Deepwater Horizon, the Exxon Valdez and Prince William Sound, and fire-breathing water faucets in homes in Dimock, PA, and elsewhere, may in fact be selling us a bill of goods.

The prudent and responsible public policy approach to this issue requires that we take a deep breath, study the pros and cons, and proceed cautiously. After all, the shale plays holding these resources are going nowhere.

If nothing else, the arrogance and greed exemplified by the oil and gas industry and its leaders should send a loud and clear message to our policymakers to move with caution and exhibit an intellectual and scientific curiosity that all too often is missing in our policy debates. Otherwise, the dinosaurs will win.

Article 69

June 20, 2011
Tilting at Windmills

I had the unique opportunity to juxtapose the past and future neatly one week as I took time from my travels down Route 61 in north-central Pennsylvania to visit the remnants of the town of Centralia. The only thing that remains of a town that once sat upon a fiery cauldron of anthracite coal is a well-cared-for cemetery and a barren street grid that once supported a community of individuals, but now paves a path through overgrown patches of weeds.

It does not even qualify as a ghost town; that would imply abandoned buildings. There are none; all that remains are the carefully-laid streets to validate that, at one time, the weeds they now border were once lined with houses and the life that accompanies them—children, dogs, lawns, picket fences, automobiles—things like that.

There are holes in the ground from which you can see smoke. When you place your hand over these, you are taken aback by the extreme heat generated from below. But the remarkable thing about this place is not the fact that life once existed and prospered here, but that as one gazes at the ridge tops that reach to the sky just a short distance away, the magnificent sight of windmills gently turning in the breeze offer hope that a more promising future awaits.

In "Centralia: Where the Future Meets the Past," I describe my wonder at this strange meeting of two conflicting technologies in such close proximity that a skilled photographer could capture the two in a single photo. This is not only the future, it is the present, and the thrill of watching these two forces meet gives me great hope that there is a bright future ahead if we have the political will and vision to make it a reality.

Posted June 20, 2011

Centralia: Where the Future Meets the Past

Sometimes in life, there are things that you are not prepared for. Sometimes the cruel ironies of life lend themselves to sheer incredulity, and sometimes they create visuals that simply cannot be described by the most carefully chosen words. And oftentimes life's absurdities, usually assisted by mankind, simply defy even the most vivid imagination.

This past weekend, as fate would have it, I traveled to Bloomsburg, PA, home of one of the state's universities, to deliver a speech on climate change. Utilizing the scenic beauty of north-central Pennsylvania's mountainous terrain, I found myself traversing the winding roads of Columbia County past the surreal ghost town of Centralia. Today it is little more than a series of asphalt grids winding through overgrown weeds, a testament to a town that no longer exists.

This was anthracite coal country, and at its peak, the town boasted over 2,000 residents, thriving in an economy governed by what lay underneath—a seemingly never-ending supply of coal whose extraction provided jobs and an energy source that powered a nation and eventually the greater part of the world. Today there are ten or so hardy residents who refuse to vacate despite the overarching powers of the state to use eminent domain to condemn the town.

For those not familiar with the story, in 1962, the town sat on an underground inferno when abandoned mines caught fire. The resulting mix of heat and toxic fumes eventually doomed the town. The fire burns to this day, and is projected to burn for another 250 years. So is this what Thomas Friedman had in mind when he talks about "fuels from hell"? You could easily pass what was the town of Centralia as you make your way up Route 61; there are no signs identifying that you are passing on the outskirts of a ghost town. But if you leave the road and travel along several of the streets in the weeds, you can find yourself on top of a hill, right next to a cemetery that appears to be well kept to this day, if the flowers and American flags are indicators of such.

Upon mounting the hill, you can witness for yourself smoke rising from underneath the ground. When you go up to the earthen chimneys and place your hand over the opening, you are immediately taken aback by the intense heat rising from beneath. It is eerie and fascinating at the same time. There are very few reminders of life here, nothing to indicate that homes once populated the streets and the sounds of children once pierced the air instead of carbon monoxide. But that was the past; it is no longer anything but a chapter in the history of Centralia. The book has closed on this town, and we can only hope that one day soon the book will close on the fossil fuels that fueled the town and the nation and, for that matter, the world.

I delivered my presentation to a group of scientists that day, imploring them to help facilitate a shift from the old economic paradigm based upon fossil fuels to a new economic paradigm based upon renewable energy. Ironically, the energy resource that once supported this town ultimately destroyed it. Ironically, I came face to face with the reality of the story on the same day I delivered my ninety-sixth presentation, imploring anyone who will listen that our future demands we shift away from fossil fuels and embrace the "fuels from heaven" that provide inexhaustible, emission-free sources of energy.

But the ironies do not end there. As I made my way back down the hill, I came face to face with a dozen or so edifices adorning the adjoining ridge tops; imposing and graceful, majestic and functionally magnificent, their very presence striking a pose in the summer-like blue skies over Pennsylvania as if to defy the conventional wisdom that alternative renewable energy is something off in the distant future. There along the ridge tops stood windmills, gently turning their blades of promise into energy. The juxtaposition of these two starkly divergent energy sources simply could not be more perfectly captured than having a picture of the smoke rising from below blending in with the whirling of the blades.

The moment captured a snapshot of the two paths we can follow: one, pinning our children's futures on that which lies underneath, providing short-term relief and ultimately long-term destruction; the other taking advantage of the benefits of nature, the wind or the sun, which promises both short- and long-term benefits for a productive and healthy world.

The choices underscored in this vivid picture bring into clear focus the depth of our commitment as a generation to actually leave the world in a better way than in which we found it, or at the very least no worse. The problem is not our addiction to oil; it is our addiction to fossil fuels. Unless we reaffirm our commitment to our children, as reflected in the lessons of the energy debate, we are simply deluding ourselves and choking our children on the fumes of fossil fuel futility. They will have every right to resent us and condemn us as a selfish and spoiled generation more interested in their own indignant entitlements, and a hypocritical, overindulgent class of individuals whose platitudes about caring and love did not match their actions.

To borrow a quote from muckraker Lincoln Steffens, "I have seen the future, and it works." In this case, I have seen the past and the future works better because the future is here now. The lessons of Centralia illustrate both the past and the future, and nowhere are they more applicable than in our decisions to break away from our dependence upon fossil fuels, because in the end they will destroy us.

Article 70

July 5, 2011
Promises, Promises

In "A Dangling Conversation," I take the opportunity to reexamine Obama's inaugural address to see if those of us who were inspired by his boldness and substantive rhetorical pronouncements had misread his commitment to a big and bold agenda. We had not. There it was, in black and white, and yes, we all heard what we heard.

What we had not yet encountered, however, was the ferocity of an opposition that was not interested in governing but in obstruction. Many of us had been less than thrilled by the compromises reached through this brush with willful paralysis, but in the light of political realities, Obama has found himself in a very tough bind and, under the circumstances, has managed as best he could.

Given this situation, I implore the administration and the president to route his message around the obstructionists and take it directly to the people. I would bet the farm that the people, in their frustration and anger, are willing to give him a chance to enact his agenda as long as it is messaged correctly, clearly stated, and understood.

I understand that this advice is the product of a frustration springing from an opposition uninterested in compromise and dead-set on crashing the system. I am still tremendously confident in the president and his agenda, but feel that the troops need to see him more invested in taking on these wayward miscreants than trying to deal with them. It is a conundrum, but time is wasting.

Posted July 5, 2011
A Dangling Conversation

There is a raging debate currently underway in the progressive community over the extent to which the president either has or has not lived up to the promises delivered during the 2008 campaign and in subsequent speeches. It has left many of us wondering if, in fact, it was we who misread the words, values and, ideals expressly outlined in the historic election of the nation's first African-American president.

There are those who rightly point out, as I have done repeatedly in this forum, that the weight of the issues awaiting his arrival was of such a magnitude that it would surely test the skills and talents of Atlas himself. There are also those who argue that the resolute and determined opposition whose avowed goal was to deny him success surely has altered the calculus upon which he has had the ability to make good on his promises.

But when you strip all the arguments of their merits, it seems to me that the lingering suspicions about this administration among progressives and independents and the legions of under- and unemployed, whose fears of both the present and the future keep them awake at night, are not grounded in whether he has done too much, but rather whether he has done too little. And the depth of exasperation in the public at large places at risk a mature and responsible response to a perceived choice between the lesser of two evils, the quality of the opposition notwithstanding.

There is a current estrangement between the people and their elected leaders that is reflected in poll after poll. Paul Simon, the musician, captured the sentiment in the verses of "The Dangling Conversation," describing the lost communication between two people during a late afternoon non-conversation as follows: "Like a poem poorly written, we are verses out of rhythm, couplets out of rhyme, in syncopated time." This is the current state that passes for dialogue in our political culture. It is important—no, imperative—that a strength borne of conviction, vision, and wisdom emerge from the ash heap of recrimination and political calculation. Otherwise, the wrath of an angry populace may exact a high price indeed on the course we ultimately chart for those who will be left to pick up the pieces of our dysfunction.

I, for one, was drawn to Barack Obama early on because he spoke boldly of the need to tackle the myriad problems both inherited and imminent, and because he appealed to the very unique aspect of American exceptionalism that makes us feel that we indeed can tackle any problem or set of problems if we just roll up our sleeves and get to work. I have found myself recently questioning whether or not we progressive supporters projected too many of our own values on an individual whose centrism was neither masked nor hidden from us along the way. So I returned to the speech Obama gave on that cold day in Washington, D.C. upon his inauguration two-and-a-half years ago to see if I had, in my exuberance, only heard what I wanted to hear.

To both my relief and dismay, I have concluded that no, we did not mistakenly paint the president with our own brush; what was said that day would be as acceptable today as it was then. To wit:

The state of our economy calls for action, bold and swift…We will build the roads and bridges, the electric grids and digital lines that feed our commerce and bind us together. We'll restore science to its rightful place and wield technology's wonders to raise health care's quality and lower its cost. We will harness the sun and the winds and the soil to fuel our cars and run our factories. And we will transform our schools and colleges and universities to meet the demands of a new age…Now, there are some who question the scale of our ambitions, who suggest that our system cannot tolerate too many big plans.

No, we did not misread Obama; we supported such pronunciations of boldness and bigness. A substantial majority of voting Americans evidently also supported the idea that what was needed was a massive overhaul of a system that had for too long suffered from deferred maintenance. This was the promise, and the American people were ready for it. The politicians were not, but with brash leadership, they would discover the wrath of the people if they stood in the way. What happened?

The administration somehow underestimated the power of its own pronouncements. The half-a-loaf mentality of Congress, combined with the we-can-be-as-stupid-as-we-want-to-be mentality of the loyal opposition, extracted concessions that belied the boldness and bigness of the hope and change the American people clearly embraced. The vacuum created by timidity and disappointment gave rise to a successful hijacking of the opposition by Tea Party populists, who apparently wish to return to a time that never existed. And today we find ourselves in a state of paralysis, most clearly playing out through the debt-limit debacle. The cumulative impact of half-measures and ideological nuance portends profound consequences in both the short and long term, politically and substantively.

So, where to do we go from here? Mr. President, on behalf of those who were energized to knock on doors for you; those who reveled in your optimism that we could tackle big and complex problems; those who still believe in you and your sense of empathy, equality, fairness and compassion; those who truly believe that you embody the true ideals that the Founding Fathers stood for—now is not the time for appeasement, but rather the time to reinvigorate the American people behind a leadership that clearly defines right from wrong, a leadership style that fulfills the words you spoke on that cold day in January: "In reaffirming the greatness of our nation, we understand that greatness is never a given. It must be earned. Our journey has never been one of shortcuts or settling for less."

We diminish our greatness when we settle for less; it is not the American way, and there will be a price to be paid for doing such— maybe not in the immediate short term, but certainly in the long term. We have already settled for far too little. The stimulus was not too large, health-care reform was not too revolutionary, financial reform was not too tough, our energy strategy is not too expansive, the housing market is not too robust, and the middle class is not growing.

We still believe in you and want you to succeed, but more importantly, we want a better life for our children, and in their honor we will not allow ourselves to settle for less. You had it right all along; stick to your guns—metaphorically speaking, of course—and don't worry about being too strong. People just want to be treated fairly, and right now they see a system that rewards unfairness. This must change, and you must change it. That is the change that people hope for.

Article 71

November 17, 2011
Thinking Big!

I wrote this article when I was communications director for the California High-Speed Rail Authority. This, the largest public-works project in the history of the United States, was under withering attack on a number of fronts, largely centering on timing and cost issues. Was it a large project? You betcha. Was it a difficult time to be undertaking such a large project? It sure was.

But in "Why We Can Afford High-Speed Rail," I attempted to lay out a defensible rationale for the undertaking based on a cost-benefit analysis basis, and supported the contention that we could not afford not to think big given the long-term trends which projected that the state's population would grow by more than fifty percent over the succeeding four decades.

Additionally, the project was environmentally smart; running on 100 percent renewable energy, it would reduce carbon emissions by relieving congestion on the state's clogged freeways, and would create both short-term and long-term employment. The project represents the kind of visionary, long-term thinking that had been lacking, and addressed issues future generations would confront.

Our infrastructure has been neglected for far too long, and that includes our outmoded public transportation network and the lack of high-speed rail, an investment currently being made in more than twenty countries throughout the world, and which has been effectively operational and profitable in Japan for over a half century. The project represents an opportunity for the United States to compete in an increasingly competitive global marketplace.

The political difficulties surrounding the project, particularly given increasing cost projections since it was first approved in a state-bond referendum in 2008 made moving it forward an iffy proposition. California Governor Jerry Brown was convinced that it was a wise and prudent investment, and strongly pushed for its advancement. The legislature was a different story, and the future of the project hung in the balance.

There was tremendous local opposition from communities in the path of the proposed alignment, and the conservative opposition from areas of the central valley was well positioned to push for its defeat. In addition, there was considerable political opposition from the congested Northern California peninsula, where additional right-of-way to build independent tracks to support the high-speed project would disrupt property.

But the project exemplified the kind of thinking that was not being pursued in this country, and it was long past time to join in the twenty-first-century transportation game. The governor had the vision to put his political capital on the table, and the battle lines had been drawn.

Posted November 17, 2011
Why We Can Afford High-Speed Rail

Long-term planning, visionary thinking, and the courage and wisdom to act upon what is in the best interest of society, regardless of the short-term consequences, political or otherwise, are the hallmarks of a progressive society. Our state and our nation have been built upon the bedrock of healthy competition and prudent risk-taking. It is what has made us an economic powerhouse. And given the demands facing this nation over the next several decades, it is incumbent upon us to prepare for the challenges of an increasingly flat and interconnected world. Transportation will play a major role in connecting us to the future, and we must prepare to do so today.

Given the current economic and budgetary environment and the political polarization that has gripped our society, we increasingly find ourselves stuck in neutral, incapable of moving forward, paralyzed in the face of large problems requiring big solutions. And as we sit idly by, our global competitors continue to march boldly into the twenty-first century. Some say we cannot afford to compete, but in actuality we simply cannot afford not to compete.

A prominent issue facing California and Californians at this moment is a decision on whether to build a high-speed rail transportation network connecting north and south and all points in between. Recently, the California High-Speed Rail Authority issued its 2012 draft business plan, outlining a solid financial blueprint for moving forward on construction of America's first bullet train. The plan is grounded in fairly conservative economic assumptions, and is a realistic portrayal of the current funding environment in Washington, DC. It reflects an economic roadmap that is as bold as it is competitive, and it is needed now more than ever.

The plan is sober and realistic in its approach. For instance, with respect to federal funding, which will be required to build the project, the plan assumes sixty-one percent federal investment, rather than the traditional eighty to ninety percent federal match in traditional major transportation and infrastructure projects.

Also, the plan does not assume additional federal funding, on top of the $3.3 billion already identified, for the next three years. By building the project in discrete, distinct segments, no construction will commence unless funding is identified. Once the project is operational, within ten years hopefully, private capital will contribute to the project. The citizens of California have voted on nearly $10 billion in bonds for the project. Truly, the project will incorporate the quintessential assets of a public/private partnership, and represents a coordinated and comprehensive public/private investment in our future.

As with any large infrastructure project, the costs over the next two decades are large; think of the Interstate Highway System, or the state university system. However, it is wrong and misguided to isolate the $98 billion cost of this system in a vacuum. On a straight-line cost-benefit analysis, the benefits far outweigh the costs. For example, in order to accommodate the large population increases in the state over the next forty years (38–60 million), the costs of meeting infrastructure needs through building 2,300 additional lanes of freeways, four additional runways, and 115 additional airline gates would run to a staggering $171 billion. And it is not feasible to realistically consider expanding airports in major cities like San Francisco or Los Angeles. Building more freeways invites more congestion and more automobiles, worsening time delays and the environment.

This "business as usual" approach would exacerbate already intolerable traffic congestion and airline delays, would continue to add an additional 3 million tons of carbon dioxide into the atmosphere annually, and increase hours lost on sitting in traffic by 146 million hours annually. The diminution of our quality of life would be an unacceptable consequence of short-term thinking. And, as noted above, the costs of such an approach would be considerably greater than building high-speed rail.

From strictly a cost perspective, we would be paying more and getting less, and one does not need to have an economics degree to realize that this is an unwise investment. And the term "investment" is the key here. There are good reasons why twenty-four countries around the world are in the process of building high-speed rail. And while some countries, like Japan, have been operating bullet trains for nearly half a century without a single fatality, we have the ability to learn from those successes and incorporate the latest technology and business practices into the California system.

In a recent article ("High Speed Rail: Too Much, Too Late," Nov. 9, 2011), the writer, on several occasions, questioned whether or not we could afford high-speed rail, referring to it as "an expensive upgrade." In response, I would argue that what we are not talking about here is an expensive upgrade, but rather a wise infrastructure investment that will generate operating revenues and a foundation for the future economic well-being of the generations that will follow us. It is penny wise and pound foolish to rely on an antiquated infrastructure designed for the mid-twentieth century simply because we buy into the misguided notion that we cannot afford to compete. We simply cannot afford not to compete.

The author freely admits that now is not the time to think big, and that immediate needs, such as education and health care, dictate that we rein in our vision. But once again, this does a disservice to the goal of all that we should leave the world in at least as good a shape as we found it. We simply cannot allow ourselves to be cowed into submission by accepting that we cannot face more than one problem at a time. Under that scenario, we will address neither. Besides, the simple economic fact is that time is money, and the longer we wait to build the system, the more it will cost. Inflationary factors, the escalating costs of composite materials such as concrete, copper, and steel, (largely driven by increased demand from places like China, which is in the process of building 9,000 miles of high-speed rail), and realignment due to development all weigh in on the cost of delay.

Henry Ford once said that "If I'd asked people what they wanted, they would have said faster horses." In light of our precarious economic state of affairs, thinking small merely perpetuates mediocrity. And lest we not forget, there are immediate short-term benefits to construction of high-speed rail, including over 100,000 job-years in the next five years alone. It is estimated that over the life of the project, in excess of one million job-years will be created.

California stands poised to lead the nation into the economic realities of the current century and provide future generations with a transportation network that will both enhance their quality of life and give them a competitive edge on the global economic scene. High-speed rail will contribute to our growth, not stunt it. Every system around the world has experienced net operating revenues once constructed. Ridding our highways of congestion, reducing greenhouse gases into the atmosphere, and increasing the economic productivity of workers by relieving stress and time lost in traffic, relying on power produced by 100 percent renewable energy, and spawning transit-oriented development around rail hubs, creating both short-term and permanent jobs, and generally fueling a movement to get us out of our automobiles all are positive benefits for the present and the future.

Yes, there are multiple problems that require our attention, and big thinking, visionary leadership, and the courage to implement a long-term agenda are what are needed. Actually, the time could not be riper for high-speed rail.

The Evolution of Revolution:
An Attack upon Reason, Compromise, and the Constitution

Article 72

December 30, 2011
Under Siege

We often find ourselves trying to balance the competing needs of opposing sides in an attempt to keep the peace. And while compromise is an important aspect of our political system, it can cause enormous dissatisfaction and put individuals under fire.

Obama had often found himself trying to be a mediator, only to reach agreement and then get pummeled from all sides. I must admit that as a progressive who had accumulated a heavy dose of frustration over the years, my patience was worn thin, and there were times when I was unhappy with the resulting policy, which was something less than half a loaf.

I have tried to temper my frustration with the knowledge that Obama inherited a holy mess, and with the new realities of politics and governance since the Tea-Party insurgency presented uncharted waters to Democrats and the administration. So, with 2011 about to close, and upon entering a year which would bring what was shaping up to be a hotly contested presidential election, I felt compelled to pen another poem outlining the treacherous territory that Obama found himself in.

In "Friendly Fire," I attempted to capture this new political environment. I was certainly fully engaged and supportive of Obama, but given the state of the opposition, this was not a courageous or tough position to take. We all wanted Obama to succeed, and some of us had definite ideas on how to proceed—meaning taking off the gloves and calling out the opposition as obstructionists whose positions did not have the best interests of the country and its citizens at heart. The poem was intended to strengthen the president's resolve. Mr. President, this one's for you.

Posted December 30, 2011

Friendly Fire

Infatuation with the middle ground
Is neither safe or very sound
If at the end of the day you find
Your lack of choice renders you benign.

For those who risk choosing sides
Develop courageous bona fides
That provides them certain nobility
Rather than fruitless utility.

And while the risk is surely great,
The excitement it brings can help negate
The anxiety that accompanies choice
When one is willing to raise their voice

Against those things viewed as wrong
In terms stretching from short to long.
For when the stakes are very high
Such is the time to seriously try

To change the world and make it right
Regardless if that change just might
Diminish prospects for respect
From those who choose to neglect.

The fact that you have chosen to define
Exactly where to draw the line
Distinguishes you from those who refuse
To take the leap and actually choose.

But such distinction comes with a cost
A fact of life that cannot be lost
Upon those who venture into the abyss
That borders uncertainty and risk.

And while the nobility you seek as you conspire
To ascend to heights ever higher and higher
He who refuses to choose will not inspire

But is bound to be killed by friendly fire.

The Evolution of Revolution:
An Attack upon Reason, Compromise, and the Constitution

The Fourth Year-2012

Article 73

April 13, 2012
Recalibrating

The California High-Speed rail project was now under fierce and unrelenting attack over the escalating costs which had been unveiled just five months earlier. There was intense political jockeying within the legislature, and its fate was uncertain. Under these circumstances, the project was subsequently revised to accommodate concern about costs, and a new business plan was released to accommodate those concerns.

For a communications guy, this was a problematic and unsettling development. It was a huge project, an engineering feat unparalleled in modern history, and there were so many moving parts that simple description was difficult. Additionally, coming out with a revised business plan on the heels of the previous one led to suspicion that there was considerable disarray within the ranks of the authority in charge of the project, and constantly shifting cost estimates further affected its credibility. Mass resignations further led to the suspicion that the project was on the wrong path.

In "High-Speed Rail on Right Track," I attempted to dampen rampant speculation that the project was on the wrong track. It was a classic example of the difficulties in pursuing large-scale, politically controversial, long-term, visionary projects in a time of frustration, mistrust, and economic uncertainty. Although it was a big idea, the project was a microcosm of what Obama had faced in the previous three-plus years. It's a tough time for big ideas.

Conceptually, high-speed rail is just the type of long-term investment in the country's transportation infrastructure that reflects a vision of where we need to be as an integral part of an increasingly competitive global marketplace. Implementation would require an enormous push from Sacramento, however, and that in itself was problematic given the growing list of competing demands, partisan sniping, and the large costs of a project that would not see completion for another two decades. All of these issues were compounded by escalating costs, which had increased the price tag to double or triple the original estimates.

But it was the right thing to do, and the governor deserves credit for pushing the initial implementation phase over the top of a very steep political mountain.

Posted April 13, 2012
High-Speed Rail on Right Track

The California High-Speed Rail Authority is listening and has heard the complaints, criticisms, and suggestions of local and state officials, individual citizens, and communities, and concluded that many of those concerns are valid. Subsequently, the authority has put forth a revised business plan that makes significant changes in the draft document released just five months ago for consideration by both the board and the public.

The revised plan adheres to a pledge by Governor Brown to construct the country's largest infrastructure project better, faster, and cheaper. It is better because it fully utilizes existing rail infrastructure, in response to community concerns about building additional dedicated track and widening right-of-way in dense urban areas. It is faster because it makes investments in local rail improvements that will benefit commuters while the system is being built. It is cheaper because by making these modifications and reducing the time it takes to make the system operational, the overall cost is reduced significantly.

Thus, in a decade, Californians will be able to travel on a high-speed rail system that will connect the two mega-regions in the north and south through a growing central valley. This connectivity will bring enormous economic benefits in both the short- and long-term to all regions of the state. In the short-term, it will mean 100,000 job-years of employment over the next five years in the central valley, a region with the highest unemployment in the state. In the long-term, it will continue to position California as a leader in the twenty-first-century global economy by having the option of a world-class transportation system.

High-speed rail will help address the infrastructure and transportation demands of a state that is expected to see its population rise from 38 million currently to between 50–60 million by mid-century. High-speed rail will be a viable and competitive option to meeting the mobility needs of an expanding population, but will also do so by enhancing Californians' quality of life. By reducing the need to build additional highways or aviation facilities to accommodate such growth, huge environmental benefits will accrue, such as reducing 320 billion vehicle-miles traveled over the next forty years, saving 3 million tons of carbon emissions annually, reducing by 146 million hours annually time spent sitting in traffic, and reducing automobile fuel use by 237 million gallons each year.

The revised business plan addresses several criticisms leveled at high-speed rail head on. For instance, much has been made of the cost and the lack of a dedicated funding source for a project the size and scope of which has never been seen before in this country. While federal stimulus dollars ($3.3 billion) have been secured for the initial build out of the central valley component, the state legislature is being asked to appropriate $2.7 billion from voter-approved Proposition 1A passed in 2008. While additional federal funding is anticipated to be available to help complete the project, proposals to use cap-and-trade funds as a backstop until these funds are secured helps address concerns about funding uncertainty. Once operational, it is expected that private sector investment will help offset the costs. Thus, a funding source has been identified. In addition, because the project will realize cost savings due to its accelerated construction schedule and the reduced costs associated with blending services with existing rail lines, the total costs are projected to be $68.4 billion. In a previous plan, a fully dedicated track system from San Francisco to Los Angeles was projected to cost in excess of $98 billion.

The adjustments made in the revised plan show a willingness on the part of the High-Speed Rail Authority to be responsive and responsible. What it means to Californians is that they can be assured that the project represents a wise investment of scarce public resources, an investment that will reap tremendous benefits now and in the future. In seventeen years, you will be able to board a train in Los Angeles' Union Station and arrive in San Francisco's Transbay Transit Center at a cost of eighty-three percent of an average airfare. In today's dollars, the cost would be eighty-one dollars, one-way.

The revised business plan also addresses many financial concerns, such as whether or not the projected ridership numbers will yield an operating profit without a subsidy. A world renowned panel of experts has worked with the authority on a number of scenarios using realistic, credible, and conservative assumptions to validate that indeed the numbers stand up. In each of the scenarios presented, a high, medium, and low set of ridership assumptions based on different yearly projections, the number of riders surpasses the number needed to break even. In other words, the system will operate on a profit and not require an operating subsidy.

Some have questioned whether the revised business plan will meet the requirements laid out in Proposition 1A. In other words, will blending operations with local rail systems allow the system to achieve the two-hour-and-forty-minute travel-time stipulation by traveling at speeds of at least 200 mph from Los Angeles to San Francisco? The answer is yes. It has always been a given that when entering dense urban areas, the trains will need to reduce speed; this is true whether you use blended tracks or dedicated tracks. The revised business plan comports with the requirements in Proposition 1A and is therefore consistent with what the voters approved in 2008.

Some have opined that they support the concept and not the project. The revised business plan has carefully incorporated solid suggestions made by lawmakers and the public in order to assuage those concerns. There will be some who continue to oppose the project, but it will not be because of a lack of responsiveness to costs or legality. This plan represents an honest effort to respond to the needs and concerns of all Californians, and it will not please everyone. But it is the right thing to do, at the right time, and in the right way.

Article 74

May 25, 2012
Concerned

The presidential campaign was shaping up to be a nail biter, and Romney was always the individual I feared the most. I was especially concerned that his success in business would hold greater sway over a frustrated populace than it should, particularly given the type of business he was in. He had overseen leveraged buyouts of companies that were then restructured and put on a path to profitability or declared bankrupt. In either case, Bain Capital received large commissions and, in many cases, jobs were outsourced. By every calculus, this should have worked against his candidacy in a time of high unemployment and growing income inequality, but Romney had positioned himself as a successful businessman, and most folks were unaware of the intricacies of being a buyout king.

He was an attractive candidate and had proven to be fairly moderate as governor of Massachusetts. The fact that he is a Mormon little affected his candidacy, and his religious faith combined with his political pedigree—his father had been an establishment Republican governor of Michigan—together with his ever-present large family gave the appearance of a well-grounded, financially successful, American-dream kind of candidate.

But that was the old Romney. A new Romney emerged as he struggled to gain the nomination of a party revolutionized by an ultra-right-wing faction which had a disproportionate stake in the primary process. My concern was unfounded, it turned out, that anger and frustration would lead people to make irrational decisions which would go against their own best interests as we had seen in the two George W. Bush elections. But my worry was that independent voters would find his moderation attractive and, combined with disappointment and dissatisfaction from progressives who might choose to sit the election out, and minorities who might not come out in the numbers they did during the 2008 election, in the Democratic fold, the election would be tight.

In "The Disaffected Class," I tried to advance arguments against casting a vote that would go against the best interests of the most disaffected class, described as refugees from the former middle class. Specifically, I was concerned about how Romney's specialization, which was reaping profits from the misfortunes of others, made him qualified to address those who had suffered misfortune. It seemed that he was the wrong guy for the job, and that the rational choice was to continue with the guy who had your best interests at heart. Of course, I had witnessed irrationality at work in politics over the years, so my concern was not misplaced. But this was my thinking at roughly midyear, as the campaigns were unfolding.

Posted May 25, 2012
The Disaffected Class

It is with a mixture of bemusement and bewilderment that I watch the current machinations of the presidential political campaign and question the seriousness and resolve of a large portion of the American people. As an individual who had spent over three and a half decades devoted to the propositions that government, one, does matter; two, can make a difference; and three, can work, it had always struck me as odd when I hear people rationalize their choice of candidates based on qualities that have little or no bearing on their ability to do the best job.

Currently we are engaged in a preview of the fall election that will pit two candidates with rather distinctly different experiences and approaches to solving the deadly serious problems affecting our society. And while this allows the serious voter to weigh two competing options as to how best resolve the problems, I am more concerned with the impact such choices will have upon those who are either too frustrated or too cynical to clearly consider the options. I fear that this contingent has swelled significantly over the past decade or so due to the government's deceitful mishandling of foreign affairs (wars) and the economy (the financial meltdown, growing income inequality, chronically high under- and unemployment, lingering recession).

Many if not most of these individuals in what I refer to as the disaffected class are refugees from a shrinking middle class. The American Dream has either been foreclosed upon or is dangerously close to being out of reach for these folks, and they are angry, as well they should be. They believe they have played by the rules and are being penalized for doing so. They worry about their kids and what kind of world they will inherit, and in many instances worry about the world they have already inherited, one steeped in personal debt and dimming prospects for living wage jobs.

The disaffecteds are beneficiaries of progressive social policies and steadfastly believe that the government, like them, should be fiscally responsible. This does not mean that deficit spending is per se bad or wrong, but rather that in time of recovery you pay back your debts. It is the payback part of the equation that has not been addressed seriously, and the failure is a bipartisan one. We are already seeing signs of retreat on the so-called supercommittee trigger mechanisms that await whoever gets elected in January, which begs the question, if our elected leaders are not serious, why should we, the voters, be serious? And of course, the catch-22 is always, well, you put them in those positions of leadership in the first place. How does this happen? Seriously!

In far too many instances, a deeply frustrated electorate throws their arms up in disgust and walks away. In some instances, they vote against rather than for something or someone. In other instances, they simply vote against the status quo, figuring that anything is better than what we have. Let me confine my comments here to this last category of folks, because it is here where I fear we run the greatest danger of actually exacerbating our current problems, and it is this group I believe that will hold the key in what is likely to be a close election. And given the degree that the influence of money in our political system has been legitimized by the *Citizens United* ruling, it is likely that an extremely polarized electorate will be the norm rather than the exception for years to come. So how do we make a rational choice?

As I watch the current campaign for president unfold, I am particularly dumbstruck by this notion that because Mitt Romney made a boatload of money in relatively risk-free investments, there is the thought that he would be a good commander-in-chief. Let's just step back and analyze this for a brief moment. Even dismissing the fact that Mitt has tried his hand at the governing thing and failed miserably, there seems to be little logic to the proposition that because he is wealthy, he would be a good president. In fact, it would seem to me that those of the disaffected class might even find this a grossly disgusting argument in light of their economically uncertain outlook.

Capitalists and the private sector are in business for one reason: namely, to make and maximize profits. No more, no less. If you do not make a profit, you do not stay in business—unless, of course, you are a large financial institution. Government, in a democratic society, exists to protect and advance the common good. Thus, by maximizing the opportunities available to the greatest number of individuals, society can prosper and grow. Somehow, the radical right wing of the conservative wing of the Republican Party sees in this proposition a socialist plot to change America. Read your beloved Constitution.

Can anyone envision the reaction in the private equity world if a community organizer applied for the position of CEO of a firm such as, oh, I don't know, Bain Capital? My guess is the individual would not fare well in the interview process, meaning the person would not even make it to the interview stage. Why in the world would the reaction of serious public policy proponents to Mr. Romney's application to be leader of the free world elicit anything other than a dismissive wave of the hand? This is not a knock on any profession or on capitalism or the business world or the private sector; it is merely a realization and recognition that some folks have special expertise, and experience in certain fields of endeavor are not easily transferable to others.

Certain people are not cut out for certain jobs. Given the requirements of the position of president of the United States, maximizing opportunities takes precedence over maximizing profits. So to those who are questioning the current state of affairs and are looking to register their disappointment, do not be so quick to shift gears merely for the sake of changing speed, and instead carefully analyze the potential of slipping into reverse and leaving transmission parts splayed across the road. I would no more want my trusted auto mechanic to perform a root canal than I would want to have an extraordinarily successful profiteer reengineer our social safety net. When viewed from this perspective, a rational choice can also be a vote for change.

Article 75

August 6, 2012
I Am Not Young Enough To Know Everything

In "What Our Kids Can Teach Us," I reject the premise that adults have proven to the next generation that we have been and are responsible, and suggest that there are many things we should be learning from our children. This view, of course, alienates me from my friends who are parents and it may be a little too harsh, but let's look at the mess of a world we are handing over to our kids. They have every right to be pissed off at our collective failure to leave them a world in as good a shape as we found it, let alone better than we found it. Additionally, they have license to question many of the values and truths we learned from our parents.

For instance, our children have every right to question the value of a college education given the lack of economic opportunities available after they graduate, and the amount of debt they accumulate to get it. It is similarly their prerogative to question our degradation of the planet and our quest for material things. They also have an interest in questioning our decisions on budget priorities and war. Kids who are now eighteen or older have never lived in a time when our country was not at war with someone.

I believe that we ought to listen to them as much as we expect them to listen to us. We may learn valuable lessons that will help us help them. I am constantly amazed at things my children teach me. Even when I am initially skeptical, I eventually capitulate and glean important ideas, perceptions, and values from the way they look at things. It amazes me that both my kids think I have been a pawn of a system they find so disgusting. This, of course, will come as big news to most of the folks I have butted heads with over my long career in public service. But once again, we need to listen to our kids, because they are the ones who will have to try to make sense of the mess they are going to inherit.

Posted August 6, 2012

What Our Kids Can Teach Us

A good friend of mine who is also a fellow parent posed this question the other day to her Facebook friends: how would they recommend handling a mother-daughter talk on what it means to be an adult and assume the responsibilities and posture of an adult? Now ordinarily I do not ensnare myself in deep reflections shared with the Facebook universe on what are ostensibly very personal and important conversations, but on this one I simply could not resist.

What I found so intriguing was the premise that being an adult, assuming the responsibilities and posture of an adult, implies that those things automatically carry a degree of gravitas that elevates the adult to a position of superiority, at least intellectually, to that of the child, who, in this case, is college age. The self-congratulatory smugness that accompanies such an assumption is probably every bit as damaging as any potential advice that could be dispensed by the parent, who, of course, is the adult.

Therefore, I reject the premise. And I am reminded of Oscar Wilde's suggestion that "I am not young enough to know everything," so I would reject a premise predicated on the notion that either the child or the adult is in a better position to prescribe the appropriate roles and responsibilities of being an adult. As a father of two college-age sons, let me offer the following: our kids have very good reasons for rejecting our advice and wisdom without serious caveats, the most important being that while we experientially have many things to offer them, they also have much they can offer us.

I am constantly amazed at the things I learn every day from my kids, but many times the things I learn are also cause for great concern. I have spent my entire professional career of over three and a half decades dedicated to the pursuit of public policies that will benefit the greatest number of citizens, but particularly geared to help those who can least help themselves. So yes, I am the quintessential bleeding-heart liberal. Yet I am also part of a generation of baby boomers who have royally screwed up and are in the process of turning over a world that is far less appealing than the one we inherited.

On many occasions I have lamented in public speeches that I cannot pinpoint when the "we" generation turned into the "me" generation, but collectively, my generation, proud to have been spawned by the "Greatest Generation," has turned out to be the greediest generation. Nowhere is this more apparent than in the environmental degradation we have engaged in, encouraged, and of course bequeathed to future generations. We have failed every metric of sustainability; we are on a climatic collision course that will have dramatic consequences for the air we breathe, the water we drink and countless species that will simply disappear from the planet, and there are serious concerns over whether the planet will survive, suitable for human habitation.

We are dangerously close to reaching a tipping point which, once crossed, will place us at the mercy of our ability to adapt, and remove our ability to mitigate dangerously adverse trends. We are in the throes of a global financial recalibration, and have come face to face with a level of economic inequality never before experienced by mankind. Financial success has always been guaranteed to only those few lucky enough to have been born into the right families, but opportunity for success has been the hallmark of an American society dedicated to the prospect that with hard work and a little luck, you too could make it. For my generation, a college education was a fairly reliable barometer that one could achieve a level of material comfort and contentment. Today our kids are losing faith in the value of a college education under the weight of staggering financial-aid responsibilities and a lack of employment opportunities at the other end. It is now estimated by some that upwards of eighty-five percent of college graduates are forced to live with their parents upon graduation.

Today's generation is well aware of the fact that our government and its institutions cannot be trusted to be responsive to their needs, is out of touch, dishonest, corrupt, and does not level with them, whether it is the war on drugs or the seemingly interminable wars in Iraq and Afghanistan. Those same political institutions are dysfunctional when it comes to handling just about any issue of substance, suffocating from a political polarization that renders them impotent with respect to the ability to reach compromise.

In my day, we once did not trust anyone over thirty; today's generation has a hard time trusting anyone, least of all those so-called responsible adults they see running the show. There is a palpable air of distrust, cynicism, anger, and despair that has permeated the world that our kids have inherited, and they have every right to be wary of adults. For it seems that to be an adult, to be responsible, to be in charge, as it were, you need to forfeit your ability to be creative, compassionate, and caring, and there is a widespread rejection of the legitimacy of those in power.

What I find most dispiriting is that the reaction from a large contingent of today's generation is to withdraw from rather than engage these inequities and inequalities. To many of today's youth, the fight for right is a fool's errand and not worth the cost. It is critical that we reverse this attitude; otherwise the downward spiral will continue unabated.

There are many things we can learn from our kids, who by virtue of the information revolution that has accompanied their development are far more aware of many things that we adults either have forgotten or ignore. The more appropriate question is what our kids can teach us about the roles and responsibilities of being an adult, because collectively I do not believe we are sufficiently qualified to dispense advice given the track record we have amassed.

Information is indeed power, and the power of the information readily available at the click of a mouse has rendered today's youth far wiser than their years. This does not mean that we adults do not have much to offer by way of accumulated experience and wisdom, but it must be tempered by the sobering reality of today's world. And that is what our kids know well.

Article 76

August 10, 2012
Pennsylvania Two-Step

As the reelection campaign of Barack Obama entered autumn, efforts to suppress the vote were gaining steam in many states. In Pennsylvania, where I had spent eight years serving Democratic Governor Ed Rendell, a blatantly repressive maneuver to keep the vote down in highly Democratic areas, such as Philadelphia, was moving forward with the enthusiastic support of the Republican-controlled legislature and the Republican governor.

From the West Coast, I watched this travesty unfold with horror, and found it difficult to understand how such efforts were possible at this stage of our country's evolution and advancement. This was clearly an attempted return to a time when active suppression efforts, like literacy tests, poll taxes, and intimidation, were common in the south, and de facto segregation efforts like red lining to keep Blacks out of certain neighborhoods were commonplace in northern cities.

I was particularly struck by the cutthroat utility and efficiency of these efforts. They were meant to inhibit—yes, inhibit—voting. That sacred right which is at the core of our conception of a free society, and which much blood was spilled to advance, was now under attack by the party having a hard time relating to a majority of the populace felt the only way they could win would be to rig the game by changing the rules.

What is most disheartening, however, was the cruelty and mean-spiritedness with which these heinous activities were concocted and dispatched. Already the conservatives had sought advantage through gerrymandering, which awards them inordinate representation. And as of this writing, there are attempts to manipulate Electoral College rules to change the way those precious votes are awarded state by state.

In "Keystone Cops," I draw attention to the shenanigans underway in the state of my birth and to which I had spent eight years as a devoted public servant. Here were their elected leaders in full retreat from the war to ensure equality, justice, and freedom. How can these faux patriots have strayed so far from the DNA of this democratic republic? It is a sorry spectacle, and we must remain vigilant to ensure that these efforts are exposed and stopped.

The desperation of a party that has lost the popular vote in five of the last six presidential elections and only maintains a majority in the US House of Representatives due to an unconscionable rigging of Congressional districts which flies in the face of majority rule has put them on a course to subvert the will of the populace state by state. It is exactly this type of chicanery that makes most Americans recoil in disgust at our political system and its henchmen.

Posted August 10, 2012
Keystone Cops

As a transplanted Pennsylvanian now safely within earshot of the Pacific Ocean, I can only gaze with sheer horror on the utterly detestable state of affairs unfolding in my former home state. While some might argue you could take your pick of travesties, whether it be the Penn State imbroglio, the fracking tragedy unfolding statewide, or the absurdity of taxpayer subsidies for one of the most profitable multinational corporations on the planet (Shell) to build an environmentally dangerous ethane cracker plant while rationalizing the need for unconscionable social services cuts that adversely impact the poorest of the poor, I would argue that the most fundamentally egregious course outlined by the legislature and governor with respect to voter suppression cuts to the very core of a mean-spiritedness that has no place in our society.

In the 1987 movie *Good Morning, Vietnam*, there is a scene that has always struck me as devastatingly simplistic but poignant because it calls attention to the importance of maintaining one's integrity without resorting to treachery. In the scene, Sergeant Major Dickerson informs popular disc jockey Adrian Cronauer (played by Robin Williams), with dripping distain and obvious satisfaction, that he is being relieved of his duties. Listening to the conversation around the corner is his commanding officer, crusty Brigadier General Taylor, whose only concern is keeping morale high among the troops, and with single-minded professionalism realizes he too needs to arrest a potentially explosive situation.

The general pulls the sergeant aside and informs him that he has decided to relieve him of his duties and transfer him to an outpost in Alaska. When the sergeant balks, the general lays this gem on him. "Dick, I've covered for you a lot of times 'cause I thought you were a little crazy. But you're not crazy, you're mean. And this is just radio."

One decision was governed by meanness, a first cousin of jealousy; the other was dictated by duty, a direct descendent of honor.

We are taught early in life not to be mean, but through the socialization process, meanness is often trivialized and, in some instances, even given the imprimatur of being tough, in many instances necessary. This perversion of values may rank second to "Greed... is good" as an indication of just how far off course we have drifted from the ideas and ideals enunciated by the Founding Fathers in their construction of this republican form of government. Meanness is personal, a vindictiveness that can lead to counterproductive outcomes that punish far more individuals than originally intended. The recently passed voter identification law in Pennsylvania, a punishment in search of a crime, defies logic, common sense, and is antithetical to sound public policy.

Meanness is a fatal character flaw that becomes toxic and contagious when inserted into public policies that are meant to benefit the whole of society, those who vote for you and vote against you. As public policy makers, you have a responsibility to all the citizens, not just those who support you. Where and who is the general is this real-life tragic drama? It certainly is not the governor, nor any member of the Republican-controlled state legislative leadership. In point of fact, a prominent member of that leadership has been shown repeatedly gloating over how voter suppression legislation will ultimately succeed in what is really important; namely, a Republican victory in November. With great relish he publicly checks it off of his legislative to-do list.

Someone needs to tell the state house majority leader he is not crazy but mean, this is just politics, and relieve him of his duties. He has lost all perspective—or has he? Remember US Senate Minority Leader McConnell proudly proclaiming that the most important thing his party can accomplish is to see the president fail? So maybe there is a concerted effort to imbue the people's business with a foreboding sense of meanness on the part of the Republican Party. I hope that is not the case, but someone or something must put an end to this destructive nonsense. They are not crazy, just mean.

I mean, mean! Civility and comity are the touchstones of a functional political discourse. At this point, our system is dysfunctional. You can fight hard, and should, for your core values and beliefs, but at the end of the day the battles must draw to a close and the people's business must be paramount in the course of action that is taken. This cowardly charade should be denounced by responsible elements in the

Republican Party, but where is the outrage? One might be left to draw the conclusion that the price to be paid for such statesmanship is far too great in political terms than is worth it. If that is the case, the state of our political system is indeed dire.

Maybe there will be a reprieve from the courts; maybe even those people who are allowed to vote will demand a cessation to such pettiness. Being mean is not being tough; it is the epitome of intolerance, and intolerance breeds indifference. And therein begins the slippery slope towards alienation, cynicism, frustration, anger, and withdrawal. It is a slope that will have us slide backward to a time when the erection of barriers was more important than their obliteration, and a place where exclusion trumped inclusion. This is not an ideal to strive for, but rather an outcome that should enjoy widespread bipartisan rejection.

Article 77

September 11, 2012
Memories

All of us who are old enough to remember will always remember where we were on September 11, 2001. I was in New York City that morning, and each year the events seared into my memory are reflected in my mind like mountains in a crystal mountain lake on a bright sunny day. I have written about my experiences on a number of occasions, but find that a fresh reminder is appropriate and important so those memories never wither.

In "Some Memories Will Never Fade Away," I briefly recount my experiences of that day and its aftermath as a cathartic exercise, if not an important reminder to those who were not old enough to appreciate the gravity of what happened. More important, however, is that we learn from the mistakes made in reaction to the horror that rained from the skies that day in New York City, Washington, DC, and in a field in Somerset County, Pennsylvania.

Much will be written about the misadventures in Iraq and Afghanistan, and the tremendous squandering of good will and empathy that occurred worldwide as other nations felt our pain and watched in horror at what had befallen us. But on this day we remember those families directly affected by the tragedy and how, for a short time, we all felt as though we were one family, one community, grieving yet resolute that we would bend but not break.

Posted September 11, 2012
Some Memories Will Never Fade Away

Eleven years ago yesterday, I was awakened by incessant sirens piercing the New York City morning. Even for New York, the sounds seemed oddly out of place and extraordinary. Nineteen floors above Lexington Avenue at Fiftieth Street, the noise was palpable. Since I had a late morning meeting, I had decided to sleep off jet lag from the cross-country flight I had taken the day before, and was in no hurry to awaken any sooner than I had to.

Upon turning on the television and witnessing a world suddenly turned upside down, I was paralyzed for a good half hour. My immediate thoughts turned to my wife and two young sons whom I had left in Santa Monica just twenty-four hours ago. Despite the hour, I phoned home and instructed my wife to keep the kids out of school that day. When she asked why, I merely responded, "Because we are under attack."

The incongruity of the perfect autumn day and magnificent azure sky juxtaposed against the billowing smoke rising from the tip of the island captured the yin and yang of life itself. Walking down Lexington Avenue—not on the sidewalk, but actually down the street—toward Times Square was a trip down a surreal void; time and life stood still.

It took me five days to get home, and the hugs were especially warm and long. As we bounded on a New Jersey Transit train south towards Philadelphia, with faces pressed against the window watching the Manhattan skyline sorely damaged on one end, seemingly listing under the weight of the damage that had been inflicted upon it, the fade-out seemed to take forever, as if in a slow-motion Peckinpah film, and then somewhere near Elizabeth it simply vanished from sight. But the searing sight would be forever etched into my memory and is there to this day.

And incredibly, magically, in ways that defy all emotion, life goes on.

Article 78

September 11, 2012
Now Is Not the Time to Change Horses in Midstream

As I have done during the last four Democratic National Conventions, I spent nearly a week in Charlotte, North Carolina as part of the podium operations team, making sure the four-day event would go as smoothly as possible and present the Democratic case as effectively as possible, giving the American people a clear choice of the vision they will be asked to decide upon in November.

It was a thrilling and exhausting experience, and the energy and optimism at this convention rivaled any that I have attended since 1976 (I have been a part of eight). Being part of a successful event unrivaled in its orchestration and presentation is almost as exciting as being part of a successful political campaign.

Democrats had every right to revel in the success of the convention. Of course, many—me included—were still concerned about the Republicans' use of maneuvers such as voter suppression, which might skew the election, but we were all feeling satisfied that we had helped put the party's best foot forward. The on-stage players certainly delivered.

Bill Clinton stole the show as he laid out a masterful fact-based, comprehensive, and comprehendible economic and political-history lesson that was a treat to witness first hand. Joe Biden carefully and poignantly rolled out the administration's accomplishments. The first lady, who had become a superstar, eloquently put a human face on the issues. And the president was as steady, steadfast, and composed as ever, a trademark that anyone familiar with what he had faced during the previous four years can only express astonishment at.

In "No Change Is Our Best Hope," I reflect on the experience and come to the realization that it was is not just about winning; it was about a vision for the country. Barack Obama's vision corresponds to a majority of the values and ideals held by a nation that is weary, but changing before our eyes.

Comparing substantive policy pronouncements from both conventions is probably the closest we come to civic discourse in our nation. Debates have their role as well, but the overall theme of three or four days of delineating differences between the course directions of two competing philosophies reinforces our ideas of leadership. The lesson for me, after having watched one convention and participated in the other, was that it was not time to change direction.

As we left Charlotte, we were tired and satisfied that we had done our jobs well, but now the campaign would begin in earnest. I was still nervous about our chances and had lost considerable faith in the judgment of the American public, but I had no doubts that we had the better formula for moving the country forward, and that things would be much better with President Obama at the helm.

Posted September 11, 2012
No Change Is Our Best Hope

So I have taken a weekend to decompress and try to put a little distance between the event and something approaching a realistic if not objective assessment of it. For eight days, I and dozens of my colleagues worked behind the scenes of the Democratic National Convention in Charlotte as part of the podium operations unit that is charged with ensuring that the three-day event flows in a seamless way. The mere logistics of ensuring that hundreds of speakers, musical talent, and group ensembles such as the forty-six veterans who appeared onstage following Senator John Kerry and Admiral John Nathman, or the thirty women members of Congress or the nine women Senators are where they are supposed to be and ready to enter stage right on cue is a daunting one to say the least. But thanks to a dedicated crew of volunteers, a mix of seasoned political veterans, rookies, and in-betweens, it all happened on-cue and seemingly without a hitch. And while the orchestration is every bit as messy backstage as making sausage, the important thing is the cooked product and, in this instance, it tasted great.

The commitment and dedication of those toiling to produce this product notwithstanding, I believe the success of the recently completed convention was the product of a vivid amplification of the different visions of where the candidates and their respective parties wish to take the citizens and the country. This was the eighth Democratic convention I have attended since 1976, and while each had its own distinctive flavor, I can truly say that by far the energy permeating Time Warner Arena last week surpassed all of the previous meetings I have had the pleasure of attending.

There is very little if any room for ambivalence when assessing the path each candidate would have us traverse over the next four years. One path would continue the progress we have already measured on the devastated economic landscape inherited by this administration; the other would represent a foolishly radical deviation that would plunge us back into the abyss. It is clear that our best hope lies in the path of no change. These distinctions were vividly on display as former President Clinton took us through the most politically thorough analysis of the consequences of each course of action being offered in this year's election. And for those who would purport that the Obama Administration has not produced any meaningfully constructive accomplishments over the past four years, Joe Biden eloquently and firmly laid out an impressive list of fact-based and irrefutable milestones that you may not like, but cannot deny happened.

And lest there be any confusion whatsoever, this administration's commitment to international and national security issues, long thought to be the Achilles heel of the Democratic Party, now stands as solid and impermeable as at any time in the last fifty years. Just ask Al Qaeda—if you can even find an operative who will publicly claim to be such.

On the question of the economy, there were no excuses and no backing away from the fact that it is not where we want it to be, but once again the facts are that we are better off than we would have been without federal government intervention. The president has made no bones about the fact that more needs to be done and we need to finish what we have started. To deviate from our course now and degrade into the past failures which have mightily contributed to us getting here in the first place would be borderline insane.

But what struck me most about the presentation of this president's resolve and steadiness was the fact that there was no whining. It would be very easy to talk about the wretched mess that was inherited and the substantial gestation period that preceded its buildup. While it would have been factual and many might argue warranted, it could have been construed as whining, and nowhere within the context or content of the proceedings could the Democrats or the Obama Administration be accused of whining.

No, it is very clear that this election will be won or lost on the issues that need to be addressed looking forward. Let there be a discussion of not where we are or how we got here but rather where we want to be and how we get there. This is really what concerns those who fear uncertainty and worry about the world which their children will inherit.

So the message coming out of Charlotte is unequivocal: namely, focus on the future, look forward not backward, and make your decisions based upon whose vision better reflects the ideals and aspirations of an American society grounded in fairness, equity, opportunity, and sustainability. To pretend that the path is an easy one insults the common sense and innate intelligence of the American people. But it is also critical to accept that the path to success will require a level of cooperation and civility that has been nonexistent for the greater part of the past couple of years, and will require a level of participation that sends a clarion call to all elected officials that partisan shenanigans will no longer be tolerated.

It is for this reason that Republican electoral strategy has focused on voter suppression in key battleground states in order to blunt the will of the people. When you are bereft of constructive ideas, you resort to obstruction, evidenced by the unprecedented employment of the filibuster, a sinister maneuver that unabashedly distorts its intended use by the Founding Fathers.

So let the discussion begin in earnest, and for its part the media owes it to themselves and the American people to focus on content and the issues and veer away from their entertainment-obsessed predilections. And let the American people be the arbiter of what is in their best interest based upon the facts of the respective presentations, not the fiction of the moneyed interests that would bury the issues under a pile of profit. These are tall orders indeed, but hope and change is still alive.

Article 79

September 13, 2012
Another Important Day

A good friend, Rick Siegel, read my piece on September 11, 2001 and gave me a call with an idea he had, which was to try to create momentum for making September 12 a National Day of Unity. To him, that was a day during which we all pulled together, and partisan squabbles were reduced to what they are—inconveniences.

I was taken with the idea, and told him he should submit it to the Huffington Post. He asked if I would collaborate with him on an article, and I agreed without reservation. The product of that collaboration is reflected in "Making September 12 'National Unity Day.'" We offer it as an opportunity to show the world that we may bend, but will never break. And in today's political environment it is something all should be able to get behind, regardless of who offers it. On the day after the tragedy, we all joined as one country, one community, with a collective resolve to rebuild and recuperate and move forward. We may have been more united on September 12, 2001 than at any other time I can remember. Rick's idea was a good one, and we fleshed it out and published it so we will see if it gets any traction in a political system and/or from a public that is as polarized as it ever was.

Posted September 13, 2012
Make September 12 "National Unity Day"

The current political environment is riven with partisanship, and the subsequent polarization of the country lends itself to an air of pessimism, cynicism, and distrust. Whether it is the result of or in reaction to the systematic dysfunction in our governmental institutions and processes is debatable, but what is beyond debate is the fact that we as a nation are striving mightily to confront the myriad problems attendant to an economy that is slowly and deliberately trying to get back on track.

Crisis is a two-sided coin displaying disaster on one side and opportunity on the other. We Americans have defied great odds in our short history, and the spirit and dogged determination that exemplifies this nation and its collective citizenry always, somehow, manages to manifest itself. What is needed today is a reaffirmation of our strength and will. While September 11, 2001 may have been one of our darkest days, September 12 truly showcased our resolve to recover and recommit ourselves to the inevitability of a new dawn.

On that day not only New Yorkers, but all Americans, summoned the courage and strength to let the world know that you may bend us, but you will never break us. No one is going to destroy us, our culture, or our spirit. You may hurt us, but we are going to show you exactly what makes America great. We are going to pick ourselves up, dust ourselves off, be better and stronger than before, and, yes, rebuild.

This is the character of a great nation. If September 11 was our worst day, September 12 was our best. We came together. It was not a Democratic or a Republican resurgence, it was an American resurgence. We looked to a sitting president for leadership and clarity. And on that day, we started the long process of healing. Politics took a back seat to perseverance, patience, and politeness. We smiled at one another, we wished each other well, notoriously impatient and aggressive New York drivers pulled aside to let fire trucks and ambulances go by, and they didn't even try to pull behind the speeding vehicles to get past other traffic.

To recapture that spirit, we would like to offer that September 12 be recognized forever more as National Unity Day, a day dedicated to remembering that we are all in this together: young, old, right, left, conservative, liberal, white, and black. Whether or not it should qualify as a holiday should be an issue for politicians and elected officials of both parties to decide, but in the spirit of comity, let us set aside a day when we can all remember the best this country has to offer.

This very well could signal the beginning of a post-partisan system of governance that if even for only one day sets aside petty bickering and devious maneuvering in which one side attempts to upstage the other. National Unity Day—can there be disagreement over either the need or the significance of it? We surely hope not.

So let the movement begin!

Article 80

September 28, 2012
The Franchise

No more insidious perversion of American justice exists than denying or inhibiting the right to vote to large segments of the population. Yet at this point in the campaign very serious concerns were rising from many points on the map that a concerted campaign was being waged to suppress votes, specifically those of minorities, who would overwhelmingly vote Democratic. This was particularly true in places like Pennsylvania and Ohio—two Rust Belt states that were key pieces in the blue playbook.

Still anticipating a close election and scarred by the shenanigans of 2000, I was concerned. It was clear that the Republican political machinery was also anticipating a close election, and they were not going to leave any stone unturned. I am no stranger to getting out the vote and Election Day activities geared toward getting identified support to the polls. This is all a part of the give and take of any campaign, but overt activities aimed at suppressing the vote, even by electioneering standards, was wrong.

In "Fight Back: Vote!" I expressed my dismay and concern that this latest bit of trickery might swing what many expected to be a close election. After the 2000 election debacle, nothing should be left to chance, and the warnings were being broadcast by news outlets across the country. How could this be happening? We were reverting to third-world, banana-republic-style suppression.

If they couldn't win the election legitimately, our new patriots had determined that it should be hijacked or stolen. After all, they had already taken over one of the major political parties, and reports of the infusion of large undisclosed amounts of cash to further these efforts started to gain attention as well.

The only way to combat this assault would be a backlash against such overt corruption that could only be carried out by the perseverance of those being disenfranchised. They would need to be prepared to endure severe intimidation, long lines at the polls, and resolve to have the strength of will to make their voices heard through the ballot. This was one of the last remaining vestiges of democracy remaining in the post–*Citizens United* Supreme Court decision era. If ever there were a time to stiffen resolve and fight back by showing that you could not be intimidated, it was now. Of course, I assume the other side had anticipated that Obama could not command the level of support that had catapulted him into office four years earlier. The only way to dispel that would be to expose their strategy and really piss people off. In this instance, anger would need to trump fear, and nothing can energize and channel anger like telling people they do not matter. The way to fight back would be to vote. In reflection, I sincerely believe that the attempts at voter suppression and the amount of coverage it received towards the end of the campaign stiffened resolve among minorities to endure whatever hardships were entailed in order to have their voices heard. In this case, the maneuver backfired and spurred more participation than if there had been no attempt to thwart the vote. This is a personal view and, as best I can tell, not supported by any evidence, but the horror stories of people waiting long hours in line in certain minority precincts anecdotally seems to support the contention.

Posted September 28, 2012
Fight Back: Vote!

There is a malodorous stench in the air as we enter the final six weeks of the current election season, and it emanates from an insidiously well-funded campaign to quash the most basic of all American rights: namely, the right to vote. A carefully orchestrated campaign has been afoot by well-heeled interests representing the wealthiest corporations and individuals in this country to suppress, depress, and flat-out deny a large swath of Americans the right to voice their opinion through the ballot box on the direction of the country and the promotion of values that accompany a swiftly changing population.

The abject fear and disdain of those who see hope and change as an enemy of the status quo has permeated the politics of this millennium and fostered a political and societal polarization that has rendered our governmental institutions incapable of functioning at anything approaching an acceptable level of efficiency or effectiveness (witness the abysmal approval ratings of Congress, on the verge of dipping down into single digits), let alone acceptability.

That a substantial portion of the electorate is willing to countenance and support such dysfunction is symptomatic of a wholesale perversion and distortion of the intentions of the Founding Fathers, and the living document that inspired the greatest democratic experiment the world has ever known. That these same individuals would characterize their efforts as patriotic is sadly laughable. In light of the current state of what passes for civil discourse or the lack of it, what is even more remarkable is the extent to which the Obama administration has succeeded in stanching further bleeding of an economic wound that quite easily could have been fatal. The final insult currently underway is an insanely destructive assault on civil liberties levied against a rapidly changing demographic that will see the nation become a majority minority-society before mid-century.

What interests are served by these tactics? Who benefits, and at what cost? As best as anyone with an ounce of intelligence or compassion can figure, the country as a whole and an overwhelming number of its citizens will foot the bill for the moneyed interests that have benefitted from decisions like the *Citizens United* case, and have profited handsomely off the misery of the under- and unemployed. It is outrageous and simply un-American. Yet foot soldiers that have been recruited to the cause, powered by the rise of the Tea Party, will not benefit from the inevitable growth in the gap between rich and poor, and will actually end up paying for it with the loss of government programs that they actually depend upon, read: Social Security, Medicare, and Medicaid nursing care costs. But the fear of change is so threatening to them that they appear to be willing to forego not only their own self-interest but also the long-term interests of progress for the larger society as a whole. Could anything be further from the ideals upon which this country has stood over the course of its existence?

But there is a way that ordinary, common citizens can fight back and actually prevail, and that is to defy these denizens of disaster their just deserts by ensuring their collective voices are heard on Election Day, and in those cases where early voting is still permitted, to vote early. Regardless of the obstacles that may be erected to deny you this right, too many have died, sacrificed, and fought to ensure that your voice is heard. The most effective way to combat this attack on your rights is to vote in overwhelming numbers against those who wish to deny you an opportunity to participate in the American Dream.

This is an open call to fight back, fight back against those who would perpetrate the most serious injustice since poll taxes and literacy tests operated to keep those who most needed representation from getting it. Fight this modern version of Jim Crow that is not only aimed at minorities, but at those who find themselves being forced from the middle class. Fight back against those whose vision of America is compromised by their never-ending quest to control others and secure unnatural wealth and riches from the labor of others.

Fight back against those who consciously prefer profits over people. Fight back against those whose vision of America is one that never existed, namely a montage of images that portray a homogeneous society nurtured and supported by an opportunity-fed capitalism that had no limits. Fight back against those who promote fear and insecurity, who label altruism and compassion as socialistic concepts. Fight back against those who deplore government as a conduit of dependency rather than a vehicle for social and economic mobility that can indeed benefit the greater society and economy as a whole.

Fight back against those whose idea of individualism and self-reliance is dependent upon a corrupt tax system that incentivizes hoarding of wealth instead of reinvestment. Fight back against those who advance privatization of basic rights like health care, education, food, and shelter to the detriment of millions who cannot afford them.

You can do this. In the great American spirit, you have the power to turn back this tsunami of intolerance and ignorance by flexing your indignation. The only thing it requires is the will and commitment to say enough is enough and cast your ballot for a more hopeful tomorrow.

While I am a Democrat, I would argue against such injustice, regardless of who was fomenting such. In this case, it just so happens to be a Republican Party that bears no resemblance to its former self, a party that has been hijacked by a vocal minority so far out of touch with the plight of everyday Americans that is has no credibility in a discussion of where the country either is or should be going. The choices facing the American people are clear, and the way to send a clear message to the world that we continue to stand on the principles of equality and justice for all those in our society is quite simply to vote.

To all those who are angry and wish to voice their resentment against business as usual, this is your chance. Show the world that your voices are as strong as your commitment to fairness and that being an American means standing up for yourselves and what is right. Vote!

Article 81

October 5, 2012
Chill, Everyone!

The world of political punditry was turned upside down after the first presidential debate between Barack Obama and Mitt Romney. To say that Obama had an off night would be kind; he was not the sharp, calm, and rhetorically masterful candidate we had come to admire. But these things happen. Candidates are human beings, and we all have our moments. Luckily this dud of a performance came early in the debate calendar, so there was time to recover. Everybody needed to just take a deep breath and relax.

I watched the debate at the Santa Monica Democratic Party headquarters with my good friend Melissa Fitzgerald, and we both left with a collective "uh-oh." But we also left feeling that there was time to recover. A lot of us were disappointed, and at this date still believed that the election would be a close one, and so the ability to reel in those who had not yet made up their minds was crucial. For those of us who have been part of or witnessed campaigns over an extended period of years, a key lesson is not to overreact. Unfortunately, overreaction prevailed in this instance. I thought Chris Matthews was going to have a coronary on air. I felt like calling him to tell him to take a deep breath. Four years earlier he had admitted on air that Obama's rhetorical skills had sent a tingle up his leg. Well, keep those thoughts, is what I would have told him.

When you remove the performance aspects of this debate, you discover that it did go a long way toward highlighting the distinct choices each candidate presented by looking at and resolving deep problems. For those who had already made up their minds, such distinctions only reinforce and validate their selection of a candidate. A bad performance, not a catastrophic one, can be excused in light of how each candidate will address real problems. The man had a bad night; it can happen, it did, and it was time to get over it and move on.

In "It's About Winning, Not Whining," I attempted to corral

overreaction and bring the situation into a clearly focused perspective. Of course, if this were to repeat itself, there would be cause for real concern, but in the absence of a complete breakdown by Obama, the expectations were that he would recover and not only do better next time, but shine. So everybody needed to relax, rally around the candidate, and keep the faith.

Posted October 5, 2012
It's About Winning, Not Whining

Okay, everyone—right, left, center, pundits and populace alike, undecided voters (however many that can be at this point)—everyone just take a chill pill, a deep breath, collect yourselves, and assess where we are after Wednesday night's debate. Welcome to the real world.

For anyone who has spent ten minutes around a campaign, particularly a presidential campaign, it is a genuine fact of life that they take on their inevitable ebbs and flows, they are subject to the vagaries of timing and events, spurts of advertising, occasional gaffes, and yes, the candidates are still human and experience all the things that humans experience—good days, bad days, thrills and disappointments, good luck and bad luck, and, yes, the unexpected.

I have watched the metamorphosis of the current campaign with an unusual amount of stoicism, partly due to my advancing age and partly due to what has become the ritual of overreaction on the part of partisan pundits who do not even attempt to disguise their preferences. There has been a pernicious giddiness over the past month among liberal commentators over the missteps of Mr. Romney that I have found particularly disturbing. And it was reinforced by the vastly superior performance by the Democrats at their convention in Charlotte when juxtaposed against the inane ranting of Clint Eastwood and his chair in Tampa, but started to take on an aura of invincibility that was brought to a screeching halt after the first debate Wednesday night.

Similarly, conservative pundits are currently overplaying the significance of a perceived Romney victory that night. When compared to the decidedly low expectations they had so fastidiously championed leading up to the event, Romney only had to stick to a carefully crafted script and not venture either an original thought or an honest answer in order to be declared at least worthy of being on the same stage with the president. If this constitutes victory, then I will be magnanimous enough to grant them their victory.

But the whining and hand-wringing being directed Obama's way is simply ludicrous. The campaign was not either won or lost after one debate. There is more than a month and three more debates until the election. The political polarization that has gripped this nation is very real. It was always going to be a close election, despite what the polls and the pundits say. The overwhelming majority of the voting electorate has already made up its mind; in several states, voting has already begun. Trolling for votes among the undecided and fiercely independent voters is the name of the game from here on out, and last night's performance is not sufficient to tip the balance sheet. Voters who are still undecided at this point deserve far more credit for their concerns over the far-reaching impact of the decision they will be faced with on November 6.

There are stark differences in the approaches offered by the candidates, and to an extent the debate helped illuminate those differences. Regardless of how you judged either candidate's performance, Romney firmly believes that the private-sector and the profit-maximizing economic marketplace is the most appropriate venue for policy formulation, whether it be health care, energy and the environment, education, defense spending, you name it. Obama believes that the federal government should play a constructive role in divining policies that benefit the middle-class and those who have been rocked by the economic calamities that were a direct result of policies that placed profit over people. Obama believes, like Lincoln, that we are one country, and that when we all benefit, the country benefits as well. Romney believes we are a confederation of fifty states where each has the God-given right to determine how it should treat its citizens. So if Massachusetts has universal access to health care and Alabama does not, that is the way it is supposed to be.

Obama believes that restoration of the middle class will come as we pull together to distribute benefits in a way that defies and reverses the growing income inequality that has been occurring for the last several decades—at least since the early 1980s. Romney believes that reducing tax burdens on the very wealthiest in our society will not only help them but have some positive benefits for the working classes as well, but income inequality is just a byproduct of an economic system that should shower the rich with government benefits (read: corporate welfare) that will trickle down to the workers at some point.

These differences have been carefully laid out over the course of the past six months or more, and hopefully will be fleshed out ever more vividly in the month to come. Unless one of the candidates makes a monumental and irretrievable mistake over the next month, voters will be presented with two very different views of the world and the future when they enter the polling booth on November 6.

If anything, the fact that the race will be close and the extent to which last night reinforces that perception, last night's debate ought to serve as a clarion call to those who are predisposed to the thoughtfulness and deliberation outlined by the president to action. Now is not the time for whining, but for winning. If anything, the reality of a close race ought to inspire and invigorate those who see a vision for the country that is competitive yet compassionate, strong yet sensitive, principled yet pragmatic, and adheres to the importance of compromise that is a foundational precept of our representative democracy.

So stop the wallowing, dispense with the bellyaching, and get fired up and ready to go.

Article 82

October 26, 2012
Out with the Old, In with the New, and
Back with the Old Again—I Think

Mitt Romney had shown that he could roll with the tides and shift with the currents and eventually make his way to shore. In his six-year quest for the presidency, he had changed positions more times than even he was able to recall, and in the final debate, he showed that he would revert to old positions if that presented a more viable path to victory.

I was very concerned about a Romney candidacy. Of course, I was primarily concerned that the old, somewhat Moderate Mitt from Massachusetts might make an appearance and challenge Obama on his inability to correct the economic mess left at his doorstep. But the dynamics of the Republican Party are such that any semblance of moderation is seen as weakness and will be rejected. Hence, Moderate Mitt had to give way to the Conservative Chameleon. At some point, the Tea-Party insurgents who now control the party must have voiced concerns about which Mitt would prevail, but their greed allowed them to set aside their convictions in the belief that anyone was better than Obama.

In "The Conservative Chameleon," I strive mightily, tongue-in-cheek, to advise those true patriots to withhold their vote for this charlatan due to the moderation he exhibited in the last debate. As weak as the first debate was for Obama, at least the stark differences in policy were on display. In the three weeks since that debate, Mitt had an epiphany or his pollsters realized that positioning him as a moderate, even at such a late date, was essential to help close what they could see was a persistent gap.

I felt that the election was still going to be close, but that momentum was clearly on our side. Obama had not only recovered from the initial debate imbroglio but had gotten a burst of speed, like a runner kicking into gear in the homestretch, and the cumulative polling data suggested that he was holding a steady lead.

It was no time to rest on a lead but, as in all campaigns, the ebbs and flows had finally settled in one direction, and in was in ours. Mitt could yet prove to be a voter-suppression machine within his own party. Independents that may have been inclined to give him a look must have experienced dizziness at the constantly changing narrative and dialogue and positioning of this candidate. He had more than two faces, and you never knew which one would appear. He was truly a chameleon.

Posted October 26, 2012
The Conservative Chameleon

The debates are over. The campaign now enters the home stretch, and in two weeks we will know whether President Obama is successful in securing a chance to finish the job he started four years ago. It has become painfully clear that such a prospect will send many folks into a state of apoplexy and will drive even the most devout evangelical Christian to question the wisdom if not the existence of the Almighty.

The latest incarnation of Mitt Romney, a peace-loving, accommodating, caring, and compassionate capitalist who once crowed that he was more liberal than Ted Kennedy on gay rights, and pushed through the Massachusetts legislature the most far-reaching attempt at universal access to health care in the nation, a template for Obamacare, by all rights should shake the Tea Party patriots to their very core.

Has the moderate Mitt risen from the grave and been resurrected during the waning days and hours of the campaign? Has he had an epiphany? Has he awakened from his long slumber? Has he finally broken free from the shackles of a neoconservative straightjacket? Or is this merely a cynical political ploy to thoroughly confuse so-called low information voters into believing that he is actually capable of taking the reins of the most powerful nation on Earth?

Let me make it abundantly clear, I do not believe that he is either temperamentally or intellectually prepared for the job. But should the unthinkable happen, I think that the last laugh may actually be on the far-right wingnuts who have sold their collective soul to the devil, a Faustian bargain which posits that anyone but Obama is worth prostituting one's principles for.

Of course, what really matters to these self-indulgent, self-absorbed, and self-selected saviors of the American Dream is the preservation not of principles but of principal. Mitt has taken so many positions on so many issues that it is difficult if not impossible to discern where he will actually settle on some of the issues that top the conservative agenda. Conservatives ought to be careful what they wish for; they may get it. And with Mitt, what they may get might be far more than they bargained for—and remember who they bargained with.

Conservatives might do well to remember a history lesson from 1994, when Newt Gingrich and his "Contract with America" swept into control of Congress. Newt was a fiery backbencher and a bomb thrower of the first order. However, in the governing arena he flamed out quickly, leading the way for Bill Clinton to assume the mantle of fiscal stewardship that enhances his stature as each day passes.

Think long and hard about this, my conservative druggies. Which Mitt do you think you will get? The Moderate Mitt from Massachusetts, or the converted champion of conservatism who will sell you whatever it is you think you are buying? These are heady questions indeed, with no clear indication of what on earth the answers might be. It is a hell of a gamble on your part, one fraught with intrigue, uncertainty, and mystery.

This is an appeal to Tea Party patriots on principle: your short-term gamble may actually result in your ultimate demise. If you are a cynic, it does not matter. If you truly believe in your professed passion for the greater cause, does it not create at least an inkling of doubt that you may have created Obama in Republican form? Did you pay attention to the debate this week, or does it just not matter? Does it bother you that there was hardly any disagreement between the two candidates on substantive matters? If you are exercising your right to choose party over principle, partisanship over priorities, then it truly does not matter. But for those who have reluctantly gone along for the ride because they were left with no other choice, you might want to rethink your long-term strategic goals here.

And what if you vote for him anyway and he still loses? Does that not invalidate your willingness to surrender even further?

Too often both liberals and conservatives have been confounded by the limited selection between Tweedledee and Tweedledum candidates that offer not a stark contrast, but rather a duality of conformity that arouses little passion or hope for real change. Mitt appeared to offer conservatives a break from that eventuality at one point in his six-year quest for the presidency, but now he has come full circle to what he actually believes in; namely, a moderation and pragmatism with respect to social issues that reflects what the overwhelming majority of people actually accept.

To the current conservative movement, with Tea Party standard bearers leading the way, this must be a palpable heartbreak that will neither further your movement or change the course of the country, and by aiding and abetting such a circumstance you have substantially aggravated the problems that you so ardently believe need to be rectified.

So my advice to all conservatives who care is to rebuke Moderate Mitt, withdraw your support, and make a statement on November 6 by refusing to support this treacherous decline into depravity. Take a stand, show your true colors, show your patriotism, and teach your kids a lesson on the meaning of principle, integrity, and valor by sitting this one out. Otherwise, the joke will be on you. Don't let Moderate Mitt tread on you; show the world that you are truly a power to be reckoned with. Make your family proud. Don't vote.

Article 83

November 4, 2012
Enough Already!

As the election mercifully made its way to a conclusion, the devastation visited upon Eastern Seaboard states by Superstorm Sandy once again showed Obama at his best, calmly but decisively turning the levers of government to full power to aid the citizens and communities left devastated.

The spectacle of New Jersey Governor Chris Christie and the president touring devastated communities like political war veterans had to strike hard at the Romney camp and Romney himself. But in times of crisis, partisanship and political calculation have no place at the table.

Romney's inconceivably inopportune flip flops, not only in the waning days of the campaign, but also given the inordinate amount of time he had pursued the presidency and his lack of the most basic convictions or a clue as to how to run a government where the bottom line is not profits but people, doomed his candidacy.

In "The Mitt Mistake," I argue that it had become clear that the man was neither temperamentally nor substantively prepared for the task he sought. The juxtaposition of an incumbent president who so deftly handled the current crisis as he had the many crises he had faced over the previous four years brought out the stark differences between the two. In the end, the Tea Party got a candidate they probably did not really trust, and that lack of confidence forced the candidate to woo them in a way that would dearly cost him credibility with the public. In the end, the Tea Party and the Republican Party were going to get the very thing they feared the most—another four years of Barack Obama.

Posted November 4, 2012

The Mitt Mistake

Enough is enough. As if it has not already been amply demonstrated that Mitt Romney is capable and willing to take all sides of every issue, the latest affront to common decency, common sense, and community comes in the form of his spin around on the issue of disaster relief. Mitt is more than mercurial; he is maniacal, and his contradictions on whether government has an integral role to play in national disasters shows beyond any shadow of the doubt that he is simply not qualified to assume a position in which decisions have real life and death consequences.

Is Mitt a moderate tragically miscast as the ultraconservative crusader? Or is he a closet Tea Party patriot desperately seeking moderate credentials through a disinformation campaign designed to persuade unsuspecting independents to throw their good sense to the wind? Hopefully, we will never get the chance to find out, for such a gamble could cost us dearly. Mitt is used to gambling with other people's money, so the gamble will not cost him one way or the other in much the same way that Bain Capital profited from their investments whether the investments were prudent or not. It is a good gig if you can get it, and being president of the United States would be the best gig ever, especially for an imposter to the throne.

President Obama has once again demonstrated, in the wake of Superstorm Sandy, that he has the temperament, demeanor, gravitas, and competence to handle the most serious and complicated issues facing the nation. Romney's incessant pandering, inexplicable vacillation, and dubious competence with respect to the serious act of governing have been showcased time and again during the course of this campaign. He is little more than a weather vane, blowing in all directions, subject to the ever-changing currents of the political winds. And this week, the weather vane blew off its hinges.

While Sandy's winds were ferocious, the political winds fueled by New Jersey Governor Christie's fawning praise of the president's performance in the face of crisis left Romney once again floundering and flailing as to what the position du jour would be with respect to FEMA and, more generally, the federal government's role in assisting hard-pressed states, many in the hands of Republican chief executives, who were faced with time-sensitive and critical decisions affecting the lives of American citizens.

Romney simply has no compass upon which to reliably steer the country. He is befuddled by complex problems and has exhibited an astounding inability to grasp a concept of governance that displays confidence, competence, or any semblance of experience when it comes to tackling issues that do not involve rendering bottom-line profits. Mr. Romney, do not quit your day job; this presidency business is not for you. You are a child in an arena reserved for adults.

Your campaign will go down in the annals of history as the most fundamentally dishonest, distorted, and disingenuous display of self-promotion ever perpetrated upon the American people. Your version of integrity is little more than an appeal to the most venal and toxic doses of greed and avarice that have no place in the community of man. And there simply is no place for you in a world which is attempting to deal with the most intractable issues we humans have faced since the beginning of our existence.

I feel confident that the American public will see through the lies, the insensitivity, the phoniness, and the downright meanness of your approach to dealing with the human race. I also sense that your enthusiastic willingness to raise disingenuousness to new heights, as reflected in your adamant refusal to embrace anything other than the most temporary conviction on any issue, will cause those who will pay the price for your habitual indecisiveness to ultimately reject you.

You have lived a life of privilege and have much to be thankful for. Unfortunately, you have learned little and have squandered an opportunity to contribute to anything other than your own offshore bank accounts. You have succeeded in fooling lots of people, and shame on you. You are a natural salesman, and I have no doubt you could sell any product, whether you believed in its value or otherwise. But that, my friend, does not qualify you to lead the nation.

The Evolution of Revolution:
An Attack upon Reason, Compromise, and the Constitution

Obama Wins Reelection—Handily

Article 84

November 13, 2012
What a Ground Game!

Election night was sweet. I savored the victory at home, feeling fully confident that it would be a satisfying night. The margin of victory caught everyone by surprise—certainly those in the Republican camp. I had expected a close election all along, and was pleasantly surprised by the margin of victory and the near-unanimous capture of battleground states.

But I had witnessed something earlier in the day that gave me an insider's insight into the Election Day dynamic that would be replicated in states across the nation. I had volunteered to make phone calls that morning to other states, and was dumbfounded when I arrived at a warehouse-sized building. There I found hundreds and hundreds of volunteers with lists in front of them and cell phones attached to their ears, making phone calls to identified supporters in Virginia, Florida, Colorado, Ohio, Wisconsin, and Nevada.

I had participated in many phone banking operations over my thirty-six years in politics, but never had I seen such an effective and efficient operation as what I would be involved in. Sure, technology played a role in this, but the organization was unquestionably first rate. I was so energized and impressed that I came back later in the day to devote another three hours to the cause.

When I left that afternoon, I was absolutely convinced that the ground game would help push us over the top. Later that evening, those expectations were fulfilled. In "Three Yards and a Cloud of Dust," I recount the events of Election Day 2012. Subsequent analysis has confirmed that the Obama ground game was second to none. The Romney camp was obviously caught off guard and as dismayed as we were delirious. But not only did I find tremendous satisfaction for myself, but I felt good for the country.

Posted November 13, 2012

Three Yards and a Cloud of Dust

Woody Hayes, the legendary football coach at Ohio State, is credited with coining the term "three yards and a cloud of dust" to describe a strategy of grinding out yards on the march to the goal line. Ironic that this Ohio legend's admonition very well could be applied to the political strategy employed by Team Obama in its march to secure not only the battleground state of Ohio but in eight of the nine battleground states up for grabs last Tuesday. The ground game on display during the election of 2012 will most certainly be enshrined in the political hall of fame.

Election Day was a beautiful day in Santa Monica, CA—the kind of day where one would sneak off to the beach, take a long bike ride on the Strand, or hike in the mountains. Those who took advantage of the state's early voting by mail option certainly could feel confident that they fulfilled their civic duty and could have easily watched the national election unfold in the other forty-nine states with a sense of satisfaction that would surely be rewarded as the state increased its Democratic political advantage to supermajority proportions and with no doubt whatsoever that the grand prize of fifty-five electoral votes would easily go into the Obama hopper.

For Democrats, life was grand on this most special and important of election days. The political stars would certainly line up to reflect the changing character of the country's demographic constitution, and it would be the responsibility of the battleground states to do their part to ensure that our future would move forward, not backward.

So what did we do as Democrats on November 6? Well, a lot of us did what I did. I spent three hours that morning in a warehouse-sized building making phone calls to voters in Ohio, Florida, Wisconsin, Virginia, and Colorado, persuading them to vote for President Obama. And, not satisfied that three hours was a sufficient investment of time for the urgency of the moment, I would return that afternoon for an additional two hours of phone calls. In Santa Monica alone, over 1,350 people manned phone banks during the Get out the Vote campaign. We made over 70,000 calls on Election Day to battleground states, and over 200,000 calls over the three days before Election Day.

And statewide, over 1.5 million phone calls were made on Tuesday. The national campaign attributed Colorado and Nevada victories to the efforts by California volunteers. This is the tenth presidential campaign I have been involved with, and the ground game, the organization, the focus, and the enthusiasm clearly surpassed any campaign I have participated in.

To borrow phraseology used to accentuate the power and devastating impact of our military artillery, the shock and awe of this political campaign has left a lasting impact upon the electoral landscape that will surely be used as the barometer for all campaigns to emulate. Of course, there are many reasons why the election turned out the way it did, and I am sure that significant academic debate, research, and conjecture from pundits across the ideological spectrum will fill political airspace for some time to come. While some explanations will be subject to heated controversy and some will simply melt away under the light of abject irrelevance, the one incontrovertible fact that will emerge in any serious analysis is that the ground game employed by the Obama team was far superior to anything that either Team Romney, or anyone else on the planet, for that matter, has ever seen.

Team Obama will forever be credited with a brilliant organizational strategy backed up by a flawless implementation delivered by troops whose dedication, commitment, and seriousness caught the opposition flatfooted. And if the formulation, implementation, and management of the campaign are any indication of the competence the administration will employ as it seeks to govern the country for the next four years, the country is in capable hands indeed.

So all Americans can take heart; these are serious times that require serious and difficult decisions, and there is no doubt that the people have clearly given their endorsement to the Obama Administration to finish the job they have already started. The election was a triumph of policies over politics. So in the best interest of the people and the nation, let us redirect our energies now to the substantive issues that deserve our undivided attention. It is time for politics to take a back seat to the business at hand; namely, the construction of a framework for dealing with the real problems affecting real people who are really concerned about the real prospects that will confront the real America. Both candidates outlined their versions of a vision for the country; the differences were stark, and the people have spoken. Now we must act, and that will require bipartisan cooperation. It will be difficult and bruising, but it must be done.

If need be, the ground troops need to be ready to once again show their muscle to ensure that the politics of obstruction is shown the door; it is not welcome and destructive. So I guess we are all reservists on call just in case. Let us hope we are not needed anytime soon. But if we are, we've got your back.

Article 85

December 21, 2012
The Fall Will Probably Kill You!

My favorite scene in *Butch Cassidy and the Sundance Kid* is when Robert Redford and Paul Newman are trapped on a ledge, looking down onto a swiftly moving river while the Bolivian authorities approach. When Redford refuses to jump, Newman asks why. Redford replies that he cannot swim. Newman, incredulous, laughs and says "Are you crazy? The fall will probably kill you."

So here we are, poised on a cliff. But it is the fiscal cliff, and Boehner and Obama are faced with a similar dilemma. Boehner insists that any compact with Obama will not float with the loonies in his caucus. Well, Mr. Speaker, you wanted this job; now you have to lead. And if your troops will not follow, you need to quit or get new troops.

And this is the current state of the political system. As much as he must hate his life on some days, Speaker Boehner wants to keep his job, and so he desperately hangs on to the horns of an insolvable dilemma. His job is to be the chief negotiator with the enemy—the president. But his troops insist that if he shows any sign of compromise, they will revolt. So the fight is on, and nothing short of unconditional surrender is acceptable. And here we stand, waiting for something to bring these folks to their senses.

In "Still Here and Waiting," I again encourage realization of the world as it is, not as some believe it should be. The world did not end on December 21, 2012, as some had prophesized, and we need to figure out a way to move forward. I do not feel sorry for the Speaker, but I do pity him. He is in a difficult situation and he has no good options, especially given the intransigence of a large part of his troops. But this is exactly why we need statesmen and leaders to help navigate tough decisions; otherwise, paralysis will remain the order of the day. Not even a decisive and sizable repudiation at the polls could convince a gerrymandered gaggle of House members to accept reality; they were still encapsulated in what Bill Maher refers to as "the bubble."

And still we wait.

Posted December 21, 2012
Still Here and Waiting

So today is judgment day, and the Speaker of the House probably wishes that the Mayans' prognostications proved true. But we are still here, and the real judgment day has come for Boehner and the Republican Party. It is deliciously tempting to launch a broadside at the tan man, but the stakes are too high for too many, the consequences too serious to slink to the level of the Tea Party snakes who worship obstruction and vow fealty to an ideology steeped in economic insanity, political vengeance, and self-hatred.

One cannot feel sorry for Mr. Boehner because, like an untold number of those in his party, they have decided that political power is both more seductive and more important than the perpetuation of a democratic system of governance that has steered this nation for the past two centuries. Addiction can rob one of their senses, sensibilities, sensitivity, and security, it can blind even the most loyal parent to their responsibilities to protect their children, and in the end it can kill them. At this point, the cancer spreading through the Republican Party body politic has rendered it deathly ill.

The Republicans have no one to blame but themselves. They have willingly engaged in a Faustian bargain with the likes of Grover Norquist, Rush Limbaugh, Sean Hannity, and Karl Rove, and are seemingly trapped in a web of spectacular deceit while the nation struggles to cope with an inability to solve some of the most destructive and intractable problems facing its citizens since the 1930s. Meanwhile, they have allowed an extremist wing of the party dictate a course and agenda that has made sensible governance an endangered species.

Compromise, contrary to the inane rhetoric of the cult of the new conservatism, is so delicately yet purposefully woven into the fabric of our institutions of governance, so essential to the infrastructure of democracy carefully laid out by the Founding Fathers in the Constitution, so integral to the steadfastly incremental nature of change exemplified by our system of checks and balances and Federalism that the frontal assault directed against it almost rises to the level of treason. We may not like the pace of normalcy, but we have discovered that we are essentially dysfunctional without it.

There is a way out of this quagmire, and that is for Boehner to step up to the plate, summon whatever courage and compassion for public service that led him to choose elective office in the first place, and piece together a coalition of support that is good for the country and the overwhelming majority of citizens who will suffer the adverse consequences of inaction. It carries great risks for him personally and professionally, but those risks will pale in comparison to the damage he and his party will suffer when faced with the wrath of an already angry and impatient electorate.

The fiscal cliff could be the advent of a new era of post-partisanship. From a strictly political perspective, it is tempting to root for a total implosion of the Republican Party. From the standpoint of practicality and compassion, however, the short-term damage is not worth the long-term benefits. The time to think about our long-term stability is long overdue. We have all suffered from partisan gridlock, and even politically sophisticated observers are tired of it.

My students learn that our public-policy process is shaped by compromise, a messy legislative process analogous to sausage-making and incremental change. Yet they are constantly bombarded by examples of political gridlock that deflate any hope and confidence in a functioning system of governance. It is this blatant disconnect that has sunk approval ratings in Congress to all-time lows.

So, Mr. Speaker, the ball is in your court, the mantle of leadership rests squarely upon your shoulders, and whether that burden will prove too heavy depends upon the skills you have learned over your years of service. I hope you are up to the task. But if you continue to allow irrationality to rule in your caucus, you most certainly are destined to be remembered as a leader who could not even lead his own troops, let alone help fashion constructive remedies for a nation.

Article 86

December 28, 2012
Trapped!

In "From Contraries to Bizarro World," I again employ film analogies to describe the surreal world of the Republican caucus and the characters that populate it. Speaker John Boehner is trapped in a world with no exits. He refuses to exercise leadership that puts country above party and thus finds that he is hopelessly trapped in a world where conflict, the enemy of compromise, is the primary default option. Yet, his world is a bubble trapped inside a real world where conflict is the preferred default. War should always be a last resort; yet in the contemporary political environment of the House, it is the preferred option of the insurgents. This now characterizes the political leadership of a nation desperately in search of solutions, not platitudes.

How long will this go on? How long will it take for reason to replace reticence? Paralysis must give way to action for society to blossom and thrive; otherwise, we will continue to thrash around like fish out of water until our strength is exhausted.

Posted December 28, 2012
From Contraries to Bizarro World

Welcome to Bizarro World, where black is white, up is down, good is bad, day is night, and right is wrong. The proverbial pickle that Speaker of the House John Boehner is in right now is a consequence of the Bizarro World zeitgeist that has mystically mesmerized those miscreants known as Tea Party patriots. In their worldview, Obama is not president, and majority rule is a quaint custom that only carries weight when a majority actually shares your point of view.

In the 1970 epic film, *Little Big Man*, there is a scene where Dustin Hoffman interacts with what he describes as the most dangerous kind of Cheyenne, a contrary, who does everything backward and hence drives himself crazy. The contrary in the story, Younger Bear, is mortally embarrassed over the fact that Hoffman's character, a white man, actually once saved his life.

In the House of Representatives, Boehner's number two is Eric Cantor, who comes as close to the Younger Bear character as anyone, and he is the acknowledged shaman of the Tea Party acolytes. This, of course, casts as unsettling and uncomfortable a political relationship imaginable, and Boehner is now torn between two worlds: an imperfect world of reality, and a deeply flawed world of Bizarro. With Cantor tethered to the Speaker at every appearance, shadowing his every move, involved in all strategic discussions, and poised to catapult into the Speakership at the faintest hint of a misstep, Boehner is rendered powerless and paralyzed, incapable of action at a time when his country needs his participation to avoid stumbling into a fiscal abyss.

Bizarro World is a creation of a comic strip, popularized in the immensely popular Seinfeld television series chronicling a comedian, his friends, and their collective stories about nothing. It is a comedy, and supposed to be funny. The world of the contrary is portrayed in a movie film that seriously reflects upon the ironies of the mass destruction of Native American culture. The current trap that has violently clamped its steel jaws on the Speaker requires him to either lie down helplessly or gnaw his way free. Of course, this is an immensely distasteful choice, but action is required nevertheless. And until the reverse polarity that has gripped the Republican Party is actually reversed, we the people will pay a very heavy price indeed.

The Speaker is trapped for sure, and his cries of pain echo through the political landscape. In Bizarro World, they are treated as sounds of weakness. In reality, they are seen as a cry for help. There is a course that will allow the Speaker to extract himself from the grip of miscalculation, misfortune, and misery, but it does not come without political cost. That cost will benefit the country, but it will seriously damage his standing among the contraries and Bizarro characters that populate his world.

A fairly novel notion that is as old as the nation itself and relatively accepted as a prudent course of action in any democracy is to allow for a majority vote. Not a majority of the majority, but a true majority of the whole. To some this may seem to be a simple solution and one steeped in common sense, concepts that spurn scorn and ire among the creatures of the netherworld. But we must accept the hard, cold realities of the consequences that action—or, in this case, inaction—will reap upon a nation and society worn ragged by the excesses of greed and the economic inequalities that have trapped them for too long now.

In Closing

The election of Barack Hussein Obama in 2008 was a revolutionary and historic event in the history of the nation. His reelection in 2012 can be seen as a revelatory incident; it conclusively validated the changing face of America. The alliance of voters that propelled him to a second term dramatically reveals the New America, one that continues to shift demographically to a darker hue. No longer will candidates be able to ignore this reality unless they wish to draft their own political obituaries. And while his major first-term accomplishment will be the signature health-care reforms enacted in The Affordable Care Act, history will record that, in all likelihood, his stimulus bill forestalled an economic depression. Even so, we have been saddled with the deepest economic recession since the 1930s. But it could have been worse.

During this period, I was involved in various political positions that cap a nearly four-decade-long journey through politics and policy. The views expressed herein are mine and are intended to reflect a deep and abiding commitment and dedication to public service, as well as a concern for the world our children will inherit.

An interesting thing that struck me as I was poring over these eighty-six articles was that my discussion of the 2012 presidential campaign makes no mention of one of the pivotal incidents that influenced its outcome; the Romney forty-seven percent comments recorded at a private dinner for large donors in Boca Raton. I never intended this to be an analysis of the campaign, or most assuredly that incident would have been included. But as I questioned my decision process for not feeling piqued enough to comment on it, I discovered that I did not find the comments that striking. Disturbing, yes; a revelation, no.

I suppose I'd readily discounted the idea that given Romney's wealth and life of privilege, and his constant pandering to a party increasingly consumed with granting tax breaks to the wealthy and cuts to social programs for which he had no affection, empathy, or time, I never considered those remarks startling enough to comment on. In retrospect, I wish that I had, but I figure that is the way most rich Republicans think.

I hope that readers will find value in the concepts and ideas expressed herein. They are embedded in experiences I have had and witnessed and a thought process that springs from a deep desire to make the world a better place for the largest number of people possible. I remain dedicated to this ideal and hope that it is reflected in all I do, personally and professionally.

In my grandest dreams, I hope this book sparks a public discussion of the value of public service and government and the role we have to advance and support each other. I have tried to encapsulate into these writings the values I have learned over a career dedicated to public service, and truly hope that public policy students, academics, activists, and ordinary citizens who have an abiding interest in their communities and their world find value in the thoughts and ideas expressed herein.

It is easier to diagnose problems than it is to prescribe effective remedies. What I have attempted to do in these writings is to not only identify deficiencies in our system but also offer suggestions as to how to correct those deficiencies. I have consistently drawn upon experiences throughout my professional career and my life and used lessons learned to help in my understanding of problems while relying upon a core set of beliefs to help solve them. There are very few inviolable truths in life, and my ideas have shifted over the years. However, my ideals have remained rock solid. Some may disagree with my diagnoses and remedies, but few would disagree with the basic premise that dedication to public service should be based on the desire to make the world a better place for the greatest number of people possible.

If one senses a growing exasperation with the Obama administration over the course of these writings it is because it is so. Of course the alternative scenarios, McCain or Romney offered little or no hope of fulfilling the basic premise mentioned above so my support for the success of the President is still unwavering. However, there have been many disappointments along the way. I will leave a discussion of those items for another day. The exercise here is intended to identify shortcomings in hopes of maximizing course corrections. But let there be no doubt that I have serious reservations with many of the policies that have taken shape over the past five years, not the least being the lack of an intellectually honest energy policy.

So if this effort is successful in energizing a healthy public debate on that one issue alone it would be a substantial contribution to the betterment of all. We need more profiles in courage among our elected leaders, from the President on down, we need long-term strategic thinking, we need to restore confidence in our leaders and our institutions, we need to remove the obscene amounts of money that have corrupted our system from both elections and the policy-making processes, and we need to place the public interest above special interests.

To do these things will not be easy, there is no delusion here, but they can be done. Our problems are man-made and therefore man can resolve them, to borrow from President Kennedy's words at American

University over a half century ago. And time is not an ally; in fact it is very much an enemy. We like to talk a good game about our devotion to our future generations, but to be blunt we are passing a cruel sentence upon them if we do not deviate from the current path we are on. So let the debate begin.

My only admonition to those who may be inspired by these written words is to get involved, speak out, and stay involved throughout your lives in making this world a better place for those who will follow. If I touch only one person then this book will have been a great success.

Acknowledgements

The idea for this work rests squarely with my friend Gail Steinbeck, who over the years has been tremendously supportive of my efforts, along with her husband Thom Steinbeck, to vent my frustrations via postings in The Huffington Post.

The Evolution of Revolution:
An Attack upon Reason, Compromise, and the Constitution